Praise for *The Professional*

The financial services industry and the role of the financial advisor along with it are in a hyper state of evolution. To be candid, advisors who do not make the shift from "salesperson" to "professional" in regard to the scope of their services and the role they play in their clients' lives will find themselves on the outside looking in. *The Professional Financial Advisor* is an excellent resource, worthy of shelf space in advisors' offices across North America.

—Dennis Moseley-Williams, Consultant, Pareto Systems

A growing number of Canadians are concerned about the sorry state of investment counselling in this country, but it has taken a rare breed of bird—an insider with a conscience—to both identify the problems and propose solutions. John De Goey's book may not win him too many friends among advisors [...] but it will earn him thanks from small investors who, for too long, were convinced that somebody was picking their pockets. De Goey not only names the pickpockets, he identifies the best methods of eliminating them.

—John Lawrence Reynolds, author of *The Naked Investor*

Increasingly, consumers are seeking real value from their financial advisors. Consumers want a transparent partnership founded on trust and full disclosure. Separating financial advice from financial products provides benefits to both parties. John De Goey repeatedly illustrates how the "professionalization of financial advice" is a winning position for everyone. He demonstrates how prudent and knowledgeable advisors can save consumers time and money through this common-sense strategy. Consumers and advisors imperil their success if they avoid this profitable trend.

—Dale Ennis, Publisher, *Canadian MoneySaver*

The ongoing health of any industry or organization is enhanced by periodic self-assessment, even when the results of that review are not always kind. John De Goey has presented a probing critical assessment of the world of financial planning, along with his passionate prescriptions for what ails it.

—George Hartman, author of *Risk Is Still a Four Letter Word*

In expressing his views about the tenets of truly professional advice-giving, John De Goey has steadfastly maintained a point of view that has raised the ire of some but should be of interest to all advisors and the investors they serve. De Goey deserves credit for stoking the flames of debate on such controversial issues as the structure of advisor compensation and the integrity of professional advice.

—Darin Diehl, Publisher, Executive Editor, StockHouse.ca

Advance praise for *The Professional Financial Advisor II*

Many talk and write about fees but often forget the other parts of the equation: value provided in return and professional standards. John De Goey hits the nail squarely on the head. The candour and passion with which he presents and discusses these issues is refreshing.
—Dan Hallett, CFA, CFP, President, Dan Hallett & Associates Inc.

You don't have to agree with everything John De Goey says to concede that he plays in a higher league when it comes to ethics and doing what is right for the client.
—Rob Carrick, the *Globe and Mail*

A wise, provocative, and well-written book. It makes a convincing case that success comes from the application of the sound principles of professionalism.
—David H. Maister, author of *True Professionalism* and co-author of *The Trusted Advisor*

John De Goey's insights into what he terms "embedded compensation" and compensation biases made an important contribution to the development of the Fair Dealing Model and the articulation of the FDM and its goal to eliminate futile regulatory requirements while promoting true professionalism in the financial service industry.
—Julia Dublin, Barrister and Solicitor, Alyesworth LLP

There are a number of distinct schools of thought on how securities are priced and traded on the secondary market. For example, value-based analysts, technical analysts, and efficient markets proponents all make different assumptions about the usefulness to investors of different types of company, economic, and market information. It is important for an investor to understand these differences and to select the approach that reflects their views. This book provides some useful insight on security pricing.
—Eric Kirzner, Professor and John H. Watson Chair in Value Investing, Rotman School of Business, University of Toronto

John De Goey is the consumer's friend because he raises issues that many advisors don't care to address—issues like how advisors are paid and why there isn't a consistent education standard for advisors. An educated consumer is an informed consumer. *The Professional Financial Advisor* is required reading before turning your life savings over to an advisor.
—Deanne Gage, *Advisor's Edge*

John De Goey effectively updates us with tremendous insights into the plight of the financial services industry and the unbundling of sales from financial advice. In particular, his unique perspective on the development of financial planning as a profession is not only interesting but also extraordinarily relevant.
—Cary List, COO, Financial Planners Standards Council

The PROFESSIONAL
FINANCIAL ADVISOR II

The PROFESSIONAL FINANCIAL ADVISOR II

How the financial services industry hides the ugly truth

John J. De Goey

MPA, CIM, FCSI, TEP, CFP

INSOMNIAC PRESS

Library and Archives Canada Cataloguing in Publication

De Goey, John J., 1963-
    The professional financial advisor II : how the financial services industry hides the ugly truth / John J. De Goey.

Includes index.
Previous ed. published under title: The professional financial advisor.
ISBN 1-897178-29-8

1. Financial planners--Canada. 2. Investment advisors--Canada.
3. Financial services industry--Canada. I. Title.

HG179.5.D44 2006   332.6'2'0971   C2006-903473-7

The publisher gratefully acknowledges the support of the Canada Council, the Ontario Arts Council and the Department of Canadian Heritage through the Book Publishing Industry Development Program.

Printed and bound in Canada

Insomniac Press
192 Spadina Avenue, Suite 403
Toronto, Ontario, Canada, M5T 2C2
www.insomniacpress.com

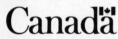

Disclaimer

The opinions expressed are those of the author and not necessarily those of Burgeonvest Securities Limited. The opinions and generalizations by the author concerning professionalism within the financial services industry reflect the lack of homogeneity among numerous providers of financial services from differing industries (insurance, banking, financial planning, and investment) and with differing standards of conduct. For advisors who are regulated by the Investment Dealers Association of Canada, some of these generalizations about professionalism are not accurate.

With respect to opinions relating to modern portfolio theory and passive versus active management, an attempt has been made to discuss these complex academic issues in simple terms. As such, the discussion does not fully reflect the breadth and depth of opinion and evidence regarding these topics, nor can it be expected to. Everyone's investment and retirement plans must be created to satisfy their particular situation. Therefore, it is recommended that the reader treat the information in this book as general in nature and consider getting advice from lawyers, accountants, financial planners, and other related professionals.

For Sophie

Contents

Introduction

In the three years since the first editon of this book was released, there has been only moderate progress in the Canadian financial services industry. We still have a balkanized regulatory framework and consumers still have very little meaningful recourse when it comes to restitution for wrongdoing. Judging by industry scandals, one might also conclude that the unsavory elements of the industry will likely continue to do things "the old way."

Then again, consumers and advisors are growing increasingly fed up with the status quo. A growing number of leading-edge advisors are doing what they can within their own practices to respond to a growing demand for professionalism. Some of those attributes that are lacking in many advisory relationships are becoming key differentiators. Matters such as transparency, the alignment of consumer and advisor interests, independent academic research, and a clearer focus on cost are all coming to the fore. Up to now, part of the problem has been the lack of suitable products and platforms: it's pretty difficult for advisors to move to a more professional paradigm if the industry is still predicated on a culture of sales.

This edition has been updated, but since the first edition was based primarily on advocacy for the future, there wasn't a whole lot to do. Updating factual data is not why there's a second edition; finding new approaches to old problems is the purpose of this new edition.

The real change in *The Professional Financial Advisor II* is in its focus. In essence, while the first edition was a challenge that called for a revolution, the second edition is more of a guide that describes an ongoing evolution within financial services. This approach seems more suited to the world we live in. People who know me know that I prefer to take a positive view. As such, this edition also aims to be more of a light and less of a judge regarding stakeholder behaviour.

Speaking of evolution as opposed to revolution, the continued evolution of the three trends I spoke of in the first edition are clearly continuing: the "all things considered" approach (called *convergence*) seems to be taking hold as the prevailing paradigm for advice; the idea of charging for financial advice after removing product compensation (called *unbundling*) is definitely gaining momentum; and the trend of some people doing things for themselves but with specialized oversight (called *disintermediation*) is alive and well too. This latter trend can be seen as the Home Depot mindset of personal finance: "You can do it. We can help." The trends of convergence, unbundling, and disintermediation are all at work as the financial services industry works to distinguish between those who merely sell products and those who add value through professional advice.

As with the first edition, I'll continue to lump all advisors and planners together with traditional brokers and salaried employees and call them all Financial Service Providers, or FSPs.

The creation of a true profession will involve a variety of factors. In fact, there is still some uncertainty about what the salient attributes of professional financial advice should be. Unlike the first edition, which was heavy on detail and targeted people in the business, this book is less presciptive and focused more on the ordinary consumer. The goal of getting all stakeholders on the same page remains unchanged, but this time there is a real effort to show how consumers and FSPs can work together to effect positive change for everyone.

Although certain challenges to the status quo are still present, the emphasis now is on looking at what the best FSPs are doing in order to capitalize on trends—for both their own sake as well as their clients'.

The lack of progress is due largely to self-regulatory organizations (SROs), advisory firms, and product manufacturers, all of which have vested interests they would prefer to protect. Taken together, I'll refer to these stakeholders as "corporate interests" throughout the book. Essentially, the corporate interests of the financial services industry, while never referencing certain things explicitly, cause people (FSPs, consumers, journalists) to think and act in a certain way. It is an approach that has allowed corporate interests to prevail at the expense of other stakeholders.

The existence of "asymmetric information" means that ordinary consumers often end up as victims of circumstance. When the laypeople are only given part of any story, it's difficult to imagine them making wise decisions. Astonishingly, there are considerable gaps in the knowledge base of most FSPs too. Corporate interests have a way of getting what they want by inference and innuendo. This is quite insidious and highly deliberate, since it leads to larger profits (for both product manufacturers and distributors) and fewer lawsuits (for SROs and the firms they represent).

Consumers and FSPs generally do what they think ought to be correct, even though the industry seldom comes out and explicitly says what that is. Many FSPs are too entrenched in defending a value proposition (that of picking stocks or picking people who pick stocks) to ever become the truly independent professionals they aspire to be. Employers perpetuate this value proposition further.

If you want more background on how corporate interests maintain dominance, I recommend you either read Joel Bakan's book *The Corporation* or watch the documentary of the same name. If you want to get a quick sense of what insiders with a social conscience go through, you may want to rent the movie *The Insider* and focus on the challenges faced by Russell Crowe's character. It is the corporate element of the financial services industry that is doing the most to impede progress.

The key intermediary in all of this is the FSP, who is conflicted in trying to serve two (or more) masters. As former OSC Executive Julia Dublin has said, FSPs are the "ham in the sandwich" of the industry. Many FSPs find themselves caught in the middle, wanting to do what is right for their clients, but brought to heel by the tyranny of mortgage payments and the need for job security. Stakeholders that are fat, happy, and extremely profitable within the status quo are hardly likely to embrace any change that threatens those attributes. Not all FSPs will be able to recognize the problem. Fewer still will be able to act in their clients' best interests even if they do recognize the inherent conflicts.

It will take a rare breed of FSP—a "STANDUP (Scientific Testing And Necessary Disclosure Underpin Professionalism) Advisor"—to cut through the noise to get to the heart of the problem. The encouragement of all advisors to follow the lead of a few trailblazers and be STANDUP Advisors offers a vision that many believe is both desirable and inevitable.

There's an acknowledgement in this edition that FSPs are by no means a homogeneous group. For greater clarity, I have chosen to compare and contrast the practices of the best advisors (STANDUP Advisors) with those of the advisors most entrenched in the status quo for reasons of self-preservation, or "SPANDEX (Sales Pitches And Non-Disclosure Eliminate eXcellence) Advisors."

It's easy to tell the difference: STANDUP Advisors do what is best for their clients, while SPANDEX Advisors serve corporate interests. Like the material they are named after, SPANDEX Advisors are both flexible and highly durable but not particularly valuable. They need to be done away with, but their durability is a significant part of the problem. Many (probably most) FSPs are neither; I simply use STANDUP and SPANDEX as extreme ends of what is ultimately a fairly wide spectrum.

There are a number of STANDUP Advisors who are tired of waiting for the industry to voluntarily transform itself into a profession. Rather than wait, they've decided to forge ahead— and good for them! However, they are facing an uphill battle because corporate interests, SPANDEX Advisors, uninformed consumers, and much of the media have lined up against them. Collectively, consumers, consumer advocates, and STANDUP FSPs are up against a monolithic industry that is well entrenched, self-satisfied, and highly profitable. The industry has no motive to morph into a profession, in spite of whatever rhetoric you may have heard to the contrary.

In light of such pervasive and well-financed opposition, how can STANDUP Advisors possibly hope to succeed? For one thing, sunshine is the best disinfectant. This book focuses on two attributes of professionalism that almost no one would dare to challenge: Scientific Testing And Necessary Disclosure. The acronym *STAND* was used briefly in the first edition, too, but I wanted this edition to be more proactive and empowering regarding positive change. I chose the acronym *STANDUP* to make a clear statement against the inertia that good FSPs have endured and to put a clear emphasis on real professionalism.

I'm encouraging all FSPs to act like STANDUP Advisors in the hope that consumers in turn will appreciate the gesture and reward those FSPs who accept the challenge with more and better business relationships. I believe consumers will gravitate toward STANDUP Advisors once they understand the problem. Change can come either by having FSPs voluntarily change their behaviour (which is highly unlikely, given what they are up against), or by forcing corporate interests to change their behaviour (also unlikely).

Many FSPs can see and read the evidence and decide for themselves how to offer advice. The most important thing is that FSPs ultimately become professionals—the "how" is secondary.

I also wrote this edition to help consumers get more from the FSPs they work with. In order to do so, they'll need a fuller understanding of the biases that corporate interests put into the business and that are such a pervasive part of financial services in the first place. Critics have suggested that I am anti-advisor. What nonsense! I am decidedly in favour of quality advice. I am also on the side of consumers, emprical evidence, and disclosure. Any FSP who cannot differentiate between conflicted advice that favours corporate interests and unbiased advice that favours consumers is clearly part of the problem. I am decidedly in favour of STANDUP FSPs and opposed to SPANDEX FSPs. As I said earlier, FSPs are by no means a homogeneous group.

This book will ask people to consider the value of both active management and financial advice. In both cases, readers are encouraged to either take it or leave it—depending on how they come down on each question—and there is evidence on both sides of both debates. Contrary to what many stakeholders would have us believe, the questions are mutually exclusive.

I am of the opinion that most FSPs add value and most active managers (i.e. people who actively trade stocks) subtract it. Many

FSPs have an identity that is wrapped up in a value proposition tainted with corporate motives, making it difficult to extricate the value proposition of quality advice from the value proposition of security selection.

Many financial services companies maximize profits on the assumption that active management adds value. While the evidence on this is sketchy, there can be little doubt that the use of active management enhances the corporate bottom line.

Unfortunately, most people are unaware of the evidence in favour of a more passive investing approach. To make matters worse, the media, aided and abetted by an army of SPANDEX Advisors, has led consumers to equate active management with financial advice, and passive management with a do-it-yourself (DIY) approach. Again, this is a facile simplification. These determinations can *and should* be reached independently.

At issue here is the notion of value for money. When it comes to stock picking, price and value can be quantified fairly reliably. Conversely, the value of good advice is much more difficult to measure in a meaningful way. At any rate, these are separate decisions where one conclusion ought to have absolutely no bearing on the other. Many people, especially members of the media, make an unnecessary link, suggesting that passive investing is for do-it-yourselfers and active investing is for those working with an FSP. Worse still, many SPANDEX FSPs buy into this joined-at-the-hip line of thinking.

Going forward, the question of genuine independence will be seen as the critical missing link in completing the transition from a culture of sales to a culture of professionalism. The industry's compensation models clearly undermine the principle of independence. It may well be that the biggest change that has to occur is the total eradication of embedded compensation. People who offer financial advice want desperately to be seen as independent champions of their clients' best interests, even though many currently feel in their hearts that they aren't. I firmly believe that most FSPs have good intentions.

There are a number of advocates across the country who want meaningful consumer protection, and for all the right reasons too. In other words, those pressing for change are generally more concerned with societal welfare than personal gain, but to date, advocates have been too few and too poorly organized to get real results. Many share the assessment that corporate interests are a major part of the problem.

On the flip side, if a consumer's situation is exceedingly simple or the FSP is not genuinely adding value, firing that FSP and pocketing the difference may well be the best thing to do. The decision to use or forgo using an FSP should be no different than the decision to use or forgo using an accountant. It is largely personal and situational.

I believe most people would be better off with a qualified FSP, but I also believe that there is a considerable minority that could do quite well without one. For those people who would be better off acting as their own advisors, they should be given every opportunity to do so with regard to both investment and insurance products. No matter how valuable quality advice may be, it is the height of arrogance to suggest that good advice is so universally useful that everyone should be forced to pay for it whether they want it or not.

The fundamental premise of this book is that *real professionals provide services that are in their clients' best interests*; a sales motive should never compromise a professional advisory role.

There's nothing wrong with sales as a calling in life, it's just that the term "professional salesman" is a virtual oxymoron. As the profession evolves (led by STANDUP Advisors), the sales representatives (SPANDEX Advisors) will need to be shown the door. Until then, the ugly truth is that we're dealing with a perverse kind of conspiracy, a conspiracy of ignorance so secret that the co-conspirators don't even know about it themselves!

When I was in graduate school, a professor of mine suggested that the term "change agent" was really a sanitized corporate euphemism for "shit disturber." I fancy myself as a change agent in the best sense of the term. If we're not purposeful, the industry might fall short of transforming itself in ways that are in everyone's best interest. I hope this book can be a constructive touchstone for what needs to happen as part of this change.

We have a fabulous opportunity to transform the financial advice channel into an integrated, holistic and bona fide profession, complete with all the trappings of other professions. The industry can be recognized as such only when the concerns raised in the pages that follow are addressed.

Throughout this process, there are a number of questions that will need to be resolved. What might the financial services landscape look like in the future? More to the point, what *should* the industry look like? Perhaps most of all, readers should consider what they believe the hallmarks of a qualified *professional* Financial Service Provider ought to be.

Paying transparently for genuine professional financial advice will require everyone to rethink both the role of the FSP and the value of that advice. The transition will be challenging, but it has to come. We need societal recognition that rendering comprehensive financial advice can and should be transformed into a professional activity in every sense. Perhaps we can call it the "world's youngest profession," even if many people think its credibility today is on par with the "world's oldest profession."

We have some very real and deep-seated problems that need to be addressed. In the end, politicians, regulators, FSPs, consumers, the media, companies, and industry associations will all need to voice their concerns in a dialogue on the creation of this new profession.

Until now, much of the discussion has not involved apples-to-apples comparisons of business models, services rendered, product recommendations, or the alignment of interests. Many hurdles need to be cleared before the associated respect and confidence accorded to any true profession can be won, but there can be no doubt that an evolution toward a more forward-looking and client-centred profession is clearly under way.

John J. De Goey
Toronto, August 2006

Part One
Preparing FSPs

Becoming a Profession

The past gives us experience and memories; the present gives us challenges and opportunities; the future gives us vision and hope.
—William Arthur Ward

The Chinese word for *change* is comprised of symbols for *risk* and *opportunity*. Many people also like to cite the famous Chinese curse, "May you live in interesting times." One can safely surmise that there is indeed change going on in the financial services industry and that we most certainly live in "interesting times." The question this raises is, "How will we deal with it?" especially since the framework of financial advice rests on rapidly shifting sands.

Despite this, there are many in the financial services industry who are equally fond of the phrases, "The more things change, the more they stay the same," and, "When all is said and done, more will be said than done." In the past, most people in the financial services industry had titles that described their compartmentalized roles. As the distinctions blurred and everyone became involved in everyone else's business, old titles seemed increasingly inappropriate.

Where Did We Come From?
Until the late 1980s, the dominant model for retail investor portfolio design was one of working with a stockbroker or insurance agent who earned commissions while constructing a portfolio of individual securities or selling insurance products. Clients paid handsome commissions for the buying and selling that occured as a result of that advice. On the investment side, people really had no choice but to work through full-service brokers because discount brokerages were just coming into existence.

The problem with a transaction-oriented business model was that it rewarded all transactions—good, bad, or otherwise. More trades meant more commissions for the broker. The problem, of course, is that transaction costs and taxes often correlate negatively to investor performance. The cardinal rule of the industry is that advice should be offered with the best interests of the client in mind, so that meant there was a disconnect.

In the past generation, many people switched from using individual securities to mutual funds. A large number of these people, however, still do not know exactly how mutual funds work, what they cost, or how FSPs are compensated, yet there is presently over $600 billion invested in mutual funds in Canada. The system has worked well enough, but there are rumblings that the time has come to start working on a wholesale overhaul.

In general, the industry has moved from giving away the advice while charging for the transaction to virtually giving away the transaction while charging for the associated advice. It is evident that people are coming to realize that, in the age of disintermediation, the only viable value proposition for FSPs is one of superior advising.

Attitudes Constrain Progress

Offering comprehensive financial advice *is becoming* a profession. Some people reading this might be thinking that giving financial advice already was a profession. That's what people in the industry would have us believe. They refer to Financial Service Providers as "trusted advisors" since offering trusted advice seems like an entirely professional thing to do.

But this approach merely exposes the presumptuousness in the industry. Many FSPs seem to think that if they refer to themselves and their peers as professionals often enough, the public will over time come to view them as precisely that. To some extent, this approach has worked. There's only one problem: actions speak louder than words. While progress has certainly been made, we haven't established a true profession yet. In fact, we're not even close.

Since the financial services industry is rooted in a background of product sales, the predominant mindset in financial services remains one of selling. I recently wrote a column in the *National*

Post in which I pointed out that this mindset persists. I got a number of snide comments from SPANDEX FSPs and a number of kudos from STANDUP FSPs. I must have hit a nerve.

Most FSPs routinely refer to their "book of business" as opposed to their "professional practice," which latter is the term used by other professionals. Old habits die hard. In order to complete the transition, FSPs need to shed the last vestiges of their heritage, ridding themselves of sales-related paradigms once and for all.

These attitudes have been put in place by product manufacturers, advisory firms, and regulators. Old course material used to refer to FSPs as "sales agents" and, frankly, that's what they were. Today, there's a war going on within financial services. The best FSPs are far more comprehensive than mere sales representatives, and they want both the tools necessary to do their jobs and the recognition that goes along with doing it. Unfortunately, there are also a number of old-school "dinosaur" FSPs who have not changed and are doing everything in their power to impede progress. Sadly, in spite of the lip service corporate interests pay to the former group, their infrastructure, product approvals, new product development, compliance procedures, and other framework policies continue to favour the dinosaurs.

There are a number of areas where old and new are in conflict. Fundamentally, we're talking about a progress versus status quo dichotomy. To be absolutely clear, this is a book that is firmly committed to progress and common sense. A number of challenges lie ahead. Here are three:

1. Industry Associations and Professional Standards

Every profession has its own association for individual practitioners. Not to be outdone by the ongoing regulatory turf war, a number of industry trade associations have sprung up, vetting the professional standards and competencies of individual FSPs. This is surely the clearest evidence of a young profession.

There is a broad consensus on the general attributes of what constitutes a professional FSP, but also a whole lot of backbiting about who will monitor those attributes and protect consumers along the way. To make matters worse, FSPs needn't join any of these organizations if they don't want to. What good are standards if a person can simply opt out of being governed by them? Not all FSPs are created equal and STANDUP FSPs generally join these organizations while SPANDEX FSPs generally do not. Currently, FSPs can opt in or opt out of their commitment to professionalism. Most consumers don't seem to care.

All of the competing organizations purport to be the true source of professional standards and enforcement. Their attitude is, "Would the others please get in line to reduce consumer confusion?" Even then, many organizations do not properly audit or enforce the standards they set. This is sort of like having posted speed limits, but no traffic cops.

The issue of standards is dicey enough. This is because North America is so far ahead of virtually all of the rest of the world that international standards are essentially worse than useless—they are dangerously misleading. In North America, there are thousands of people who are trying desperately to become true professionals by obtaining the designation of choice for qualified financial advice: Certified Financial Planner (CFP). The problem is that most other nations have virtually no CFPs at all because much of the rest of the world is just getting around to setting the most rudimentary standards possible. Agreeing on common standards first and then raising the bar once everyone is on the same page is all well and good for nations where there's little training to begin with, but in North America, low international standards effectively mean no meaningful domestic standards.

The disparity between de facto North American standards and those likely to be adopted for the rest of the world will soon put us in a very tricky situation. We'll have thousands of FSPs in North America presenting themselves as "ISO Certified" (i.e. meeting international financial planning standards), even though those standards will be laughable.

Consumers are at risk. North Americans need to recognize the magnitude of this situation immediately. With all due respect to other countries, they have lower standards than we do. The international Financial Planning Standards Board has recently established a permanent committee to propose, review, and validate changes to the certification scheme for the CFP mark worldwide.

In 2006, the committee will establish an international competency profile for professional financial planning, international financial planning practice standards, and relevant work experience requirements. The committee will also form an education working group to examine the feasibilty of a global core curriculum for personal financial planning once the competency profile has been established.

Canada is taking the lead in the globalization of planning competency by donating its own competency profile as a starting point. This profile identifies specific competencies (performance-based skills, abilities, and professional judgments) that are expected of all CFP registrants in Canada. The eventual establishment of a truly international set of professional financial planning competencies will be a huge leap forward for the international planning community. It will ensure not only that all Certified Financial Planners will be held to consistent competency standards but also that a consistent definition of what it means to be a professional financial planner can be implemented throughout the international CFP community.

By and large, a professional in another part of the world is not on par with a professional from North America. Consumers recognize this intuitively, but since financial advice is such a new field and not yet a true profession, these same consumers could easily be duped into believing that the international standard and the North American standard are one and the same. The bottom line is that there could be thousands of FSPs calling themselves "professionals" and "ISO Certified" in a couple of years even though most of them will not measure up to the standards set internally by their own professional associations in Canada.

2. Proficiency

How are consumers going to determine which credentials are most appropriate if the financial services industry can't even agree within itself? Consumers understand that if they go to see a physician, they should expect to see a diploma displayed prominently in the office, attesting to the fact that the person they are seeing is an MD. If they go to see a lawyer, they would look for a law degree hanging on the wall. The same goes for dentistry, accounting, engineering, and architecture. Professions hold themselves to a consistent standard as set by consistent and rigorous training, suitable experience, peer review, and ethical conduct. This in turn gives consumers a degree of confidence about a minimum level of competence. There is no such standard regarding financial advice in English-speaking Canada.

With the recent coming together of various financial disciplines under the umbrella of holistic wealth management, different trade associations have each come to espouse their training as the best, most comprehensive, and most suitable. There should be no surprise here, since we're really talking about survival. Any organization that has a primary responsibility to train and licence practitioners would be ostracized if their training was revealed to be inferior to what was offered elsewhere. Besides, each organization believes its product and training solutions to be most appropriate.

For instance, insurance educators and licensors believe insurance products and solutions should be emphasized, while securities educators and licensors take a diametrically opposed view. There's no consensus on what constitutes appropriate advice because there's no consensus regarding what constitutes appropriate training. Designations flow from these perspectives and consumers end up getting advice based on product-oriented solutions as opposed to client-centred solutions.

At the turn of the twenty-first century, there were about twenty designations available to FSPs who wanted to demonstrate competency in some field of financial advice. Aside from boosting the egos of those FSPs who held them, many people in the industry felt the situation was outright embarrassing. What self-respecting profession can't even agree on what is required to join? Today, the industry is coalescing around the Certified Financial Planner (CFP) designation conferred in Canada by the Financial Planning Standards Council (FPSC) as the title that most accurately denotes an FSP who can offer qualified advice to the public. This doesn't mean the other designations are substandard, only that they often convey competence in a more specialized area. The FPSC mandate is to "benefit the public and the financial planning *profession* by establishing and enforcing uniform professional standards for financial planners." (italics mine)

There are presently over 80,000 CFPs worldwide. Canada, at about 17,000, has more CFPs per capita than any nation on earth. In spite of this, there are some who insist that the CFP is not the appropriate standard to which FSPs should be held. These groups often do not want the CFP to be adopted because they are fearful that their existing registrants will be unable to handle the rigours of becoming a CFP. Without saying so explicitly, they want a lower standard.

3. Unbundling

This is a concept that has only caught on with a handful of (mostly) STANDUP FSPs at present, but is already successful in the U.S. Simply put, unbundling allows investment products to be made available without any embedded compensation for the FSP (i.e. commissions and trailing commissions are built into the ongoing cost of owning a managed product). As a result, there can be no second-guessing the FSP's motive. Clients no longer have to wonder, Is this guy recommending the product because it's best for me or because it will pay him more than others? In short, it is doubtful if true professionalism (including product independence) could ever be attained without unbundling.

The *industry*, as it is inappropriate to refer to it is a *profession* at this point, has already gone through a partial transformation. Conventional stock brokers made (and many continue to make) commissions on both the buy and the sell recommendations that were accepted by their clients. As such, there was a clear bias to trade.

Paying a prescribed fee is likely the best way to eliminate this bias. Ironically, this might involve paying an FSP to "do nothing," but if "nothing" (i.e. deliberately not trading) is the right thing to do, then everyone should hail this as significant progress. The aim here is to develop a framework where the FSP's motive (and corresponding advice) are aligned with consumer interests and cannot be called into question.

Until late in 2000, most mutual funds recommended by FSPs were available only in a format that paid the FSP in some way. At the end of that year, mutual fund companies began to offer funds with no embedded compensation (and correspondingly lower management expense ratios, or MERs) to the public. These are called "F Class" funds ("F" meaning "fee"). Around the same time, a wider number of exchange traded funds (ETFs) became available in Canada. These also feature no embedded compensation. Unlike the U.S., where F Class funds and ETFs have a significant market share, Canadian FSPs have been slow to start using unbundled products.

I know many FSPs that would happily move to an unbundled practice format if only there were enough good unbundled products to recommend and their employers would provide platforms to use them. Manufacturers and distributors (i.e. the firms that employ FSPs) say they have been slow to develop these products because demand is low. It's an "if you build it, they will come" conundrum that defies clear culpability. However, there can be little doubt that for STANDUP FSPs who want to do the right thing, a smug industry that caters to the lowest common denominator seems to be penalizing them for being early adopters.

The idea behind unbundling is that FSPs can charge a separate fee for the advice being offered but that the compensation that had previously been embedded in the product would no longer be allowed to cloud the issue of suitability. Again, acceptance from FSPs has been disappointing to say the least. Most investment products today are still sold with embedded compensation going to the FSP for completing the sale. This is especially disappointing for do-it-yourself (DIY) investors who want to use advances in technology to engage in disintermediation. These people often end up paying their discount broker for the (non-existent) "advice" costs that are built into certain products.

Embedded compensation is closely related to tied selling, the idea that access to a given product or service is predicated on doing something else that you might not want to do. For instance, bank loans used to entail as a necessary condition the use of the lending bank's products, while some planning firms to this day offer more comprehensive wealth solutions, provided that you use their investment products along the way.

Many FSPs rightly want "shelf space" as bona fide professionals in the minds of consumers. They position themselves as professionals who can wisely discern suitable options in a sea of complicated financial choices. Without unbundling, however, that positioning usually rings hollow. Embedded compensation creates bias, the antithesis of professionalism.

The financial services industry needs unbundling because *unbundling creates trust*. However, SPANDEX FSPs generally don't want to have full and frank conversations with their clients about how and how much they are being paid. It's easier to sell things when you don't have to have a discussion about what they cost.

The best FSPs know all about the importance of trust. They know that without trust, an FSP can say whatever he wants and his clients still won't likely believe him, even if what he says is measured, appropriate, and fundamentally true. There is a clear need to suspend self-interest when offering financial advice, and unbundling does this. There's a certain kind of unimpeachable integrity that comes from being able to say, "There are three options here; the pros and cons of each are as follows and no matter which you choose, I'll be paid the same. The best option is the one that works best for you."

Without trust, advice is suspect. It has been said that the fundamental job of the FSP is to create a space where the truth can be spoken, heard, and believed. Unbundling does this and the transparency that stems from unbundling has obvious additional benefits. Most people had probably never heard the term "corporate malfeasance" until the new millennium. Going forward, there will almost certainly be a premium placed on good governance and transparent business relationships.

This trend will almost certainly filter down to the relationship between FSPs and their clients. Consumers demand more these days. They want to know what they're paying for and what services should reasonably be expected in return. To make informed decisions, consumers know that apples-to-apples comparisons will have to be made and that the facts will need to be placed before them in terms they can understand. Most people understand that everyone needs to earn a living and simply request that the value of the services rendered be equal to or greater than the fee being charged.

Until now, the financial services industry has been fraught with convoluted disclosures made on a rather ad hoc basis, allowing a number of FSPs to work without ever having to explain how (or how much) they get paid. Most consumers can check records to determine how much they paid their dentist or lawyer or accountant over the past year. The same level of transparency and disclosure will soon be required of all FSPs.

The FSP of Tomorrow

To understand what the FSP of tomorrow will look like, we'll first have to consider the FSP of today. Most FSPs have a background in sales. I marvel at how much new FSP training is rooted in selling techniques: how to increase appointments, improve "closing rates," and deal with objections. Do doctors, dentists, lawyers, and accoutants spend most of their first few months learning sales techniques as newly minted "professionals"?

The old (SPANDEX) paradigm of sales is reflected in such phrases such as "eat what you kill" and "ABC: Always Be Closing." Mercifully, that paradigm is giving way to a more contemporary kind of thinking; ABC now stands for "Always Be Consulting" and enlightened (STANDUP) FSPs are now making a *genuine* effort to overcome the limitations of their early career training. It should come as no surprise that the psychological aspects of offering financial advice are now coming to the fore.

Where Consumers Fit In

There is a wide range of consumer demand for financial services in the marketplace. One-stop shopping can be a dicey objective in a world of "different strokes for different folks." It is difficult for FSPs and their firms to deliver a consistent "brand experience" when consumer wants and needs are all over the map. Some consumers want more detail on statements, while others would be quite content to get fewer statements altogether since they often don't open them anyway and generally see reporting as a nuisance.

When considering retail financial planning advice and services, a continuum can be drawn that demonstrates the problem. On one extreme, we have people who want to do everything themselves and find any contact with the financial services industry a nuisance; on the other, we have people who do virtually nothing for themselves, choosing instead to abdicate their responsibilities altogether. Both extremes can be dangerous. Here's a quick glance at this continuum:

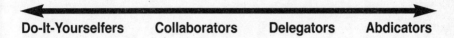

Do-It-Yourselfers   **Collaborators**   **Delegators**   **Abdicators**

While most people would agree that it is reckless to totally abdicate responsibility for their own financial well-being, there are certainly those who do it. These are people who find the whole business of money, investing, taxes and estate planning too overwhelming and distasteful to merit serious consideration.

Most consumers find themselves somewhere in the middle of the continuum and are generally inclined to some degree of collaboration, with an increasing likelihood of working with an FSP as they move to the right. The challenge for FSPs is that many are trying to be all things to all people, working with whoever comes through the door. They would likely be better off if they focused on one psychographic subset of the population: the delegators.

Note that abdicators are even more likely to do as they are advised, but the best FSPs want their clients to feel a sense of ownership; abdicators don't make for fulfilling client relationships. If FSPs are offering stewardship to clients who appreciate it, everyone feels more fulfilled. Just as physicians would rather have their patients quit smoking of their own volition than prescribe a patch, rendering advice is more rewarding when there's a sense that people receiving advice really want to take destiny in their own hands rather than be prescribed band-aid solutions.

When we get to the chapter on financial advice for those who need it, readers might wish to refer back to this continuum. There's no single best way to determine whether one should work with an FSP or not, but as a general rule, the further right you go, the greater the likelihood you'll need an FSP. Just how much progress have we made so far, anyway?

Preparing FSPs

Men are men before they are lawyers, or physicians, or merchants, or manufacturers; and if you make them capable and sensible men, they will make themselves capable and sensible lawyers or physicians.

—John Stuart Mill

There can be little doubt that we are in the final stages of the creation of a new profession focused on providing financial advice. People have been giving financial advice for years without it being a bona fide profession, just as people built structures before there were certified engineers. Over time, the need to formally train workers and standardize the building work being done moved from being a good idea to being entrenched as a requirement for doing business. What about financial advice? On the surface, it might seem that today's FSPs can be considered professionals. Then again, maybe not. There are thousands of people selling mutual funds today who have taken a week off work to study for and successfully complete the mutual fund licencing exam. Just how rigorous does professional training have to be?

The great number of people who introduce themselves as true professionals despite having met no demonstrable or relevant proficiency requirement underscores the importance of all serious professionals requiring recognized designations.

Passing the CFP exam would offer demonstrable evidence of comprehensive training. Of course, other professions require up to two years of apprenticeship or internship training. Doctors serve internships, and it seems the financial industry is moving in a similar direction.

In the future, formal academic programs will have to be revamped and expanded so that the coursework represents broad exposure to a number of related disciplines. Self-study licencing courses would never be permitted for law, accounting, or medicine. The depth and breadth of knowledge simply requires formal classroom training. Besides, the stakes are much too high to consider offering anything less to the public. Licencing people to sell products without arming them with the wisdom that comes from proper context and a well-rounded education is a tenuous proposition. Real progress is being made in laying an academic foundation, but much remains to be done.

At present, there is no mandatory second hurdle that one needs to clear by demonstrating an applied competency in the field of financial advice. There is nothing similar to medical or accounting internships, bar exams, or professional engineer exams for graduating CFPs, and they don't exist for people entering the industry with less than a CFP designation either.

The bottom line is that professionals get respect. People listen to what they have to say because they are experts in their fields. They studied long and hard to gain the knowledge required to perform their roles and other people look to them to tell them what to do. The phrase "Trust me, I'm a doctor" is filled with assurance and the presumption of knowing what's best for the situation at hand. When your accountant hands you a bill for services rendered and you scoff at the price, she might very well simply shrug at your scoff, as if to say, "What do you expect? That's what professional services cost."

Compensation Reconsideration

Let's consider what an appropriate compensation structure for a *professional* FSP of the future might look like. Would it involve commissions? Certainly not. Doctor's don't earn commissions. Would you respect a doctor's opinion if one treatment paid him 20% more than another? Whatever the compensation format is, it should leave the FSP beyond reproach regarding potential ulterior motives. As soon as the client can call the FSP's rationale into question, professionalism is compromised and credibility lost.

There are two ways the problem can be solved. The first is to do what lawyers, accountants, and other professionals do: charge a transparent hourly fee. The good news for an FSP who charges $200 an hour is that anyone who pays that fee is most likely to pay attention to what is proposed or written. Furthermore, the likelihood of acting on the advice is also high. Who in their right mind would pay that kind of money for recommendations that were merely interesting? The meter is running and time is precious, so there's very little bantering about taking the beagle to the vet or getting new shingles put on the roof. At $200 an hour, it's all business. Ultimately, this is where the financial services industry is heading. The second and more common way that qualified FSPs charge for their services is through an annual fee linked to the client's account size.

An FSP should have no interest in recommending anything other than what is best for clients. If clients become unhappy for any reason whatsoever, they can simply pick up their marbles and go home. In simple terms, the more the account rises, the more money the FSP makes; the more it declines, the less the FSP makes. This represents a clear performance linkage that more closely aligns the interests of clients with those of the FSP. The FSP, in turn, can go to a client and honestly say, "I succeed when you succeed"—a hallmark of true professionalism.

Meanwhile, some product-manufacturer companies offer to subsidize the marketing efforts of those FSPs who recommend their products in their ads and letters. Is it truly professional to gain access to money from "partners" while other companies with comparable products offer no such assistance? What does this say about independence? What about proprietary, in-house products? Finally, what about trips, trinkets, and trash that FSPs get from companies if they sell a certain number of products or a certain amount of a certain type of product? Is that the sort of incentive you might reasonably expect from a genuine professional who is dispassionate about products and focused on client-based solutions? It should be noted that other professionals could also clean up their acts. Think of the relationship between physicians and pharmaceutical companies, for instance. The point here is that certain elements of the status quo undermine the principles of professionalism. Having other, more established professions engage in the same sort of behaviour is hardly evidence that the behaviour is acceptable. For now, it might be best to examine the attributes one might associate with a professional advisor:

Continuing Education

If you accept the premise that the world is becoming more complex and interconnected all the time, then the people who are offering advice in light of these changes should also be keeping abreast of them. Membership organizations have made it mandatory for their members to maintain a minimum level of continuing education. Thirty hours of continuing education work is the annual benchmark. This usually includes course work on ethics and is verified with questionnaires that are signed off by members and audited throughout the year. Since the FPSC has an identical education condition, this makes the professional association hurdle a little redundant. Still, FSPs who are members of these sorts of associations while not holding the CFP designation will be held to a reasonable standard of continuing education.

One problem is that even though membership organizations are promoting continuing education and making it mandatory, joining these membership organizations is entirely optional. The net effect at present is that FSPs who want to be properly seen as professionals opt into these groups. Those who might not be up to snuff are allowed to look in from the outside and, in the process, save both their annual membership dues and the trouble of being held to a higher standard that membership entails. They flout the same principles that the organizations they avoid are trying to uphold. Most consumers are none the wiser.

When looking for an FSP, be sure to ask about their membership status within an organization committed to the promotion and enhancement of professional financial advice.

Offering Financial Advice: A Profession of Our Times

The world has become more complex and it seems everything spills over into everything else. Life is as much about maintaining a balanced schedule, lifestyle, and diet as it is about a balanced chequebook and portfolio. Everything is interrelated. If you don't eat right, you might develop health problems, which could mean time off work and could lead to a reduction in income.

As this complexity grows, people need someone they can trust to co-ordinate all the relevant aspects of their life, a "go-to guy." This person will need to either know answers or know where to find them. Financial decisions are more complex than ever because of the products, services, and concepts in the marketplace. In the 1970s, financial planning and advice were about stocks and bonds. In the 1980s, they were about real estate and tax shelters. In the 1990s, it was mutual funds and professional money management. Looking ahead, they will likely be about all of these things and much more.

The need for qualified financial advice is especially acute for professionals, corporate executives, and business owners. These people often lead busy lives and need to consider a wide range of options that take into account a wide variety of variables and possible outcomes. There may be multiple objectives where trade-offs between income, security, lifestyle, creditor protection, financial independence, estate planning, tax planning, and other matters need to be taken into account.

Let's have a look at what some of the more established professions do:

Doctors

Physicians and surgeons are among the most revered professionals on the planet. They enjoy a level of implicit trust that most other professinals couldn't even dream about.

Although these medical specialists perform a number of delicate procedures routinely, they still insist on written disclosure and consent before proceeding. It is standard procedure to sit down with the patient and explain, *in terms the patient can understand*, the risks and limitations of the procedure they are considering. What is the likely outcome for the patient if they do nothing? What is the probability of success? How long is the recovery likely to take if the operation is successful? What is the probability and frequency of failure? What is the worst that can happen? Has the patient consented to the procedure?

This is all documented in writing and the patient signs a consent form waiver acknowledging these discussions and disclosures before heading to the operating room. The chips fall where they may, but at least the decision about what to do was made with a clear and purposeful understanding of what the problem was and what the risks, rewards, and limitations were before getting started. It should be obvious that this process also protects the professional. There are many who feel those who offer financial advice should be obligated to make similar disclosures before products can be purchased.

There would still be a sales pitch element to many recommendations, but at least the consumer would see some uniformity of disclosure regarding pertinent facts relating to their choices. Other salient points that could be included in the point-of-sale disclosure might be: product cost (management expense ratio, or MER), FSP fee, and portfolio turnover (tax efficiency). Improved disclosure might stifle sales a little in the short run, but it would also add some much-needed trust and transparency.

Most FSPs recommend products based on superior short-term performance, even though there is evidence that short-term performance is not indicative of long-term performance. Over longer time frames, the percentage of funds that beat their benchmarks decreases. Very few FSPs disclose these points and few consumers think to ask what might "go wrong" as well as what might "go right."

Once these considerations are clarified, the FSP should act in accordance with the client's wishes. The most crucial point here is that professional advice should be predicated on the evidence garnered from rigorous testing and the best information available, not a sales pitch. The FSP should have no conflicts when offering opinions or advice and should obtain verifiable consent to proceed, knowing that all material disclosures and explanations were made before doing anything. Without a proper sign-off, what happens if something goes wrong?

If a surgeon explains every reasonable facet of a procedure to a patient but does not receive written consent to proceed and something goes wrong, there may be a substantial liability. Why should the standard be different for your financial health?

Dentists

Dentists are reliable and systematized. Say what you will about the operation they have going on, but they provide a model of consistency where appointments are concerned. First, the hygienist does the relatively general spadework, then the dental surgeon comes in to do whatever specialized procedures are required.

At the end of each session, the next session is scheduled for about twenty-seven weeks later. How many FSPs do this? Meetings with FSPs are not something typically scheduled. One of the reminder postcards I received recently had a dentist looking at an elderly female patient and saying, "You have acute gingivitis," to which she replies, "Thank you." Some clients only need to come in once a year, but there are those who may need or wish to come in two or more times a year. There should always be a system in place to ensure meetings are happening in a consistent, pre-dictable, and purposeful manner.

Lawyers

Unlike other professionals, lawyers seem to get much less respect from the general public. There are three things that lawyers do, however, that are extremely professional: they use letters of engagement, have a set fee schedule, and carry liability insurance. All three are critical hallmarks of a true professional. Let's take a look at each and explore how the use of a similar series of documents would raise the bar substantially for those FSPs who wish to present themselves as professionals.

The Law Society of Upper Canada recently took the unusual step of defining professionalism for legal practitioners in Ontario. The Law Society states that:

> As a personal characteristic, professionalism is revealed in an individual's attitude and approach to his or her occupation, and is commonly characterized by intelli-gence, integrity, maturity, and thoughtfulness. There is an expectation among lawyers, whose occupation is defined as a profession, and in the public who receive legal serv-ices, that professionalism will inform a lawyer's work and conduct.

The LSUC goes on to itemize the various components of pro-fessionalism. The "building blocks" listed are: scholarship, integri-ty, honour, leadership, independence, pride, spirit, collegiality, service, and balanced commercialism.

The widely accepted concept of professional practice standards is gaining credence everywhere. One of the most important aspects of such standards is the letter of engagement. Here, both the nature and the scope of the engagement between the client and the professional are mutually defined and agreed upon before services are rendered. There are many aspects to this concept, including:

- identifying services to be provided
- disclosing both the nature and amount of remuneration involved
- identifying the responsibilities of both parties
- establishing the duration of the agreement
- disclosing any related ties or potential conflicts of interest (both real and perceived)
- confirming confidentiality

FSPs need to be absolutely clear about how much they charge by using a compensation disclosure document. Many clients are told to "read the prospectus" when buying a mutual fund, but most of them don't and the small but intrepid few who do, generally have no idea what they've just read when they're finished. A separate disclosure document at the point-of-sale would go a long way toward clarifying how and how much FSPs are paid.

All professionals carry liability insurance to cover errors and omissions. Lawyers deserve some credit because they are perhaps the most keenly aware of the liabilities they assume when offering their services to the public. Clients should have some assurance that they will be covered in the unlikely event there should be a major oversight or error on the part of their advisor. After all, their personal fortune is usually at stake.

Lawyers are self-regulating through the use of law societies. Ontario legislation, primarily the Law Society Act, authorizes the LSUC to educate and license lawyers and to regulate their conduct and competence. The society's bylaws set out the professional and ethical obligations of all members of the profession. Those who fail to meet these obligations are subject to the society's complaints and disciplinary process. The society is governed by a board of forty-eight directors (known as benchers), forty of whom are lawyers and eight of whom are ordinary citizens known as "lay benchers."

Lawyers are also required to use a letter of engagement when being put on a retainer to do their work. That way, there are no surprises as to what will be required and what the services might ultimately cost. In contrast, letters of engagement are currently viewed as a best practice within financial services, although most FSPs still don't use them.

Choice in Compensation Models

Most financial products today come with some form of FSP compensation included (but buried) in the price. Since completely unbundled compensation is still rare, the best we can reasonably expect from most FSPs in the interim is not only client disclosure but also client *choice* regarding FSP compensation. Two reasons why it is rare is because product manufacturers have been slow to produce unbundled products and product distributors (advisory firms) have been slow to establish platforms that will accommodate them.

Still, there are some people who genuinely prefer to work in an arrangement where the FSP's compensation is buried in the cost. Some people just resent being reminded that financial advice costs money, just as some people resented being reminded about taxes when the GST was introduced.

Unless or until commissions and trailing commissions are abolished, it is impractical to have any philosophical or moral opposition to FSPs earning them. It is absolutely their prerogative to do so if they wish. Furthermore, there are a number of products that are only available on a commission basis (life insurance, for example).

People Don't Care What You Know

Perhaps most tellingly, consumers of professional services often choose their professionals on the basis of relationships and the gut feeling they have once they come into contact with them. We're all human and no one wants to feel like a "number" or an "account" or the living embodiment of a certain number of "billable hours." There is a saying that every FSP comes to learn within weeks of starting the job: people don't care what you know until they know that you care. Although a little trite, this is generally good advice.

FSPs are often reminded that they work in a "relationship business" in which connecting with the client is more than half the battle. Unfortunately, most consumers don't have the wherewithal to make a meaningful judgement in assessing the services provided (or about to be provided) by the professional. They look at the décor of the office, gauge for a suitable firmness of handshake, and hope that the person who referred them did not have a uniquely positive experience prior to recommending the services of the person in question. All the while, the prospective client is thinking, *I sure hope I can trust this guy*.

The client has to presume that the FSP has a certain level of competency and a reasonable degree of personal integrity. Conversations are held, goals are explored, and written recommendations are made before most clients embark on a business "relationship." As a general rule, the more understanding the FSP seems, the more likely they are to get the business. This represents the triumph of compassion over competency.

The day will come when some FSPs will be asked—or perhaps even forced—to leave the industry because of their lack of competence. That will be the day when the industry has fully reinvented itself as a true profession. That day is coming sooner than many people (including FSPs) think. Every so often, one comes across a story of a small-town doctor who flunked out of medical school but somehow managed to maintain the charade of a practicing professional in good standing in spite of incomplete training. When this happens, the imposter doctor is generally viewed with pity by his former patients, who had really come to like the guy, as he is made to endure public humiliation for having been a fraud throughout his career. Statements like "He's looked after my family for twenty-four years and it's a shame that he's being forced out of medicine" are not uncommon. That's because of the triumph of compassion over competency.

What if financial services were a profession like any other? Imagine if laws were passed informing FSPs that they have five years to get a CFP or they'll be prohibited from offering comprehensive financial advice? Think of the uproar. There would be FSPs managing over $100 million in assets saying, "Do you know who I am? I'm managing oodles of money and have been doing so for twenty-four years with hundreds of happy client relationships to show for it. My company *loves me*." The FSP's former clients would do media interviews to solicit support: "It's a shame Ernie has been forced out of offering financial advice. We had really come to like the guy." If they are worth anything, standards of competency have to be enforced uniformly and rigorously across the board. That's the way it works in professions.

The point is that FSP competency and the best interests of the consumer are paramount. There can be no doubt that competency combined with compassion is preferred, but given the choice, society has clearly chosen competency over compassion. In the professions, it is better to be a brilliant technician with horrible people skills than a horrible technician with brilliant people skills. Imagine a "nice gal" in medical school whom everyone liked immensely and who had the most pleasant bedside manner in the class. Even if her grades indicate otherwise, should her professors pass her just so that prospective patients could have access to her wonderful demeanour?

Many of the most valuable benefits that accrue to those who work with effective FSPs are emotional rather than logical or intellectual. How can anyone solve human problems if consideration is only given to non-human questions of dollars, tax rates, income levels, and pension plans?

On the surface, it seems we're making real progress toward creating a profession. Then again, there are a number of problems that continue to persist. Obviously, people who offer financial advice for a living will also need to offer evidence of some base level of intellectual ability. It should be equally obvious (although this is seldom mentioned) that that base level will need to be much higher than those required today. There's so much that FSPs don't know, largely because they haven't been taught. After all, so much of what FSPs convey to those they work with is predicated on what they were taught in the first place.

Have you ever heard of someone calling themselves a physician without first going through the rigours of medical school? As mentioned previously, the trend toward holistic advice remains strong. Over the generations, the competing silos of financial services have been responsible for the training and monitoring associated with their FSPs. In recent years, the industry has moved toward a model where an FSP is allowed access to products that might not have been part of their initial core competency.

Unfortunately, there are many who believe that "we can't get there from here" if we keep on training people to be specialists in one area and generalists in others. In all other fields of endeavour, the most common way of thinking seems to be the exact opposite. We teach people to be responsible generalists first and then, if there's an aptitude and an interest, we allow for greater specialization.

For instance, there are pros and cons to both mutual funds and segregated funds. Most FSPs are licenced to offer both. Not surprisingly, those licenced primarily through insurance companies tend to recommend segregated funds, while those licenced primarily through planning and advisory firms tend to recommend mutual funds. If FSPs are licenced to sell both and both have well-documented attributes, why does one distribution channel clearly favour one product while another channel clearly favours another?

The simple point here is that FSPs, being human, tend to stick with what they know, and what they know is generally synonymous with the products they were trained to offer advice on when they first entered the business. Intuitively, many people are concerned with the implications this has for independence. If FSPs were genuinely independent, why would their product licencing from years ago still have an impact on the recommendations they make today?

Before society can become competent in financial matters, our FSPs need to be competently taught. Otherwise, misinformation, no matter how well intentioned, can take hold and lead to poor planning decisions down the road. Most people giving financial advice today were not formally (i.e. academically) trained to do so.

Many of the most important theories about capital markets that are taught in first year MBA finance texts are mentioned only as passing footnotes in Canada's securities licencing texts. On top of that, there are a number of sound academic concepts that are never even mentioned in licencing textbooks for insurance.

This is not to suggest that most FSPs have anything less than the best intentions. Rather, many FSPs simply wish to convey what they have been taught to their clients as best they can. But if what the FSPs know comes largely from *licencing courses* that will allow them to *sell products* rather than *offer competent, professional advice*, there are bound to be biases and blind spots.

This gap in the preparation of FSPs could be revealing when considering their predisposition against certain concepts and products. Unwittingly, many FSPs have become co-opted as de facto sales agents for the products offered through their initial point of entry rather than true professionals who are inclined to survey the market for the most suitable products as dispassionate protectors of their clients' collective welfare.

When giving testimony before a court of law, witnesses are obligated to tell the truth, *the whole truth*, and nothing but the truth. Two out of three ain't bad. Some believe that by not telling FSPs the whole truth when training them to advise retail clients, we only hurt ourselves by doing a major disservice to the clients we aim to protect.

You'll Need a University Education

It's dangerous that newly minted FSPs can begin offering advice the day they get their licence to sell products. Other professions have various types of internship programs in which new practitioners can make the transition from learning the mechanics to gaining context by sitting in on meetings and ultimately gaining experience by offering advice in a controlled environment of mentorship.

Financial services is a major industry and there is a widely acknowledged demographic need for qualified financial advice as people age, estates grow, and lives become more complex. Furthermore, there's a crying need to ensure that FSPs can dovetail their generally excellent technical product knowledge with less clearly defined but equally important and personal client considerations. Our universities, with their multidisciplinary academic resources, are almost certainly far better equipped to teach these skills than disparate product-based licencing bodies. Specifically, since good advice is increasingly complex, multidisciplinary, and circumstantial, new FSPs could be taught using a case study approach, with a number of activities that simulate the real world experience.

The transition will take time, perhaps five or more years. Anyone who has not attained a CFP designation by 2012, for instance, could be politely asked to leave the business of offering comprehensive financial advice on the grounds that the industry will have transformed itself into a bona fide profession by that time and the CFP will be the certification of choice. No professional accreditation means no professional status.

Of course, people who are licenced to sell products could still do so. They would simply be excluded from being called "professionals" and be expected to forgo the rights and privileges associated with that status. Such people would simply be called what they are: salespeople.

With only a few post-secondary institutions in Canada offering a post-secondary (much less post-graduate) degree in financial planning, there's room for significant expansion. Students should be encouraged to pursue a CFP much as they might pursue an MBA: as a degree leading to a rewarding career in the financial services industry in advising retail clients. Many of the core professional financial planning courses would be identical to those offered in MBA programs, so schools offering these programs would be first on the list of where CFP programs could be established.

Presently, most of the FSPs offering advice to retail clients never went to university to get direct training as financial advisors. They simply decided at some point that they wanted to sell investment products or insurance and then got licenced to do so. The responsible ones continued to get more formal training. Today's CFPs are the effective founders of the world's newest profession. Of course, they're not the only people offering financial advice.

We Need CFPs

Society needs more comprehensive and professional advisors. The best of these are generally recognized as Certified Financial Planners (CFPs). Today's CFPs are people who trained in the multi-faceted field of financial planning. They have a disposition toward assisting people in making rational decisions with their personal finances.

We simply don't have enough CFPs. Let's look at this using the time-honoured metric of supply and demand. Judging by the enrollment numbers, you would think there was an absolute glut of CFPs already. This is untrue. And you'd think that this would be obvious to all those people who might be looking at this as a career choice, since CFP types are supposed to be "good with numbers." As is often the case, people seem to gravitate toward those career options that seem "sexy" or "trendy." Right now, the Chartered Financial Analyst (CFA) designation is hot, while the CFP designation toils in relative obscurity.

People who hold the CFP designation have an unfortunate problem. The work they do is relatively mundane, thankless, and lacking in glamour. Although there's less glamour in helping families with their budgeting, savings, income splitting, and asset allocation, these activities are priceless. There still aren't nearly enough CFP-designated advisors to go around.

Practical Professional Challenges

There's a lot that goes into creating a profession. Many of the biggest challenges discussed earlier are quite distinct from the academic requirements that might present themselves. Still, there are a number of technical questions that need to be consistently addressed in the academic training provided before financial advice becomes a truly professional calling. These are matters of preference, training, and disclosure. All need to be considered. There are dozens, but here are eight of the most notable:

1. Integrating Suitable Investments with Actual Goals

The cardinal rule of the investment industry is the primacy of suitability as expressed through the new client application form, also called a "know your client" form, or "KYC" for short. These forms are mandatory when opening new accounts and must be refreshed every two years or whenever there is a material change in the client's circumstances (career change, physical move, change in marital status, etc.), but KYCs don't ask clients to document their life goals.

The objective "to retire at age sixty-five in 2017 with no debts and a retirement income that is equivalent to at least two-thirds of what I averaged in my last five years on the job and lasting for as along as I live," is seldom found anywhere on a KYC. This in spite of the fact that such a sentence would demonstrate that the client has succinctly defined financial independence in personal, measurable, and practical terms. It seems logical to make FSPs responsible for offering advice within that kind of context. We're simply dealing with an industry that is defined and regulated by product choices, not the lifestyle choices that are made as a result of those product choices.

If financial services is to redefine itself as a profession of our times, it had better be able to respond to the wants and needs of the people it hopes to serve. To that end, there needs to be a clearer integration of superficial numeric objectives with more meaningful lifestyle objectives. There might even be a continuum for trade-offs if the entire list of client objectives becomes unattainable. What could be more professional than to ask a client to prioritize her personal objectives, especially if there is professional liability associated with falling short?

2. Fee Impact on Calculations

Many people believe that true professionals need not only justify their fees but also to account for them when called upon to do so. What rate(s) of return should be used in doing financial independence calculations? Popular choices include:

- a "best guess" of how that asset class might perform over time
- historical return data for the asset classes used
- historical average return data for mutual funds in the asset classes used
- top quartile average return data for mutual funds in the asset classes used

As a simple illustration, let's say someone has a portfolio invested 100% in Canadian stocks. What rate of return should that person expect? Would it help to plan based on different assumptions for one asset class? Also, is it reasonable to use an expected rate of return that is higher if fees are charged outside the account rather than against the portfolio's return (i.e. through the mutual fund's MER)? If the expected return for the asset class is 5% above inflation and the FSP charges a 1% fee on top, should the sensitivity to the fee be used in the illustration and assumptions?

3. Return Expectations

In the 1990s, there were some unscrupulous FSPs who were

telling their clients they should plan to get long-term returns in the neighbourhood of 15% annually. Some actually used this as a client-acquisition strategy. After all, they said, that's what people had been getting for the past three to five years. Why not extrapolate that return further?

The trouble is the presumption that the long-term future will resemble the short-term past. Unfortunately, uncommonly good periods for capital markets are frequently followed by uncommonly bad periods, and vice versa. For instance, 2001 to 2002 was horrible, but 2003 to 2005 was great. Over any long-term time frame, the expected outcome for any given asset class is nowhere near as high as has been projected by some charlatan FSPs. One element of time diversification is that long-term returns tend to "regress to the mean," meaning they trend toward their historical long-term average.

Many of the most highly respected students of capital markets, including Dr. Jeremy Siegel of the Wharton business school at the University of Pennsylvania, expect long-term equity returns to come in at the 5% to 6% range for the foreseeable future. That's a far cry from 10% or more that many FSPs often assume when doing financial independence modelling for clients. Everyone should plan for retirement based on real return: the return above inflation. After all, you'll be living your retirement (and paying for it) in inflation-adjusted dollars, not today's dollars.

4. Variability of Returns

The first cousin of time diversification is variability of returns. When writing investment policy statements and doing planning projections, there is a debate that rages between two competing risk measurement models. The essence of the question is, "How do you define risk?" There are two parts to this question. The first concerns the debate between probabilistic versus unvarying rate illustrations and the second the use of either mean variance or semi-variance models.

At present, virtually all illustrations done by FSPs involve assumptions that include a single unvarying rate of return based on some assumed average. But markets are highly volatile, so the generated results may deviate substantially from actual experience. As a result, probabilistic modelling offers far more meaningful data for financial decision-making by allowing for a range of possible outcomes.

5. Applying the Rules

Like so many things in life, offering financial advice is sometimes distilled down to a number of trite little truisms. "Pay yourself first" and "buy low, sell high" are among the most popular. The industry has also developed a few simple principles that assist people in making informed (and hopefully rational) decisions. Your mortgage payments should not exceed 30% of your take-home pay, for instance. Everywhere you turn, there are rules of thumb.

Most people will have heard of the famous "rule of 72" whereby the return you get on an investment divided into the number 72 generates a reasonable approximation of how long it will take to double your money. For instance, a 6% return will double your portfolio in about twelve years, whereas an 8% return will allow you to double it in about nine years. Over the course of a working lifetime, a person might be able to get in an extra double as a result and have a portfolio that's twice as large due to the ability to withstand the risk associated with the additional 2% in annual returns.

Of course, the rule of 72 works in reverse with inflation too. If inflation runs at about 2% a year, as it has for over a decade, your purchasing power is cut in half after about thirty-six years. What is far worse, if inflation runs at 4% a year (which has been the approximate level over the past half-century), then purchasing power is cut in half in only eighteen years or so. People on a fixed income should be very concerned about inflation rates.

But here's a little gem of a "rule" that most FSPs and consumers are not aware of: it's called the "rule of 40" and it has to do with that very important factor all investors should be concerned about, namely, costs. Here's how the calculations work: Start with the number 40 and divide your portfolio's MER into it. The result will produce the approximate number of years it takes your expenses to erode one-third of your investment value. A total cost of 1.5% erodes one-third of your portfolio value in 26.67 years; a cost of 2% erodes one-third in 20 years; a cost of 2.5% erodes one-third in 16 years; and a cost of 3% erodes one-third of your portfolio's value in 13.33 years. Again, all of these numbers are just rough approximations, but they serve as useful guideposts nonetheless.

Virtually everyone in the financial services industry believes we are heading into a "low return environment" where the double-digit returns of the past will not be seen again over a substantial time frame. If the consensus of experts is correct, costs will surely matter more than ever before. How many FSPs make this simple but vital point to their clients?

Along with all these rules, there are many myths that exist in the financial services industry. One of the most pervasive myths is that costs are "unimportant" and that only the total return net of costs matters. If only it were that easy. Research the world over has shown that cost is the most reliable predictor of performance—as a negative indicator. In other words, the higher the cost, the less well investors do. William F. Sharpe has explained this point eloquently in a paper entitled "The Arithmetic of Active Management."

6. "Risk" Disclosures

Many FSPs encourage investor clients to take "a long-term view." Clients, in turn, often ask their advisors how long "the long term" really is. There's no simple answer. The short answer, however, is that risk (also called "variability" or "standard deviation") goes down over time. There's a saying in the portfolio management business that states returns are unknowable in the short term, but in the long term, they are virtually inevitable.

The most striking observation most people take away from the Andex Risk/Return Analysis is that the client experience can be extreme over short time frames but is relatively stable over long ones. Over one and three year time frames, for instance, an investor might experience extreme highs and lows. Over five and ten year time frames, the highs and lows are less extreme. Once the time frame extends beyond twenty years, however, the difference between a "best case" and a "worst case" scenario is relatively small.

2005 Andex Risk/Return Analysis
January 1, 1950 - June 30, 2005

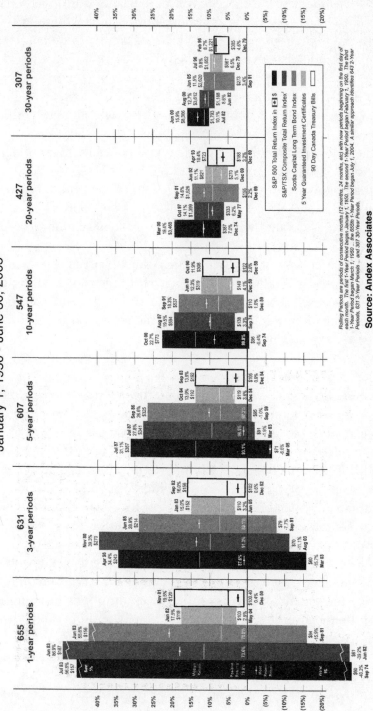

Rolling Periods are periods of consecutive months (12 months, 24 months, etc) with new periods beginning on the first day of each month. The first 1-Year Period began January 1, 1950. The second 1-Year Period began February 1, 1950. The third 1-Year Period began March 1, 1950 ... the 655th 1-Year Period began July 1, 2004. A similar approach identifies 643 2-Year Periods, 631 3-Year Periods ... and 307 30-Year Periods.

Source: Andex Associates

S&P 500 Total Return Index in $

S&P/TSX Composite Total Return Index[1]

Scotia Capital Long Term Bond Index

5 Year Guaranteed Investment Certificates

90 Day Canada Treasury Bills

Investment risk exists over all time frames but depends largely on the time period in question. Furthermore, there are many definitions of "risk," some of which are highly personal, circumstantial, and subjective. These include:

• the risk of outliving your savings
• the risk of not being able to emotionally tolerate market fluctuation
• the risk of not having the capacity to financially tolerate fluctuation
• the risk associated with underdiversification and unreasonable expectations
• the risk associated with poor or non-existent planning

A useful way of looking at the Andex chart is to match your current asset allocation with your current time frame. Most people have extremely short risk thresholds and so should consider an asset allocation that is similar to the pie chart that minimizes risk over a one-year time frame.

7. Reasonable Assumptions

Simple logic demonstrates that the average return for any investment is likely to be the return of the benchmark minus the investment's cost. For example, if the Canadian stock market returned 10.6% while a mutual fund investing in that market has an MER of 2.6%, the expected long-term return is 8.0%. Over the course of twenty or more years, a difference of 2% or more is gargantuan. The need for meaningful, professional disclosure is evident here. Many FSPs suggest they can "outperform" their peers simply by using distorted assumptions in their planning.

FSPs are generally interested in helping clients get a handle on how much money will be required to maintain a certain quality of life in retirement. Many use different assumptions in doing their own financial independence calculations simply because there is no accepted standard regarding what those numbers should be.

It is reasonable to believe that past history is as good a guide as any in making projections about the future. However, this is the point where many FSPs start to use some discretion. They do this especially where active management is concerned. Specifically, they often inflate the numbers by some amount under the pretense that active management will allow their clients to "beat" the relevant benchmark(s). This is almost certainly incorrect. The converse is far more likely to be true. According to Sharpe, the converse is absolutely certain, on average.

8. Process, Not Product

Will advisory firms ever get their story straight? They tell their FSPs that process is more important than products, but their actions tell a different story. Many even run professional development sessions where they go on and on about the importance of having a process for making investment recommendations. They talk about making recommendations using a consistent, repeatable, and unambiguous process which leads to a more scientific asset allocation that is implemented through an investment policy statement (IPS). The only problem is that sometimes when there are excellent products that use this process, they never make it to the approved list for reasons that have more to do with corporate imperatives than corporate consistency.

Virtually all advisory firms are owned by either banks or mutual fund companies. These institutions make a large portion of their profits by charging fees for picking stocks. No matter how good any asset allocation process, if it involves the repudiation of the corporate parent's core value proposition, the story usually changes. Specifically, if corporate bosses insist that FSPs are better off using wrap accounts (customized portfolios featuring asset mix, reporting, security selection, and so forth, "wrapped" into one product) to calibrate client-specific and risk-adjusted returns, why should they care if products use active investment products, passive investment products, or both, so long as the process is consistent and defensible?

And yet it seems that they care very much. Corporate decision-makers have gone so for as to establish points programs for product sales with quadruple points for these process-driven products. When pressed for a reason, the quadruple weighting is justified in terms of offering a positive incentive for advisors who make the transition from a more transaction-oriented practice to a more process-driven relationship model. That would be fine if it ended there. How do corporate bosses explain the non-approval of certain products that use that same process, but with indexes making up a substantial portion of the asset pools?

It seems that advisory firms, banks, and mutual fund companies want it both ways. They go on about process, as though it were the be all and end all, and then refuse even to acknowledge certain products that use those same processes. Things that are important should never be at the mercy of things that are unimportant.

Banks and fund companies make money by managing assets for a fee, among other things. They might also charge fees for writing IPSs, portfolio optimization, tax integration, consolidated reporting, and the like. If this is only about the process that wrap accounts bring to the table, why should the use of active or passive management make one iota of difference if the process is identical?

The financial services industry is good at offering incentives to FSPs to do certain things without ever rationalizing its own inconsistencies. Perhaps STANDUP FSPs could write to the big national firms to ask them to offer quadruple points on index-based wrap accounts too. After all, it's all about process. I wrote an article about this entitled "To Sell or Advise" for the *National Post* a while back. Many consumers contacted me to thank me after it appeared, but none of the national advisory firms contacted me to thank me for pointing out the inconsistency of their corporate messages and policies.

If a firm has a choice between championing a SPANDEX FSP who adds to corporate profits and a STANDUP FSP who looks out for clients, a process will be designed to clearly benefit the former. And then the company will go on and on about how committed it is to "raising the bar" of financial advice. Some people will actually believe them. Of course, these people will deny this vigourously and it's one person's perspective versus another's. Still, actions speak louder than words, and I have seen and heard of many corporate programs that offer benefits for sales and exponential benefits for the sale—sorry, *the professional recommendation*—of preferred (read: more profitable) products. Meanwhile, I've never seen programs that offer FSPs benefits if they use investment policy statements, write comprehensive financial plans, use a letter of engagement, make written compensation disclosure, or do any of a number of other things that are generally considered part and parcel of professional behaviour.

What Next?

As the consensus emerges on how the financial services industry will evolve over time, the next questions revolve around what needs to be done to ensure an honourable and responsible transition. What remains to be decided is how and when this change is going to occur. If everyone understands where we are and agrees on where we're going, then surely the next question must be how to get there from here.

What we're dealing with right now is a kind of "conspiracy of the uninformed" where many people who, in spite of their good intentions, aren't even understanding the true nature of the problem.

Having come this far, it seems that the best way to understand the "disconnect" between what many FSPs purport to be (professionals) and what they often are (sales representatives) is to look not only at what they are taught but also at how they are taught. A vital point of consideration might involve the research and opinions surrounding both active management and passive management.

Inefficient Markets

If a man is offered a fact which goes against his instincts, he will scruti-nize it closely, and unless the evidence is overwhelming, he will refuse to believe it. If, on the other hand, he is offered something which affords a reason for acting in accordance to his instincts, he will accept it even on the slightest evidence.

—Bertrand Russell

Having already discussed the mindset of those who work in the business of picking stocks, it should be obvious that the dominant paradigm of the financial services industry is that stock picking is not only valuable but entirely rational. As such, I believe it is safe to say that most industry commentators would agree that the vast majority of all FSPs believe stock picking can be practiced in a manner that is likely to add value more often than not over long time frames. The notion here is to "outperform" a benchmark through shrewdness, intelligent analysis, and a breadth and depth of insight that most individuals could never muster on their own. Not surprisingly, a substantial percentage of individual consumers believe this too. This is presumably why many people use FSPs in the first place.

The idea behind market inefficiency is that a person with rea-sonable intelligence and diligence can consistently beat the con-sensus view after accounting for costs. People will gladly pay someone who is thought to be an above average stock picker because no one wants to settle for average when it comes to invest-ment decision-making.

As a result of this perspective, most FSPs recommend that their clients use active management as the predominant and often exclusive way of managing money. They engage in fundamental and technical analysis, do copious amounts of due diligence, and generally think of a number of ingenious ways to outsmart their peers in an attempt to get a leg up in determining how much stocks will move, when they will move, the direction they will move, and the reasons behind the move. All these people have to do to make money is figure out where the crowd went wrong and then make buy-and-sell decisions to exploit the collective inaccuracy of the market as a whole.

The world is full of legendary stories of investors who have outperformed their benchmarks (often by wide margins) and over long time frames. Names like Warren Buffett, Peter Lynch, and Sir John Templeton are well known even to people who have never invested a dime in their entire life. Given the fantastic returns achieved by these individuals, it should come as no surprise that active management enjoys such a dominant position in the world of finance. Whether working with a stockbroker who picks stocks on behalf of a client or with mutual fund managers who do the same, given a specific mandate, the lion's share of consumers have come to share the view taken by the lion's share of industry players.

The same holds for FSPs. The majority of FSPs are proponents of active management. This is true whether they are licenced to sell mutual funds, a wide range of securities or insurance products. It is true whether the FSP in question has a designation or not. It is true whether that FSP works for a large national institution or a small mom-and-pop shop. It is true whether that FSP is fee based or commission based. In short, no matter how you segment the industry, there is a clear preference among FSPs of all shapes and sizes for active management.

The view within the industry that active management is the way to go is so pervasive that I do not believe most FSPs could do a reputable job of explaining the differences between active and passive management if their lives depended on it. But why bother being able to reliably portray one way of doing things if you know all there is to know about the other way and you are convinced that yours is the right way? Indeed. Some companies have been known to say things like:

We strongly believe consistent outperformance will result from extensive fundamental research on the equity side.

You need to have a consistency of approach. We are very focused on the portfolio construction process to ensure we have the right risk controls in place. We feel strongly this philosophy will lead to superior risk-adjusted returns with the consistency and the stability to add value over a long period.

Can't you just feel the conviction? The thing about conviction, though, is that it can be rational and based on fact, or it can be hair-brained. For most people, what comes across is the strong emotional connection that whatever these people are doing, gosh darn it, they sure believe that it works. What if the conviction were there, but the rationale was, well, a little "off"? What if you met a group of experts who said: "We strongly believe that the abominable snowman will be captured in the near future due to state-of-the-art satellite surveillance, advanced anthropological intelligence, and superior search and rescue capacity."

Please forgive the silliness of the example. If you just listened to the conviction of what was being said and ignored the content, you'd swear the person doing the talking was a credible, professional practitioner in their field. A good number of industry participants have that kind of conviction when it comes to market inefficiency. Of course, conviction and proof are different things. Unfortunately, when people are ill-equipped to discern between real insight and practitioner sleight-of-hand, conviction might be the only thing a person has to go by.

In law, it is considered prudent to anticipate the other party's line of argument before heading to a trial. That way, you'll have at least some rebuttals ready when the standard and more easily anticipated counterarguments are made. That doesn't seem to happen with financial advice.

My experience is that most FSPs would simply invite would-be clients to go elsewhere if they wished to use a passive approach and passive products. "That's not what I do" is a typical response. Would-be clients quickly come to recognize that "doing it the FSP's way" is a de facto price of admission. Irrespective of what they might think or want, consumers have been socialized to equate advice with active management. Most product manufacturers, distributors, and members of the media are happy to support this connection. To this day, I have only encountered two product manufacturers that pay a trailing commission on a passive product.

Accepting that many observers feel that embedded compensation needs to go, there is still an unevenness to the playing field. There are hundreds, if not thousands of actively managed products that feature embedded compensation for FSPs. A level playing field in this case means that products should have an "all or none" approach to embedded compensation. Where are all the embedded compensation passive products? To my mind, the best response is to eliminate all embedded compensation. The second best is to include embedded compensation for all passive products. It seems the corporate elements within the industry really don't want FSPs or consumers making apples-to-apples comparisons.

You'll note that this is by far the shortest chapter in the book. There are two reasons for this. First, there are already hundreds of books available about how to pick stocks, how other experts pick stocks, and why people should engage in picking stocks. There have been a large number of books about picking funds over the years too. I don't want to reinvent the wheel. If you want to learn more about stock picking, I recommend you pick up one or more of the many books already published on the subject.

The second reason for brevity is balance. By adding a chapter about active management, I'm offering a counterpoint to an industry that simply and utterly refuses to reciprocate. Short as this chapter is, it offers more content about active management than is found in the Canadian Securities Course (CSC) textbook about passive management—and the CSC is the course that all brokerage-based FSPs study before offering advice. Besides, I'm writing for a wide and disparate audience. Licencing textbooks are the core course material for all newly minted FSPs.

Efficient Markets

Great spirits have always encountered violent opposition from mediocre minds.

— Albert Einstein

Here's a little game to try whenever you've got a bunch of people together. It's a variation on a game I suspect virtually everyone has played. Get a big container and fill it with jelly beans or something and count them as you fill it. Then, offer it as a prize to the person who's estimate is the closest to the actual number of beans in the jar. Be sure to have everyone write down their guesses privately and to submit them to a central scorekeeper. Give the jar to the winner.

Now you can perform a little experiment once everyone has gone home. Let's call this game "none of us is reliably smarter than all of us." Simply add up the numbers guessed and divide by the number of guessers. Virtually every time this experiment is performed, there are only one or two people whose guess is closer to the actual number than the weighted average guess. In other words, the collected wisdom of a large number of decision-makers often leads to a consensus opinion that is startlingly close to the actual number—and is very difficult to top.

While there may always be a handful of individuals who are closer to the actual number than the consensus, it would seldom be the same person who pulls it off. Determining the number of jelly beans in a jar is akin to coming up with an assessment of a company's most appropriate stock price. People who believe that there are superior stock pickers out there feel it is reasonable to presume that someone's prowess at counting jelly beans might also be consistently more accurate than that of a large group.

The large majority of stakeholders (including most FSPs) have come to believe that people can predict how current events can lead to making insightful calls on the impact on security prices. This kind of information and all associated market gyrations are, by definition, unknowable in advance. Random events simply cannot be reliably predicted and exploited. Investing is about markets working properly, whereas stock picking is akin to speculation based on markets not working properly. Making decisions to buy and sell based on random events is speculation masquerading as rational decision-making. The expected return of speculation before costs is zero. Since speculation has an associated cost, the expected net return is actually negative.

The Efficient Market Hypothesis

In the 1960s, a graduate student at the University of Chicago named Eugene Fama put forward the efficient market hypothesis (EMH). EMH has three variations (based on the availability of information) and generally suggests that it is exceedingly difficult for active managers to add value in the long run after fees are taken into account because the movement of stock prices cannot be predicted.

Since there is no way to definitively prove or disprove market efficiency or inefficiency, over forty years have gone by without a resolution to this debate. I use the word *debate* loosely here. Many people in academia have had many a heated discussion about EMH. There's probably not a single finance student in the western hemisphere who hasn't learned about it.

In the last chapter, I mentioned that most FSPs are not able to reliably explain market efficiency. This is probably because they were never taught EMH. Given that most FSPs know essentially nothing about EMH, just how likely is it that they will be able to reliably advise their clients about the pros and cons of both the active and passive approaches (e.g. indexing)?

As with the belief in the existence of God, different people may be pursuaded or dissuaded by different things. Nonetheless, Dr. Fama (now a world-renowned professor in finance) has made a lasting impact in his field. Virtually everyone in the industry expects him to win a Nobel Prize in Economics in the near future for his contributions to finance.

The view here is that a mature stock market is highly "efficient" and that it is unlikely one could make abnormal profits by using all available information regarding buy-and-sell decisions. This is because everyone has the same information at the same time and it is impossible for any one manager to consistently act on the information before everyone else does. Some managers will beat their index some of the time, most managers will be able to act on inefficient information about half of the time, but all managers will incur costs in excess of indexing all of the time. Put another way, it's impossible for any one manager to *consistently* beat the market by digesting financial information and acting on it. In the past decade, exchange traded funds (ETFs) have emerged as a new type of product with a mandate to offer tax-effective access to benchmarks at a significantly reduced cost.

It follows that most pension fund managers, mutual fund managers, and discretionary brokers do not add value through security selection in their well-intentioned work. Ironically, their hyper-competitiveness against one another only ensures greater efficiency of the market. In highly efficient markets, active managers generate returns that exceed a benchmark only by taking on a similarly high level of risk relative to that benchmark.

Economists have a term that explains the added benefit of each additional unit of a product or service: "marginal utility." If you have 50 analysts, markets might be said to be somewhat efficient. If you have 500 analysts, markets might be said to be highly efficient. If you have 5,000 (and the world has far more than 5,000 analysts and researchers), you've probably moved to the point where each additional participant actually does more harm than good. Most people don't suggest capital markets are totally efficient. However, it is probably fair to say that there's a consensus among the world's leading academics that markets are "sufficiently efficient" and that additional attempts to exploit whatever inefficiencies might remain are largely a waste of time and money.

The industry mentality is that it makes sense to *try* to beat the market. In spite of this, index-based products in general and ETFs in particular have been steadily gaining market share over the past decade or so. I asked Howard Atkinson, Head of Business Development at Barclay's (the world's foremost ETF manufacturer) to provide his thoughts on the changing landscape and the recent market share gains made by ETFs. Here's what he had to say:

Largely due to the push by enlightened investment advisors who seek to offer better portfolio solutions to their clients, global exchange traded fund assets have risen from U.S. $38 billion in 1999 to over U.S. $400 billion today, and are forecasted to reach U.S. $1 trillion by 2010.

Note that Atkinson attributes the growth in ETF assets to their acceptance by "enlightened" (read: STANDUP) advisors. This is largely a phenomenon where FSPs are recommending ETFs to clients, not one where clients are demanding them from their FSPs. The best FSPs do what is right for their clients in spite of what their peers, employers, or previous product suppliers might want them to do. Swimming against the tide is seldom easy, so credit ought to be given where credit is due.

Market Efficiency and Alchemy

Years ago, I was having a conversation with an industry CEO about the efficiency of capital markets. I mentioned that I believed the balance (not the totality) of empirical evidence shows that markets are highly efficient. To my mind, "efficient" means "correct enough that it is difficult to reliably exploit any mispricings." He said that although he did not agree with my assessment overall, he did concede that the U.S. market is indeed efficient. I was surprised. After all, capital markets might be said to run along a continuum of efficiency where the most developed are the most efficient and the least developed the least efficient. As such, if there can be only one efficient market in the world, it would surely be the U.S. market. Of course, because the company he represented was a vertically integrated advisory firm where the parent company manufactures actively managed mutual funds, he also acknowledged that his company *would never admit this publicly*. His company doesn't even offer passive U.S. equity product options.

That conversation stuck with me. How many other senior management types in Corporate Canada believe that at least some of the world's markets are efficient? Why don't they say so in public? Are they embarrassed? Didn't they know that others would think they are hypocrites?

Many believe that "groupthink" is a powerful motivator of what is said and done in the world in general and the financial services industry in particular. Even as firms try to make a big deal of their "independent thinking," most tend to act in a manner that doesn't stray too far from the path of convention. How much longer can this go on? If the weight of the majority of empirical evidence seems to favour the efficient market view, why have opinions have been slow to shift? Indeed, is market efficiency a matter of fact or opinion? After all, many people continued to think the world was flat even after Magellan circumnavigated the globe, but that was during a time of deference to authority and trust in large institutions. We're not sailing toward the edge of the earth anymore—or are we?

Today's active managers (and the people who share their perspective) are much like modern-day alchemists: they are trying earnestly to do something that, based on past history, can't reliably be done. In spite of this, they soldier on, refusing to admit the preponderence of past failures.

Back in 2004, Standard & Poor's Index Versus Active (SPIVA) scorecard for indices was developed and released in opposition to actively managed mutual funds. Unlike many other reports, it was designed to be more empirically accurate, since it corrected for survivorship bias (when companies close funds with poor performance and try to pretend they never existed). Their research showed both equal and asset-weighted peer averages.

At the time of this book's printing, the most recently available SPIVA report was for March 31, 2006. It is generally accepted that the longer the time period chosen, the more accurate the data. The longest time period that was tested was the five-year period ending on March 31, 2006, and over that period, the S&P 500 had beaten 67.1% of all available large cap equity funds that were benchmarked against it. Similarly, and over the same period, the S&P MidCap 400 outperformed 87.3% of all mid cap funds and the S&P SmallCap 600 outperformed 78.7% of all small cap funds.

Over long time frames, "beating the market" becomes a finger trap sort of exercise. You've probably seen those little finger traps that can be placed on two opposing digits; the harder you try to get out, the more difficult it becomes.

Capital markets might be like that too. Analysts and money managers are always trying to outwit one another in an attempt to exploit whatever mispricings exist. As some people see it, the problem is that the more they do to exploit mispricings, the less likely it is that those mispricings will exist over time, making the "outwitting" part increasingly improbable.

If markets do a reasonably precise job of setting prices that accurately reflect all available information about any given security at any given point in time, then those prices are likely to be pretty accurate. Furthermore, since inaccuracies are just as likely to be positive as negative, it might be futile to attempt exploitation, since the mispricing is equally likely to show up in either direction.

If, for instance, markets are 85% "correct" (i.e. efficient), then a stock that trades for $10 might not actually be worth $10. It could be worth as little as $8.50 or as much as $11.50. But since no one can say for sure which side to err on, the "consensus best guess" of $10 is about as fair a proxy for fair market value that you will find anywhere. Making money by picking stocks usually requires that both the degree and the direction of any mispricing be reliably quantified.

Since there's a lot of money to be made in managing other people's money, the industry naturally attracts a lot of bright, hardworking, and insightful people. These highly motivated people are constantly competing with one another to determine which stocks are mispriced, by how much, and in which direction. The more they compete, the more they are right in identifying mispricings. The more they identify them, the more they can exploit them. The more they exploit them, however, the less likely it is that those mispricings will persist.

Note that the number of indexers is immaterial in this line of thinking. Market efficiency goes up as the number of active mangers goes up. Good stock picking exploits mispricings out of existence. Decades ago, there were a number of people who seemed to be able to produce index-beating performance numbers by picking stocks. Today, there seem to be relatively few people who can do it. Why? Perhaps it's because many years ago, markets were less efficient.

Let's say markets were only 75% efficient back then. If that's true, it stands to reason that intelligent and highly motivated people might be able to "add value" by exploiting other people's lack of meaningful information or incisive analysis. Of course, if this is true and trends continue, one could argue that markets will be 95% efficient one day. However much sense active management once made, it makes less sense today, and is likely to make even less sense still in the future.

For example, the Templeton Growth Fund is over fifty years old and has a track record that resoundingly beats its usual benchmark (MSCI EAFE) over that time period. Still, if one looks at the most recent twenty-year period, the index beats Templeton. Perhaps the new entrants have combined to make the market more efficient. It stands to reason that, directionally at least, more market participants means greater market efficiency. Perhaps Templeton built up a massive lead in the early years when markets were less efficient and has been in give back mode ever since.

Where's Alpha?

You've probably come across the famous "Where's Waldo?" books where people look at complex illustrations to try to see if a character named Waldo can be found. The corporate stock-picking industry plays a version of this little game, except with a twist: People in the industry are constantly on the lookout for "Alpha," the active management equivalent of Waldo.

In short, Alpha is the extent that performance above a certain benchmark can be attributed to superior security selection. Finding Alpha is all about beating the market and is portrayed by industry types as being akin to finding the Holy Grail. There's only one problem: Alpha is sort of like the Loch Ness monster. There have been alleged sightings, but no one has been able to definitively prove that Alpha really exists. People who think they've seen Alpha, typically end up admitting that they merely ran into his evil twin, "Randomness."

Sighting skills used in this game actually seem to weaken over time. The longer one plays the game, the worse one gets. Over a one-year period, people are tripping over all the Alpha that's out there. Over three to five years, Alpha becomes a little harder to find. Over ten years, finding Alpha becomes downright difficult. Over more than twenty years, it becomes doubtful that Alpha even exists. Like capturing a yeti in a blinding snowstorm, capturing long-term Alpha is virtually impossible task.

The thing about stock market efficiency is that it's self-correcting. Looking for exploitable market inefficiencies involves looking for ways to exploit market mispricings. The problem is that as soon as the inefficiency is found, it is exploited mercilessly until it no longer exists. In other words, the expedition team effectively causes the thing they are looking for to disappear *as a direct consequence of their looking so hard*.

Are you confused yet? So are the people who could have sworn they saw Alpha just recently. Let's say someone discovers that stocks with a year-end from January 1 to June 30 consistently outperform stocks with a year-end from July 1 to December 31. As soon as the discovery becomes known and accepted, the price of the stocks with the early year-end will go up and the price for the stocks with the late year-end will go down until the current prices of both sets of stocks fairly and accurately reflect the new information. Even if you could have beaten the market by buying stocks with an early year-end yesterday, that little trick won't work today.

Independent research dramatically shows that the likelihood of any investment manager beating their index continually decreases with time. The reason for this is the long-term drag on performance caused by management fees and expenses. If the odds are 48% or 49% in your favour that you'll win any "Where's Alpha?" contest in the short run, then it becomes nearly certain that you will lose the contest if you play long enough. It's a simple matter of probability. Active managers would never admit to their collective poor track record. It's far more profitable to round up creditors with an appetite for the bragging rights associated with "bagging the big one." It leads to more fees to be paid to the search party.

What He Said

Don't take my word (or anyone else's) regarding market efficiency. Some people are just more eloquent and credible than others. When the topic of the efficiency of capital markets comes up, there are a number of people who are far more learned and reputable than most Bay Street or Wall Street analysts ever were. Many of them have Nobel Prizes to show for their work, while others are revered as investment geniuses for their past performances. Some of the most intelligent and reputable people in finance know that if there is one simple truth, it is this: you can't reliably beat the market unless you take on more risk than the market. Let's look at a number of quotations from the following esteemed people. You be the judge.

William F. Sharpe won the Nobel Prize in Economics in 1990 for his work on the capital asset pricing model (CAPM). In "The Parable of Money Managers," he asks: "Why pay people to gamble with your money?"[1] The question is rhetorical and the answer is obvious. More on this later.

One of the most acclaimed economists of our time is Paul Samuelson, who won the Nobel Prize in Economics in 1970. Here's what Samuelson has to say about the subject:

Ten thousand money managers all look equally good or bad. Each expects to do 3% better than the mob. Each has put together a convincing story. After the fact, hardly 10 out of 10,000 perform in a way that convinces an experienced student of inductive evidence that a long-term edge over indexing is likely... It may be the better part of wisdom to forsake searching for needles that are so very small in haystacks that are so very large.[2]

Samuelson has also been quoted as saying, "Investing should be dull, like watching paint dry or grass grow. If you want excitement, take $800 and go to Las Vegas. It is not easy to get rich in Las Vegas, at Churchill Downs, or at the local Merrill Lynch office."

Of course, these are just academics. What do they know about the real world of investing? It's been said that those who suggest something can't be done should stay out of the way of those who are doing it. If it is all but mathematically impossible to beat the market, then why are there conspicuous examples of people who beat it? What about people like Peter Lynch and Warren Buffett? It turns out that even "exceptional" investors have a healthy dose of humility in their work.

Considered by some to be the greatest stock picker of all time, Lynch had the unique opportunity to select and train his own successor—and the guy he chose couldn't beat the market. So, if the "greatest stock picker in history" couldn't pick a good stock picker, what makes people think a less accomplished person can do it? In an interview with *Barron's* magazine in 1990, Lynch was quoted as saying, "Most investors would be better off in an index fund."[3]

Finally, let's see what the Oracle of Omaha has to say. Warren Buffett is perhaps the most revered man in investing today, given his long and laudable track record. Here's what he had to say in his 2004 Annual Report at Berkshire Hathaway:

> Over the past 35 years, American business has delivered terrific results. It should therefore have been easy for investors to earn juicy returns: All they had to do was piggyback Corporate America in a diversified, low-expense way. An index fund that they never touched would have done the job. Instead, many investors have had experiences ranging from mediocre to disastrous.

Going back a little further, in a 1996 letter to shareholders, he wrote:

> Most investors, both institutional and individual, will find that the best way to own common stocks is through an index fund that charges minimal fees. Those following this path are sure to beat the net results (after fees and expenses) delivered by a great majority of investment professionals.

Let's assume that "most" (Lynch) and "the great majority" (Buffett) of any group is at least 50% + 1. At that rate, over half of all participants should use an indexing strategy. Unfortunately, overconfidence rears its ugly head and *most people* (both retail and institutional investors as well as virtually all FSPs) think that Lynch and Buffett are referring to someone other than themselves. Well over 50% of the population consider themselves to be above-average drivers, too, but we all know that it is impossible for more than 50% to actually be above average. Meanwhile, the percentage of all retail assets is invested in passive strategies in Canada is still in single-digit territory.

Note also that Buffet uses the phrase "investment professionals." But if FSPs are so professional and the evidence in favour of a passive approach is so strong, then why do almost all of them recommend an active approach? Do you think it might be possible that things such as corporate culture, embedded commissions, corprate point programs, and the like might be clouding their ability to think and advise clearly?

The Yard Sale

Many people take what I'll call a "modified Bob Barker" approach to asset pricing: to them, the price is (more or less) right.

Market efficiency is predicated on lots of smart, self-interested people making decisions based on all available information. As they say, knowledge is power. It doesn't take much for "the market" (any market) to find an equilibrium. Let's say you're having a yard sale and one of the items you're selling is an old table that's been in the family for as long as anyone can remember. It's been in a corner in your basement for forty years and the time has come to make some space. You have no idea what it's worth, so you put a price tag of $50 on it in the hope that someone will actually pay that much.

After a while, a guy shows up, introduces himself as an antique dealer, and asks about the table. He offers you $50 and you feel pretty good about yourself. Just as you're about to seal the deal, another antique dealer comes skidding to a halt outside your driveway. "Wait, wait... don't sell it!" she yells. You look perplexed, but the antique dealer beside you looks downright annoyed. The lady dealer jogs over, takes a quick look at the table, and instantly recognizes it as a genuine, mint condition 1812 Laura Secord kitchen table.

"I'll offer you a thousand dollars," says the lady, not even knowing who the person beside you is.

"Two thousand," says the first dealer.

"Three thousand," says the newcomer.

"Four thousand," says the guy who was eagerly offering $50 only a minute before.

This goes on until one of them offers $6,500 and the bidding war stops. At that point, you know that no matter how many more antique dealers are driving down your street that day, your table is probably worth something like $6,500. Why?

Information has a way of helping markets find their equilibrium. The two antique dealers obviously knew more about the value of the table than you ever did. In fact, you would have been happy to accept $50 just to get rid of it that morning. The first dealer knew what the true value was, but since you didn't, he wasn't about to pay a dollar more than he had to. Why would he? Paying more to you would mean less profit for him. Everything changed when a second person came along who also knew the true value of the table. The bidding war was swift and purposeful.

In this scenario, both dealers knew a table like this might fetch between $6,000 and $8,000 at a proper auction. Given the excellent condition of the table, the bidding went above the low end of the range of the resale price. Each had to leave at least a little room for profit and each had a pretty good idea of how much other bidders would pay. Any other reputable dealer would have come to the same conclusion. Other dealers may have come along, but some would not have been willing to pay even $6,500. Perhaps a few aggressive ones might have bid the price up to almost $7,000. The point is that the final price was a pretty fair price. In its present state, that table may not have been worth *exactly* $6,500, but it was certainly worth *about* $6,500…and there's very little any other dealers could have done to bid the price even higher. This last point is the most important. In order to make money through security selection, it is not enough merely to be smart: *one needs to be consistently smarter than everyone else in order to make money.*

Stock Picking in Jeopardy!

Have you ever noticed that portfolio management is a lot like the game show *Jeopardy!*? It's not about how smart you are in an absolute sense, it's about how smart, speedy, and shrewd you are relative to the competition. People don't make big money in markets by merely being smart; they have to be smarter than the competition and faster to the buzzer (or trading terminal) in order to win in the game of *Security Selection!* And it really is a game…

"I'll take basic logic for two hundred, Alex."

"Answer: It ensures that someone with an IQ of ninety-five wins at *Jeopardy!*"

"What is, 'the consequence of all three contestants having an IQ of ninety-five'?"

"That's right."

"Basic logic for four hundred, Alex."

"Answer: It ensures that two people with IQs of one hundred and forty lose at *Jeopardy!*"

"What is, 'the consequence of all three contestants having IQs of one hundred and forty'?"

"Right again."

Now think of the same exercise, but think of thousands of people (securities analysts and traders mostly) with IQs of 140 and lightning-fast decision-making abilities competing against one another simultaneously in one big never-ending game of *Security Selection!* Someone has to win, but by definition, someone else who plays has to lose by an equal amount. Since it's all relative, and since there are thousands of portfolio managers and securities analysts who are all brilliant, hard-working, and insightful people, portfolio management is a game that's hard to win at consistently.

There will always be some people who will play for a long time and create the impression that they are smarter than average. Stock picking is a lot like that. The basic premise is that it involves (as Samuelson says) paying smart people to gamble against one another on your behalf. In this context, plenty of smart ringers will not be able to add enough value to cover their fees, which they will charge whether they add value or not.

Another way of looking at this is by thinking of the game of poker, which is a zero-sum game. Imagine six amateur guys getting together to play every Saturday night. They bring $1,000 each week, so each contestant risks up to $52,000 a year. They're all of about equal ability, so no one ever comes close to losing all $52,000 and certainly no one is good enough to win the whole $312,000 that's at stake in a year. Any money that one person wins comes at the expense of another.

One week, one of the boys decides to hire a professional poker player (for a $50 fee) to play his $1,000 weekly ante. The guy wins some money—not everything, but there's a clear skill evident. After this happens for a couple of weeks, the other guys grow tired of being patsies to their buddy's ringer, so they go out and hire sharks of their own (also for $50 a round).

In the end, the six ringers are about as evenly matched as the six buddies were in the first place. The ringers will have exploited all competitive "inefficiencies" out of the market until none exist. So, instead of carving up $6,000 a week for 52 weeks, the boys pay a total of $300 in fees every week and end up carving up only $5,700. The ringers get paid for their service, which adds no value since the outcomes revert to being essentially random. On average, the six guys end up losing about $50 a week each for their collective competitive shrewdness in hiring professionals to help them "outperform."

In doing the usual promotional media work for the first edition of my book, I sent a copy to John Bogle of Vanguard. Imagine my surprise when I got back to my office one day to find a package from Mr. Bogle. In it, there was a copy of a speech entitled "It's an Ill Wind That Blows No Good." He was also kind enough to enclose a handwritten note that read: "You've done a fine job on a critical issue, and I wish you and your book great success." He went on to say that "...I see things your way, and am also 'standing up and doing the right thing'." I've kept that note in my office ever since.

Mr. Bogle, of course, has been "fighting the good fight" of having mutual fund companies act in the spirit of stewardship for a very long time now. What never ceases to amaze me is that there are still so few people out there who are prepared to stand up and simply tell the truth. Of course, Bogle isn't the only person who has written to me over the years. Some SPANDEX FSPs use phrases like "you must be really popular with your colleagues" in a sarcastic way. I politely write back and suggest that, given the choice between being popular and being honest, I will choose honesty ten times out of ten. This is because I simply point out that there are a number of important truths that certain elements of the advice side of the industry conveniently neglect to mention when offering advice. Here's a short list of the truths that often go unmentioned by FSPs and the firms they work for:

- Most active managers lag their benchmark in the long run.
- The handful that outperform cannot be reliably identified before the fact.
- Cost is the most reliable determinant of long-term fund performance (as a negative indicator).
- FSPs consistently fail to recommend products that offer no commissions or trailing commissions, yet continue to hold themselves out as "independent."

There are others, but you get the picture. The speech that John Bogle forwarded detailed a whole series of additional circumstances that consistently benefit the manufacturers, distributors, and owners of mutual fund companies ahead of the owners of the mutual funds themselves. Yet, the mantra of the financial services industry is "the client comes first."

For a simple understanding of the rationale here, people should review Sharpe's paper entitled "The Arithmetic of Active Management," referenced at the back of this book. In a nutshell, Sharpe argues that the average active manager can't possibly beat the market because collectively, all active managers *are* the market. As such, the average return of the average active manager is the return of the market minus the average cost of active management. The only reason why any rational person would want to engage in active management is if that person had a deeply held belief that superior managers could be reliably identified in advance. We'll look at that proposition a little later.

After Costs, Indexes Will Outperform Most Active Managers

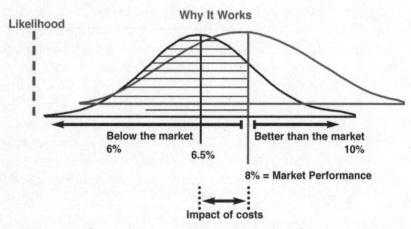

Part of what makes markets efficient is that current prices reflect a consensus view on all available information. If two people have differing views on where the market is headed, there are three possible explanations:

1. The first is right and the second is wrong.
2. The second is right and the first is wrong.
3. They are both wrong.

The one thing we know for certain is that they cannot possibly both be right. It is this competition between legitimate perspectives that causes prices to shift and settle. Few would suggest that experts are "uninformed" when they come to their opinions, it's just that it is extremely difficult to properly calibrate all available information regarding a security price. Have a look at the following headline from the *Wall Street Journal*. You may wish to refer back to it after reading the chapters "Investment Pornography" and "Behavioural Finance," since it demonstrates a number of things:

1. Gurus can disagree on what's going on at any point in time (and often do).
2. The market might move due to prevailing sentiment, which could have nothing to do with fundamentals.
3. The media loves to grab our attention with salacious headlines (which might even add to the sentiment referenced above).
4. Most consumers expect most FSPs to be able to discern which competing view of reality is "correct." Once again, although it is impossible for both views to be correct, it is possible that both are wrong.

THE WALL STREET JOURNAL.

MONEY & INVESTING

Two Strategists Expect 1,000-Point Move In the Market, but in Different Directions

HEARD ON THE STREET

By JOHN R. DORFMAN
Staff Reporter of THE WALL STREET JOURNAL

Morgan Stanley's market strategist Byron Wien is looking pretty good so far on his April prediction that the Dow Jones Industrial Average would begin a 1,000-point decline this year. So far, the Dow industrials have fallen 296 points from their May peak.

Now a respected rival has come forward with almost a mirror-image prediction. Edward Kerschner, PaineWebber's market strategist, has just told his firm's clients that the Dow industrials will *rise* about 1,000 points in the next 18 months.

Wall Street gurus often shroud their predictions in enough mist that they later can claim they were right, no matter what happens. And lately, bold market predictions have been a bit rare. But Mr. Wien and Mr. Kerschner are being unusually blunt and explicit with their 1,000-point bets. For investors, a lot rides on whose reasoning is more compelling.

Mr. Kerschner maintains that inflation is licked, and that interest rates are in a gradual but dramatic downtrend that will take yields on long-term bonds all the way down to 5% by the end of 2001, from about 7% today. Low interest rates make very healthy fertilizer for stock-market rallies.

Dueling Gurus

Edward Kerschner
PaineWebber
Predicts Dow Jones industrials will rise 1,000 points

'WE'RE GOING TO SPEND THE rest of our lives looking over our backs for inflation that is just not coming.'

Byron Wien
Morgan Stanley
Says Dow industrials are in the process of falling 1,000 points

'INFLATION IS NOT GOING to return to 1970s levels, but inflation is not dead.'

Mr. Wien's bearish stance stems from his belief that the economy will be stronger than most people expect. As companies clamor for money, ie says, interest rates will rise, poisoning the stock market. He also says that various technical market indicators are flashing red. "The 1,000 points, in all honesty, was picked for its drama," he says. "But I'm not backing off" — even though the market has rebounded by 132 points since mid-July.

If Mr. Kerschner is correct and the industrial average advances 1,000 points
Please Turn to Page C2, Column 3

For now, let's confine our discussion to differing views on market efficiency. Right away, I suspect readers might be puzzled. Not everyone who believes in market efficiency believes in taking the same approach or using the same products. The best way to describe this discussion is to say that there are people who believe markets are efficient and, thus, believe in buying an index, typically through an ETF or index-based mutual fund. Conversely, there are people who believe in equilibrium markets and in buying "enhanced" index funds that represent asset classes. In short, even people who share a basic paradigm might differ in their choice of corresponding products and approaches.

Efficient Markets in Theory

The predominant view of market efficiency is that no one can reliably pick stocks, so the most rational thing to do is to buy a series of diversified vehicles with mandates that track particular indexes for the asset classes in question. For instance, an investor might want to buy the iShare ETF known as XIC for exposure to the Canadian stock market.

Anyone who wants to learn more about ETFs should refer to Howard Atkinson's excellent book *The New Investment Frontier*, now in its third edition in Canada. The book delves into product structure, product development, tax efficiency, and even has a chapter on working with a STANDUP Advisor for those who are interested. In essence, efficient market adherents are of the opinion that:

- the number of managers outperforming the index in any one year is about equal to the number that would be expected randomly to outperform;
- the number of managers repeating outperformance is also about what would be expected randomly;
- no active manager can consistently outperform the index;
- even if there were a manager who could consistently outperform the index, he or she could not be identified in advance and would likely not be managing a retail mutual fund at any rate (if you had a system for consistently picking winning lottery tickets, would you tell anyone?).

Equilibrium Markets in Theory

A more interesting take on market efficiency comes from the father of the EMH himself. Working in concert with his long-time research collaborator Professor Ken French, Eugene Fama has expanded on Sharpe's capital asset pricing model (CAPM) by developing what he calls the three factor model, which postulates that higher returns can only be acheived by taking higher risk (i.e. that risk and return are related and that there is no such thing as "Alpha").

Over the long-term, stocks have historically produced higher returns than bonds. Over most five-year periods and almost all periods fifteen years or longer, stocks outperformed bonds. That's not news, since it's exactly what Sharpe would have predicted. According to Fama and French, the main characterization of risk is increased volatility of returns. As such, "low priced" (value) stocks historically provide higher returns than "high priced" (growth) stocks over the long term. Value stocks outperformed growth stocks over most ten-year periods and almost all twenty-year periods. Value stocks tend to be distressed or out of favour, resulting in a higher cost of capital. A company's cost of capital is equal to an investors expected return.

The main characterization of the extra risk is deviation or tracking error from the market. According to Dimensional Fund Advisors (DFA), most people don't care much about tracking error and do not use it as a measure of risk. Anyone who does think tracking error is a meaningful measure of risk should be more inclined to use ETFs or index funds. At any rate, by tilting toward value stocks, the volatility is usually about the same as the broad stock market. In a "growth" market, value stocks may significantly underperform the broad market.

Similarly, it has been shown that over the long term, small company stocks have historically provided higher returns than large company stocks. Over most ten-year periods and almost all twenty-five-year periods, small company stocks outperformed large company stocks. As one might imagine, small companies usually have a higher cost of capital than large companies, resulting in a higher expected long-term return to investors. Risk presents itself as both increased volatility versus the broad market and deviation from the broad market return.

Fama and French are the main drivers behind product development at DFA. They see it as their mandate to take the attributes of risk and return as identified in empirical research (i.e. scientific testing) to produce products for retail investors that will reliably capture those elements of risk and return.

When looked at from DFA's perspective, people should buy the index but be smart about it. As far as the people at DFA are concerned, strict index funds are largely flawed. Since they are required to buy and sell stocks at the end of the day, stocks are added or removed (index reconstitution). According to DFA, this effect is fraught with peril. Even in large liquid markets, their research has shown that stock prices are affected and that the indexer incurs this extra cost when it happens. In small or illiquid markets, the effect is even more severe. As such, DFA counsels its clients to buy patiently and pay attention to price.

Rather than rigidly adhering to an index, DFA will delay or accelerate buys and sells to avoid the excessive prices when the index changes. They will buy at a discount when other sellers are anxious to sell large blocks of illiquid shares and then wait through stock momentum to achieve a better price.

DFA also believes the industry could do a far better job of defining proper indexes to be used for benchmarking. Stocks to be included in DFA funds are based on their research into proper index construction and asset class modelling rather than simply following an externally defined index. It might be said that DFA takes an "asset class" approach to investing. The DFA philosophy also involves the opinion that:

• the market return is there for the taking
• buying the index will achieve the market return less fees
• all an investor must do is remain invested
• if the market return allows an investor to achieve their goals then take it
• by intelligently capturing the elements of risk and reward, investors can improve returns

Comparing Equilibrium Markets, Efficient Markets, and Inefficient Markets

As has already been discussed, most mutuals funds and retail investment portfolios are managed by active managers who believe markets are inefficient. These active managers perform extensive analysis on individual companies and only buy those companies that they believe will outperform. As such, they try to outperform the market as a whole. If active managers were successful, their performance would be high and it would be worthwhile paying them for their efforts. If we could identify outperforming managers in advance, they would be worth hiring.

The DFA funds use a passive asset class approach. They buy the entire asset class with a controlled risk tilt towards value and small cap. The elimination of stock-by-stock analysis allows the DFA funds to have lower fees than active managers, though their funds cost more than most index funds and ETFs. As with active management, the DFA passive approach should achieve market returns less fees. However, since DFA funds capture the return of an asset class, not a market index, they tend to outperform both ETFs and active funds, although their performance usually comes with the constraints of higher tracking error and higher volatility.

With all this in mind, a comparison of past performance probably becomes irrelevant as an indicator of future performance when looking at active products, index products, and asset class products. Some actively managed funds will almost certainly outperform ETFs and DFA funds over any given one-, three-, or five-year time frame, since the randomness of returns demands it.

It should be noted that Claymore Investments has also entered the Canadian market with ETFs that are similar in their approach to the asset class funds offered by DFA and largely based on the work of esteemed researcher Rob Arnott. Another way to contrast the index fund/ETF approach with that of DFA/Claymore is by looking at their approach. Traditional index funds and ETFs seek to replicate the performance of a pre-specified universe of securities. There are hidden tradeoffs involved in tracking an index. Generally speaking, reducing tracking error adds to other costs. In essence, ETFs and index funds pursue relative risk strategies where risk is defined as tracking error and the investment objective is to minimize it.

Conversely, the DFA/Claymore approach uses absolute risk strategies. Here, risk is defined by asset pricing theory. The investment objective is to maximize risk-adjusted returns through structure, engineering, and total cost reduction. An investor could move from the former toward the latter simply by delaying certain trades that are associated with tracking an index and accepting a higher level of tracking error along the way. This raises the question of whether tracking error is a meaningful way of defining risk.

If DFA is right and risk and return are related, then only those risks that offer higher rewards are worth taking. From a tax perspective, ETFs and DFA funds are expected to be more tax efficient than most actively managed funds since lower turnover produces lower realized taxable capital gains. Everything that can be can controlled is accounted for—and no one can control or predict stock market movements.

Here's a quick visual summary of the expectations one might have using the three theories as applied to stocks on a basic risk/return schematic:

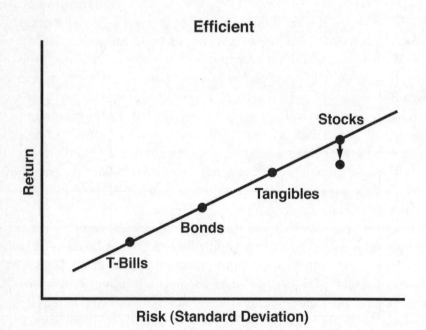

Inefficient

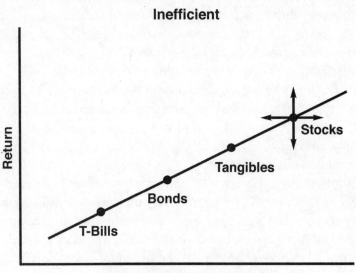

Equilibrium

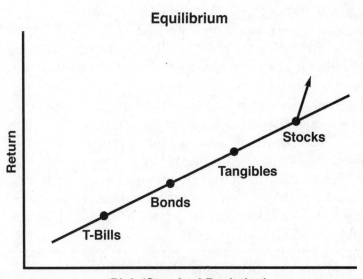

In summarizing the areas where both conventional indexers (efficient markets) and enhanced indexers (equilibrium markets) seem to agree, there are four main points:

1. Markets work, so stock picking doesn't.
2. Diversification is extremely important.
3. Costs matter (you get what you *don't pay* for).
4. FSPs bring discipline and focus to the process.

Offering Advice

No matter what any FSP might believe about market efficiency, a lot of excellent research suggests the prevailing paradigm of portfolio management (active security selection predicated on the assumption that markets are largely inefficient) is far from perfect. Even people like Warren Buffett have taken to going around saying that most people should use a passive approach. So what is it with FSPs? If even people like Buffett are advocating a passive approach, why are so few FSPs following his lead?

To be clear, the issue here is not cut and dry: some people end up doing better through active management, but most do worse. The question, therefore, is *how professional is it to counsel someone to do something that is improbable when other alternatives exist?* Again, just because something is improbable does not make it impossible. However, if FSPs have a mandate to protect the best interests of their clients, why do they consistently encourage them to do things that are likely to leave them worse off?

Part of the answer lies in compensation models. Your average FSP wants to be paid, which is of no surprise. Since corporate interests don't generally manufacture embedded-compensation passive products and since many large firms wouldn't have a proper business platform for FSPs to work from even if the products existed, a large number of otherwise well-intentioned FSPs have taken the easy way out and decided not to "fight the system."

But there's another reason. How does the goal of training FSPs in a rigorous university environment compare with what and how they are taught today? No matter how good the intentions of your average FSP might be, the simple truth is that when it comes to the "debate" between active and passive management, most FSPs simply don't know any better. Now why do you suppose that might be?

Education or Indoctrination?

People do not know what they do not know...because they do not know what they do not know!

—Benjamin Franklin

Personal beliefs are funny things. Creationists are adamant that their world view is right, while evolutionists are equally convinced that they have it right. Agnostics are the Switzerland of the religious world; they don't take sides. In many ways, agnostics are prudent, since neither the creationists nor the evolutionists can offer incontrovertible proof that their view is correct or that the opposing view is conspicuously wrong. There are precious few agnostic FSPs when it comes to choosing between active and passive money management.

Pension funds have been aware of this for years and have governed themselves accordingly. Most use elements of both active and passive strategies in designing portfolios, so we might call them portfolio agnostics. They're not interested in taking sides and being right so much as in doing whatever they can to avoid being conspicuously wrong. Like atheists who go to church regularly, they hedge their bets.

In spite of the fact that the brightest pension funds act equivocally in this debate, the dogmatists in both the active and passive camps act as though they are conspicuously and incontrovertibly right when dealing with retail clients. There is some evidence that can be analyzed on this matter, so people can look at the details and draw their own conclusions, but that evidence is far from conclusive, which brings us to questions of belief. The one thing we should all respect when living in a pluralistic society is that it is inappropriate for anyone to impose religious beliefs on others, yet many FSPs do the equivalent with respect to regarding how investment assets are managed.

People have a tendency to believe things based on what they were taught in their formative years. Finance textbooks talk about the various strategies and techniques that portfolio managers might employ in attempting to add value by improving risk-adjusted returns (lowering risk, increasing returns, or both). True scientists, of course, are more interested in how things actually work and what is accomplished in practice rather than how things ought to work in theory. Theories are nice, but theories have to hold water in the real world of actual testing. The scientist's mantra is, "Can you prove it?"

There is a further difference between honesty and full disclosure that also needs to be considered, and in spite of these fairly obvious criteria, both sides have managed to make strong cases for themselves over the years. Still, if economics were a religion, the ivory towers of academia and the gleaming towers of Bay Street would be waging a vicious war right now. The two camps essentially hate one another because each is a proponent of a specific doctrine that runs contrary to the views of the other. Academia is mostly for passive management and portfolio managers are entirely for active management.

How can this be? Aren't FSPs obligated to do what is in their clients' best interests at all times? And shouldn't they work to identify the strategies that are the most likely to be successful and then pursue those strategies exclusively? Using a medical analogy, what if your physician said the odds of success were 60% for one procedure and 95% for another? Would you be indifferent regarding the procedure you pursue since the odds are in your favour either way?

To be fair to those managers who have developed superb track records over very long time frames, there certainly does seem to be a substantial element of skill involved. People like Sir John Templeton, Warren Buffett and Peter Lynch have all inspired intelligent adherents over the years. It would be disingenuous to say there's overwhelming evidence that most markets beat most active managers most of the time without also acknowledging that some active managers beat the market handily, over long time frames, and after fees. Investment gurus seem to have clearly demonstrated their skill. What is more, they regularly articulate how they do it.

But if what these gurus do can be so readily *explained*, why has it never been effectively *taught*? In other words, if Warren Buffett's value style of investing is so compelling, why has he never had a protegé who has put up similar numbers? It's certainly not because he has a lack of protegés (he likely has tens of thousands). For a "system" to be worth anything, it has to perform consistently. Otherwise, it's not really a system.

Proponents of active management point out that passive strategies need to fully acknowledge that they will never beat their benchmark. This is absolutely true. Of course, the other side of the coin is that in *trying* to beat their benchmark, most active managers typically fail to do so and often lag by a wider margin than passive options *as a direct result of having tried to outperform*. Many proponents of active management also fail to explain this part of the story to retail clients.

Purity and turnover are also major concerns in gauging performance. Active funds almost always have cash or other asset classes in their funds. For instance, almost all have some cash component beyond the 5% or so required to meet redemptions and buying opportunities. Similarly, I know of one fully invested Canadian equity fund that has had a nearly 30% stake in U.S. equities for about five years, but still markets itself as "pure" because there's no meaningful cash component. Given the importance of the purity decision, surely this should be a source of concern.

In a world where integrated wealth management is the overarching objective, tax efficiency also becomes a primary concern. The higher the portfolio turnover, the higher the tax liability in a non-registered account, all else being equal. Any FSP who is truly conscientious about the delivery of total wealth management needs to give serious consideration to those products that can accommodate this reality. In the U.S., mutual funds are reported not only in absolute returns but also in absolute after-tax returns. Tax considerations often play a major role in the rankings, with the more efficient (i.e. lower turnover) funds often moving up considerably.

Should professionals be taught one way of looking at the world or, if the matter in question is contentious and impossible to either verify or deny, should they be taught all of the possible explanations of how things work? Moreover, should professionals be allowed to think for themsleves or should they be essentially told what to think by their "educators"?

The Canadian Securities Course (CSC) offered by the Canadian Securities Institute (CSI) is a testament to the predominance of the inefficient market worldview. The course is jam-packed with information about understanding and interpreting financial statements, everything you'd ever want to know about bonds and how to judge them, preferred shares, commmon shares, the factors affecting security prices, and various details about stock exchanges, trading, and portfolio construction, among other things.

But the CSC isn't the only course available for people who want to learn more about capital markets and how they function. Still, the textbook for the CSC is as revealing for what it omits as for what it includes. It is many hundreds of pages long, yet has less than one page devoted to the concept of market efficiency. In effect, the text acknowledges the existence of the theory but is silent on the evidence that underpins it—and the implications this evidence has for the industry. Taking the concepts presented in the two previous chapters into account, real consideration will need to be a given to the notions of tolerance and acceptance of alternative viewpoints, respect for all evidence, and censorship.

I dusted off an old finance textbook to see how the content differed from the CSC; there are considerable similarities. However, there are some interesting differences too. For starters, finance textbooks are far more detailed in working through the theory and practice of portfolio design using the principles of risk-adjusted returns as they pertain to combinations of asset classes. The thing that strikes me as being most interesting, however, is the candour with which finance textbooks talk about market efficiency. Here's a quote from the 1997 second edition of *Investments* by Sharpe, Alexander, Bailey, and Fowler:

In Canada and the United States there are thousands of professional security analysts and even more amateurs. Not surprisingly, due to their actions the major U.S. and Canadian security markets appear to be much closer to efficiency than to irrationality. As a result, it is extremely difficult to make abnormal profits by trading securities in these markets.

While the reasoning in the preceding quotation might seem self-evident to many readers, it most assuredly is not self-evident to the army of professional analysts and managers who continue to charge fees in their quest to outperform market returns—on both an absolute and risk-adjusted basis. Note that the textbook does not suggest that markets are perfectly efficient, merely that they are highly efficient. It does not say that it is impossible to beat the market, but merely that it is "extremely difficult." Furthermore, since market efficiency is primarily a function of the number of participants, it should be obvious that irrespective of how true that statement was a decade ago, it is likely even truer today.

When comparing this to the CSC textbook, we see that the industry might not be as forthcoming with information as one might hope. The CSC text makes a brief mention of the existence of EMH and explains what it is. However, it offers no commentary like the "extremely difficult" reference found in university textbooks regarding reliably selecting securities. Instead, it says:

...there have been times when investors have been able to consistently outperform index averages like the S&P/TSX Composite Index. This evidence suggests that capital markets are not entirely efficiently priced.

Is it just me, or does that sound like the educators are making a big deal out of strategies and outcomes that have historically proved to be improbable? The course material for the CSC is set by member firms of the Investment Dealers Association (IDA) and the course is supposed to be an entry-level "survey." Still, this is what new FSPs are taught before getting a brokerage licence. In corresponding with a representative of the CSI, however, I was assured that the organization is "responsible for evaluating current industry trends and requirements and ensuring the cirriculum and learning objectives meet or exceed those standards." I might also add that FSPs who are licenced through the other organizations are not given one iota of evidence regarding market efficiency in their course material. The people who designed those courses apparently didn't feel it was important enough.

Note how similar this is to the disclosure problem most consumers have with prospectuses. There's a reference being made about something important (i.e. the facts are in plain sight for all to see), but it is said in such a pedestrian manner that virtually anyone reading it would likely conclude that the information is barely relevant at all.

In fairness, hypotheses have a funny place in textbooks. If something is hypothesized but has been neither proven nor disproven, is it worth teaching? Before answering that question, let me ask another. If something is neither proven nor disproven, is it appropriate to teach entire generations of society based on the assumption that it has been proven or that it has been disproven? For instance, the existence of God cannot be definitively proven or disproven. As such, would it be appropriate to teach children as though creationism were unequivocally correct? Conversely, is it appropriate to teach evolution as being unequivocally correct?

As a society, we seem to have come to a viewpoint that if neither side can be demonstrated with a high degree of confidence, then educators should either remain silent on the matter entirely or teach both and allow students to draw their own conclusions. That may be how it works with the existence of God, but that's certainly not how it works with market efficiency. Ironically, the industry seems smug in portraying those who take a more balanced view (i.e. both active and passive have a place in a portfolio) as "extremists"—so pervasive is the view that active management is sensible management.

Education or Indoctrination?

I looked up the word *indoctrinate* and here's what I found: "v: to teach partisan or sectarian dogmas."[1] A simpler definition might be, "teaching people to take your side." Note that this does not mean that your side is either right or wrong, merely that only one side of an issue is being taught.

In universities, students in both the sciences and the humanities are encouraged to take courses that offer competing views of difficult concepts. That way, they will be well-equipped to look at information from vaying perspectives in order to make informed decisions. In stark contrast, FSPs are typically allowed to offer advice after having taken one course which is based on gaining a licence to sell products rather than having the dispassionate perspective of multiple points of view from equally valid and reputable sources.

Part of the discussion around unbundling has to focus on the merits of the constituent parts. This is tougher than most people think. For instance, there are many Christians who simultaneously possess a low opinion of organized religions and their weekly services and therefore don't attend. Casual observers might think that this form of Christianity is insincere, based on activity. But this isn't necessarily so. Belief in God and respect for the Church are different things.

In late May 2002, the U.S. federal education act was interpreted in Ohio through an addendum stipulating that, "Where topics are taught that may generate controversy—such as biological evolution—the curriculum could help students to understand the full range of scientific views that exist."

A similar amount of open-mindedness might do FSPs some good regarding active and passive management. At present, virtually all FSPs are strict proponents of the active approach, even though scientific evidence is largely, but certainly not entirely, against them. Not surprisingly, virtually all FSPs have been taught in the "traditional school" of active management. Least surprising of all, active management features embedded FSP compensation while passive management does not.

Similarly, the media would have many of us believe that consumers can fire their FSPs and pocket the savings, as if the FSPs add no value, only cost. This is a simplistic view that is only sometimes true. The part about cost is usually true and the part about added value is usually false, although there are exceptions. Under the current structure, there are some highly qualified FSPs who are actually cheaper than discount brokers. It is equally fair to say that there are some FSPs who, no matter how their services are priced, do more harm than good.

It bears repeating that virtually all FSPs recommend active

management and that active management generally involves embedded compensation while passive management generally does not. It would be difficult to support the view that these facts are not related. And to make matters worse, many advisory firms still have not set up a platform for FSPs to charge directly, effectively compromising the choice of FSPs' business models.

There's no logical reason why FSPs wouldn't recommend passive products based on merit. In other words, active management and traditional financial advice are joined at the hip by most FSPs, product manufacturers, product distributors, and the media. Note that this connectedness needn't exist, which is to say, that qualified financial advice and the decision between active and passive approaches can and should be mutually exclusive. As such, FSP recommendations can likely be better explained by prevailing compensation structures than by any form of compelling or overriding logic—including the merit principle.

The point that all indexers concede just by using the laws of probability is that there will always be a handful of active managers who beat their benchmarks handily. If coin-flipping were a skill and the whole world started flipping fair coins at the same time, someone out of the more than six billion people would come up heads thirty or forty times in a row. Would that outcome make that person a skilled coin-flipper or a lucky one? This is a simple probability based on something statisticians call "The Law of Large Numbers."

As with any discussion that cannot be definitively resolved, the perspective one takes might well come down to where one feels the burden of proof lies. The proponents of EMH cannot *prove* that the active managers that outperform their benchmarks over long time frames are merely lucky. Conversely, active managers cannot *prove* that their outperformance is due to insight and intelligence.

What about the FSPs who need to act as intermediaries and sort this all out? It could be said that a major reason why most FSPs don't recommend index-based products for at least part of their clients' portfolios is that they are blissfully unaware of the evidence favouring an index-based approach. They honestly believe active management is *always* better because that is *the only approach they have ever been taught.*

The mutual fund industry does a great job of teaching people how well they would do if they invested in mutual funds, but it is often silent about the fact that clients would likely do better still if they just owned the investable indexes that those funds were benchmarked against. The people granting licences to sell products are looking out for their own interests and perpetuating their own existence, not for the interests of the consumers of their products.

I asked Moshe Milevsky, a professor at the Schulich School of Business at York University in Toronto, to offer his thoughts about what is taught to finance students. Here's what he said:

> When finance professors in training (i.e. Ph.D. students) are in graduate school, they are continuously fed a steady diet of efficient market theory using the rigour and language of mathematical economics. And, even though some of the papers and studies they are forced to read contain empirical evidence that violates these assumptions, it is more of the exception than the rule. They graduate to professorship with a very passive (i.e. efficient) view of the world. Then, of course, they come in contact with CFA practitioners and MBA students whose raison d'être is that markets are inefficient and value can be obtained by picking securities. This is why many of the assistant and associate professors of finance you might encounter in graduate school have a schizophrenic attitude to market efficiency and indexing. Some courses might be very dogmatic while others are agnostic about the whole thing.

It may be observed that universities tend to take an "agnostic" view and teach both sides of the efficient/inefficient debate, while the CSC takes a "dogmatic" view and teaches only one side.

Who Teaches FSPs?

To get a handle on the kinds of recommendations many FSPs make, we first need to examine the kind of training they receive in order to be considered qualified to offer financial advice in the first place. Right away, we have a problem. Until now, the financial services industry has regulated the ability to sell products, while regarding advice as an ancillary function. Only recently has the industry started to come to grips with its own flawed logic.

As a result of the notion of giving advice as an adjunct to selling a product, virtually all FSP educational training has been done by the organizations that grant licences. They are predisposed to portray their products in a favourable light, yet are not regimented like a university. Training courses that grant licences to sell financial products are predictably focused on the narrow attributes of the products themselves. As a result, course graduates might know a lot about stocks, mutual funds, or life and disability insurance, but little about the broader context in which these products can be applied, disciplines like economics, law, public policy, and ethics.

Virtually all FSPs working in the industry are effectively self-taught, meaning they bought textbooks and studied them for a while and then wrote exams that allowed them to sell financial products if they passed. Unless FSPs take special preparatory courses, there is no formal classroom learning going on at all.

English Canadian regulators have tried to regulate financial advice in the past. The problem with these initiatives, which ultimately failed, was that FSPs *had to have a licence to be regulated*. If you had a licence to sell stocks, you could refer to yourself as a broker, investment advisor, financial advisor, or by a number of similar monikers. If you had no licence to sell stocks, you could call yourself anything you wanted. Regulators are set up solely to oversee product sales. They have no mechanism to monitor advice.

What Are They Taught?

Teachers have a massive responsibility because they collectively shape the opinions, attitudes, and competency of their students, who, in turn, make up our future. Students tend to believe much of what they've been taught simply because they trust their teachers. As a result of teachers' presumed expertise, there's an implicit credibility associated with many established teachings, allowing for a certain degree of intellectual imperialism.

When broadly based teaching gives way to more concentrated sales-based training, the perspective that comes from the more formal and often more rigorous approach may be lost. The healthy skepticism that normally comes from a well-rounded university education might well be lacking in the more focused "curriculum" associated with licencing courses. In these instances, teaching people about an industry can be tantamount to indoctrination regarding product sales.

This might arise through what is *implied* precisely because it is *not taught*. For instance, where are the references in licencing textbooks to the fact that the vast majority of money managers fail to beat their benchmarks over long time frames? Evidence to that effect is everywhere for those prepared to be inquisitive and dispassionate, but newly minted securities and mutual fund salespeople are essentially never taught about how rare it is for their kind to actually succeed at beating the market. In short, training for FSPs is presumptive since it teaches FSPs to presume that active management is sensible management.

This lack of balanced training creates the false impression that active management is virtually always superior to passive management. Empirical evidence offered by Nobel Prize–winning economists demonstrates exactly the opposite.

True professionals would never stoop so low as to withhold relevant information simply in order to perpetuate their own existence. Can you imagine a physician going through medical school oblivious to the principles of basic good health? What if this physician were allowed to practice without ever being told that many ailments can be addressed simply by eating a balanced diet, getting regular sleep, and maintaining an active lifestyle? With this fantastic hole in the provided training, the physician would be doing a massive disservice to his patients. Obviously, this could never happen because our society is too knowledgeable about health matters.

But what if people didn't know about basic health and relied implicitly on their physicians to guide their decision-making? Imagine if medical schools around the world came to the collective realization that much of a physician's work could be eliminated if people simply took better care of themselves? Imagine professors commiserating in the common room, conspiring to cover up facts in order to preserve tenure and their paycheques?

The added costs of mutual funds (MERs) are like that. The

industry wants people to presume these costs are sensible, justified, and add value. But in most instances, MERs can't be justified since fund performance lags the appropriate benchmark performance.

Centuries ago, the Catholic Church did some very nasty things to Galileo when he came up with hard evidence that Copernicus was mathematically right in suggesting that the earth did indeed circle the sun. Telling the truth can involve risks to one's professional reputation and personal welfare when that information threatens the power, integrity, and authority of the people and institutions that rule the roost. In the financial services industry, much of that authority is rooted in the books used to train the FSPs on the front lines and the companies that set the cirriculum in the first place.

Similarly, until Magellan's circumnavigation of the globe, many people believed that the world was flat. But even many years after Magellan's voyage, some people continued to cling to a position that had been thoroughly discredited because it took a long time for the rest of the world to digest the irrefutable evidence that changed history. Well-intentioned people who were "educators at heart" had spent generations spreading misinformation to impressionable young students.

Magellan didn't want to stir the pot so much as he wanted the truth to be known as an end in itself. Ideas that challenge authority are considered radical and their proponents are considered heretics. So there's a pattern where scientific trailblazers say things that are considered inappropriate in their day only to be proven right in the fullness of time. Unfortunately, some ideas take longer to make their way into textbooks than others. This often occurs not because these ideas lack merit or proof but because people in positions of authority actively suppress the ideas themselves. They often do this while insisting they are fighting for what is right and protecting or advancing the industry in question.

There's an old saying that if you think education is expensive, try ignorance. This is certainly true when it comes to the formal training we offer to financial FSPs in Canada. The emphasis in licencing courses is on the strategies employed by professional money managers on both the macro and micro level: government fiscal and monetary policy, security valuation techniques, and the effects on security prices if they are trading ex-dividend or cum-dividend. There's a little bit about some related planning activities like having retail investors average down their cost base or do some tax-loss selling, but it's a very minor part of the training.

Our licensing courses do not go nearly far enough. The perspective is sales-oriented and rooted in an old-school world view that money managers can consistently add value. Selling investment products and offering counsel on financial matters are far from synonymous. That's half the problem. The other half is that there has been no mandatory disclosure of the most likely ramifications associated with the actual advice given. This means consumers could end up being sold when they think they are being advised.

Most FSPs are unwitting accomplices in what amounts to a massive sham being perpetrated by the industry on investors of all sorts. In essence, this is how the financial services industry hides the ugly truth. It leaves the evidence out in plain sight for all to see and then talks endlessly about things that are unimportant. But the industry goes on and on about various micro and macro economic factors, indicators earning reports, and the like, and people are quickly seduced into thinking that these unimportant things are, in fact, important.

Active Management and Intelligent Design

How would you feel if your school board taught only evolution and not creationism? What if it taught only creationism and not evolution? What if it taught neither and let children come up with their own ideas? As fate would have it, most schools throughout the Western world have decided that the best way to deal with this sticky subject is to teach both and advocate neither.

It's too bad we're still stuck in the Dark Ages regarding market efficiency. Much like Charles Darwin on evolution, Eugene Fama has proposed that the idea of reliable stock picking is a proposition that is more a matter of faith than anything. Evidence seems to support his claim.

In any decent and progressive society, competing views are allowed to co-exist, yet Bay Street effectively teaches only market inefficiency to FSPs, who in turn offer supposedly unbiased advice to investors. That's the nub of the question about properly disclosing and disclaiming the research behind market efficiency. To many, it is every bit as factual as the evidence showing cigarettes cause cancer. As with that evidence, there are obviously exceptions, but the risks and limitations of cigarette consumption are clearly spelled out on the packaging too. There are no such disclaimers regarding the nebulous value proposition of security selection anywhere in the investment industry.

One of the defining attributes of a decent society is that people are allowed to have their own opinions. Our Charter of Rights and Freedoms has enshrined the right to thought, belief, opinion, and expression. Is the debate about market efficiency a question of fact or a question of opinion? If it is a question of opinion, then surely everyone ought to be entitled to their own view, provided it is suitably disclaimed as such. Compliance departments routinely insist that advisors offer disclaimers on their written material. Surprisingly, I have read passages written by CEOs of manufacturing and distribution companies that extol the virtues of active management but with no disclaimer about the opinions expressed not necessarily coinciding with the views of others within the organization, such as STANDUP FSPs, for instance.

The prevailing attitudes within the industry offend many people profoundly. Speech is free, but society also demands accountability for the views being expressed. As with Intelligent Design, the institutions doing the teaching should probably teach both and espouse neither. Teaching one while remaining silent on the other is not education, it is indoctrination.

Efficient market hypothesis adherents are being discriminated against, marginalized, and denied legitimate rights. As a result of this de facto oppression by a larger and stronger majority (corporate interests), EMH adherents have grown some pretty thick skin. These days, they're actually fighting back. Efficient market adherents are tired of being suppressed in the investment world and are now standing up to be counted. *All they really want is full, true, and plain disclosure of both sides of the discussion regarding market efficiency.*

We can learn a great deal about how any society (or industry) treats its minorities. In April 2006, two families in Massachussets filed a lawsuit against the public school system after a teacher read a gay-themed fairly tale called *King & King* to 20 seven-year-olds without offering prior notification. The suit said the school had "begun a process of intentially indoctrinating very young children to affirm the notion that homosexuality is right and normal in direct denigration of the plaintiffs' deeply held faith." Regardless of where your own sympathies lie, note the similarities: the issues are disclosure, prior consent, and respect for both minority views and majority views.

Having become addicted to the drug of security selection as a value-adding activity long ago, FSPs and their companies are now loathe to come clean. Besides, there are thousands of consumers out there who actually don't want to hear the truth. For some of them, it's more fun to "play the markets" even if they understand the odds are against them (which is the same reason people frequent casinos). Investing has an "entertainment value" for some. For others, they would rather not give serious consideration to the evidence in favour of market efficiency because it would be too painful for them to admit that they were "being had" all along.

Let's take a look at the questions of disclosure and education surrounding active and passive options. You can decide for yourself. I confess that I am more compelled by the evidence in favour of market efficiency. Unlike. many of my peers, however, I do not believe it is appropriate to force clients to share my view. I've always believed that people should be free to exercise their right to independent thought.

No one is saying FSPs have to come down on one side of the active/passive (i.e. inefficient/efficient) debate at all. This is especially true given that there is no definitive evidence that points to the superiority of either perspective.

When it comes to the "religious" debate surrounding market efficiency, the opposite is more likely to be true. Most FSPs are unaware of this "debate" between active and passive options and probably could not offer a meaningful account of the passive approach if they were. This in turn means most consumers are likewise unaware. How can FSPs be expected to alert consumers to a potential controversy surrounding competing views if they themselves are oblivious to that controversy?

Some of the most progressive minds in the industry don't even think people need to pick a side, since there's an argument to be made for both approaches. As a result, the real end-game of independent financial advice might bring FSPs to the point where they are indifferent to both sides. Perhaps *indifferent* isn't the most precise word, either. Perhaps *sanguine, balanced, adaptive,* or *purposeful* might be better.

At any rate, there might soon come a day when FSPs mix and match these two completing paradigms depending on various considerations. Here's what Michael Nairne, CEO of Tacita Capital Management, has to say about the subject:

> One of the emerging trends that will permanently change the landscape of the investment advisory business in Canada will be the widespread adoption of a core (passive) and satellite (active) portfolio structure. Combining a highly diversified core of tax-efficient, low-cost index and enhanced index products that deliver asset class returns with a satellite ring of active managers that seek superior returns or enhanced diversification creates a compelling value proposition to investors—lower taxes, lower volatility, lower costs, lower tracking error, more investment opportunities, and superior potential portfolio returns. A core and satellite structure requires unbundled pricing due to the barebones cost of index-based products. Progressive practitioners who construct and customize core and satellite portfolios for their clients on an unbundled fee basis are a tiny minority today—but rising awareness and intense competition will make this an ever-growing and ultimately preferred approach in the coming years.[2]

Note that Nairne refers to a multiplicity of benefits, including the possibility of both lower risk and higher return. That's something that many FSPs still don't totally grasp either. What does the research have to say about those objectives?

Modern Portfolio Theory

In the late 1950s, Harry Markowitz, another graduate student at the University of Chicago, theorized that a total portfolio approach was more appropriate than one that looked at a portfolio as a series of discrete parts. This represented a radical break-through, since he suggested that portfolios could be created that combine different asset classes in a way that would increase return and/or lower risk when compared to portfolios of individual asset classes. This approach, now known as modern portfolio theory (MPT), took a total portfolio approach to investing. Incidentally, regulators to this day still look at portfolios as being the sum of many disparate parts rather than as a single entity.

Markowitz's big breakthrough was the "efficient frontier," a mathematically derived continuum of risk/return trade-offs that prescribed a certain mix of asset classes in order to maximize returns for any given amount of risk. Of course, quantifying risk tolerance is an exceedingly difficult thing to do. It is also fraught with varied personal opinions and biases. Still, the mathematical theory became widely accepted. It quantifies the personal toler-ance for risk and then maximizes returns within that constraint. One would expect any nuances to be captured and reflected in writing and implemented through an investment policy statement (IPS). Portfolio design began a shift from art to science that is con-tinuing to this day.

A well thought-out investment strategy naturally serves as the foundation for a properly constructed portfolio. Consumers often focus almost exclusively on security selection, while ignoring asso-ciated risks and underlying asset allocation. It's like being penny-wise and pound foolish.

There are many explanations for why it took so long for aca-demic research to enter the mainstream, ranging from healthy skepticism to sloth to hubris to deliberate suppression. Although it took over a generation for Markowitz's work to be appreciated, it has since become a hallmark of portfolio management.

People are striving to build portfolios that maximize returns but hope to do so by taking on only as much risk as they can per-sonally tolerate. Unfortunately, Markowitz's ideas are still not truly appreciated since virtually all commercial applications of his logic involve the use of actively managed products, something Markowitz's co-winners of the 1990 Nobel Prize (Merton Miller and William F. Sharpe) have been particularly disdainful of. Markowitz's work is about combining asset classes to improve the theoretical risk-adjusted returns for the portfolio as a whole. It is silent on the question of whether to use active or passive approaches in doing so.

Thinking on MPT

The offshoot of this advance in thinking is that portfolio development now focuses primarily on reducing risk. Recent advances in portfolio design have rested almost entirely in the realm of risk reduction rather than return enhancement. Consumers often put too many eggs in only one or two baskets, rather than diversifying properly. Those who work with FSPs generally do a better job of diversifying, but there is still considerable room for improvement. Diversification means not only adding securities within certain asset classes but also including additional asset classes.

There are two primary types of risk within any given asset class: systematic risk and unsystematic risk. The former is simply the risk of being in the market—any market. The latter is the risk associated with individual securities. Unsystematic risk can therefore be diversified away, while systematic risk is inescapable.

Simply "buying the market" is the surest and simplest way to eliminate unsystematic risk. By buying an individual stock, an investor is assuming a high degree of unsystematic risk within a single asset class. Buying a mutual fund offers considerable diversification, especially if there are a broad number of holdings within the fund. Buying the market (or an index that tracks it) all but eliminates unsystematic risk.

Buying the market still leaves one exposed to systematic risk, which can be considerable. Fortunately, the ability to hedge one's portfolio against temporary declines can go a long way to mitigate this risk. Unfortunately, the world of retail investment management hasn't yet found a way to dovetail hedge funds into mainstream product solutions like wrap accounts.

The notion of purposeful diversification and ethical disclosure come together in the question of adding value. Asset allocation is what drives risk and return above all else. People tend to forget about allocations and strategies when markets go haywire and tend to pay very little for asset allocation services and advice. That's a shame because they are worth far more than what they are presently paying. These same consumers simultaneously overpay for portfolio management that is generally worse than worthless; they would be better off simply buying and holding the market and pocketing the savings.

Imagine a mutual fund wrap program where the total cost is 3% + GST. In exchange, clients get a comprehensive offering: advice, active asset class management, consolidated reporting, tax optimization, the works. Here's the rub: If the service includes all those elements *except* active asset class management, the cost will (or at least should) be about 1% lower, provided that all else remains constant.

Even in the very long run, some managers meet or exceed their benchmark after deducting their fees. These managers are as rare as hen's teeth. They would have to consistently outperform the market by more than their fees *in perpetuity* just to "add value." This assumes there are no taxes due in the actively managed portfolio, which would almost certainly experience a higher turnover than a passive one.

Since fees for actively managing money were introduced, firms have come to rely on the profit margins that go with it. Ironically, there are many excellent programs available today that strategically maximize risk-adjusted returns and regularly rebalance the portfolio to ensure that it remains on the efficient frontier. This is a huge value-added service, yet one that is practically given away.

The net effect is that companies and FSPs are overcharging for services that add no value while simultaneously undercharging significantly for those services that do. Why? Neither the average consumer nor the media get it. Both are focused on the market gyrations rather than the primacy of a strategic asset allocation. The relationship creates a vicious cycle. The more the media focuses on the narrow matters that explain next to nothing, the more consumers are led to believe these factors must actually be important. After all, why else would they be newsworthy?

The media is in the business of selling advertising space and advertisers pay for readers, and "top-of-mind, newsy" stories are what people generally want to read. It's a form of presumptive sale, much like the training FSPs to get into active management. If the media talks about market gyrations often enough and long enough, the average person will be effectively brainwashed into believing that market gyrations are somehow relevant to their situation.

FSPs are often sucked into discussing what most consumers and the media think is important. Rather than setting their clients straight about what it is they do, they delude their clients (and ultimately themselves) into thinking they have a better sense of where the market is headed, when it will change direction, and which stocks and mutual funds will outperform their peer group. Once they have played the game for a while, it becomes difficult to come clean.

I looked up the word *charlatan* recently. The definition I found was: "n: One who makes a claim to skill and knowledge he does not possess."[3] Since it is doubtful that anyone can reliably pick stocks in a way that adds value on a risk-adjusted basis net of fees, one could reasonably conclude that those FSPs that purport to "add value" are nothing but charlatans.

Only the most professional FSPs have the decency to avoid claiming any ability to predict these sorts of things. Sadly, most FSPs still rely on sales tactics to get new business. Most still honestly believe that top performing managers can be reliably identified (and spend an enormous amount of time trying to do so).

If there was any justice, these would be precisely the sorts of FSPs who would not last long in this industry. Instead, these sorts of FSPs have not only survived but many have actually thrived, not because what they do is useful but because so many people *think* that what they do is useful. The ugly truth that no one can reliably pick stocks is being hidden in plain sight. The evidence is everywhere for those who care to look. For instance, mutual fund prospectuses uniformly reference the fact that past results are not reliable indicators of future results.

Astonishingly, product manufacturers always point out that the metrics used by many are not reliable—and then often proceed to use those metrics anyway! What's the use of telling people that the past isn't a reliable indicator of the future if nearly all discussion about product performance revolves around how it has done in the past?

Look at it this way: What if prospectuses said "reading chicken entrails is not a useful indicator of future performance?" You can insert whatever presumed explanatory variable you want: tea leaves, tarot cards, weather patterns, you name it. The simple point is that if someone acknowledges that using X to make decisions is unreliable and then goes around making recommendations based on using X anyway, there's a pretty serious problem. Then again, we're talking about things that can't be controlled. It is generally acknowledged by STANDUP FSPs that these things are not really part of the job description anyway. Management requires control. So what, exactly, can a good FSP control? How about investor behaviour, asset allocation, the timing of taxable events, and things like that? If this is the case, investment policy statements are likely among the most useful tools an FSP could have in doing the job well.

Part Two
Scientific Testing

Get an Investment Policy Statement

To think is easy; to act is difficult; but to act as one thinks is the most difficult of all.

—Johan Wolfgang von Goethe

If financial advice is not synonymous with stock picking (or its first cousin, fund picking), then what exactly is it that FSPs do to earn their compensation? One of the great ironies of financial advice is that although security and fund selection don't generally add value, most other things that FSPs do actually do add value. It's pretty much the exact opposite of what most people think.

Money As Food

We often hear of medical professionals that refer to the need to eat a "balanced diet." That generally means eating appropriate quantities from the four major food groups: breads and cereals, fruit and vegetables, dairy products, and meat. The same could be said for building a balanced portfolio. People need to invest in judicious amounts of stocks, bonds, and cash. Similarly, there are clear elements of good health that apply pretty much across the board: exercise regularly, get plenty of rest, drink plenty of fluids— those sorts of things. For financial planning, analogous sayings include: "pay down non-deductible debt," "save a portion of everything you make," and the ever popular "buy low, sell high."

It would probably be a bit silly to extend the metaphor too far, but the general principles of "everything in moderation" and "diversify for safety" are clearly appropriate for both lifestyle and personal finance.

One can surmise from the many people today hiring personal trainers, going on any number of diets, popping any number of supplements, and practicing yoga, that there's clearly a movement afoot to "do better." The decision to get outside help if necessary is a logical extension of that desire for self-improvement and wellness. So it is with personal finances. Most good advisors are like coaches: they won't tell you what to eat or what exercises to do because, for the most part, we know all that already. Coaches and trainers motivate us to do better and hold us accountable for our behaviour. That's what good FSPs do too.

Note that stock picking and fund picking are not in the job description. FSPs make sure you invest in a balanced portfolio the way a personal trainer would make sure you eat a balanced diet. They don't care whether you eat apples or oranges, so long as you eat reasonable portions of fruit. They don't care about whether you have toast, Corn Flakes, or Cheerios for breakfast, so long as you eat reasonable portions of cereal. So it is with good FSPs. To them, the identity of individual stocks or funds is secondary to the concept of balance—they just want to make sure you're not loading up on one thing to the virtual exclusion of everything else. That's not healthy, yet that's what many people would do if left to their own devices and not held accountable by someone who can offer guidance and perspective.

Beyond that, the management of finances is much like managing anything else: you need to focus on what you can control. This should be obvious because if you can't control something, you can't really manage it. No one can control where the stock market is, or, more properly, where the stock markets are, headed in the short term anyway. But people shouldn't worry about it. Pretending to have control of things when you don't is just a way of fooling yourself with a false sense of security. I believe that's part of why financial "gurus" are still in high demand. People want desperately to be able to have control of their finances and are sometimes willing to put undue faith in those who claim to offer it. When it comes to capital markets and their behaviour, we have no control, only focus and direction.

As with physical health, there are some people who are disciplined and savvy enough to do what needs to be done so they can remain in excellent health without any coaching at all—with others, this is not so much the case. In terms of your physical health, there's likely room for improvement no matter who you are. The same goes for financial health. The question that only you can answer is: "just how much do I need a financial coach?" It then comes down to a simple (albeit speculative) cost/benefit analysis. If the value added meets or exceeds the cost expended, you should probably hire someone to help keep you accountable to yourself for your goals. Instead of doing one more rep or one more lap, you've got someone urging you to set aside an extra $100 a month or to set up that college fund immediately.

The analogy isn't perfect. There are a lot more people with financial coaches than there are with personal trainers. Still, the broad roles are rather similar. The key point, to my mind at least, is that security selection is a lot like choosing the food in a giant buffet. There's lots of selection, but as long as you use discipline and diversify, it will be difficult to make a wrong choice. Financial advisors help with that discipline, as well as with needs assessments, accountability and review, benchmarking, progress reports, and the like. But they shouldn't tell you what to eat today. Actually, the word *today* is an important nuance in the previous sentence. Properly considered, the decision should never be made based on the circumstances of the day, it should be both general and timeless.

An investment policy statement (IPS) sets out the most important aspects of a portfolio: risk tolerance, asset allocation, expected return, and so forth. It is a "portfolio blueprint" that ensures decisions are made in a consistent and purposeful manner.

Does Anyone Understand Gary Brinson?

Back in 1986, some groundbreaking work was done on the subject of the determinants of portfolio performance. Updated in the early 1990s, research done by the highly respected Gary Brinson and his team delivered the following finding: "Data from ninety-one large U.S. pension plans indicate that investment policy dominates investment strategy, explaining on average 93.6% of the variation in total plan return."[1] This research dealt with how much a diversified portfolio might deviate from its investment policy and what explained that deviation. It did not look into questions of performance and was more descriptive than prescriptive in its nature.

Between the technical language used in the study and the lack of training of most people who read it, it may well go down as one of the most misquoted pieces of scholarship in modern history. Virtually everyone in the financial services industry wanted to quote the research but few people really understood it. Unsuspecting FSPs (we have already delved into how they are "educated") were quick to jump onboard to promote the benefits of strategic asset allocation in general and portfolio optimization techniques in particular.

Corporate marketing departments, many of which were equally eager to legitimize the profit-maximizing and risk-minizing wrap accounts coming out around the same time, talked glowingly about asset allocation. Looking back, it seems corporate interests twisted the research to get it to say whatever their marketing departments wanted it to say, which usually had little to do with the actual findings. Virtually everyone involved got it wrong and it is hard to believe the industry-wide error wasn't wilfull.

Brinson's research broke down the investment management process into three sequentially made decisions:

1. Choose the asset classes to be used.
2. Choose the normal weightings of those classes.
3. Select the securities to populate the portfolio.

When it comes to investment decision-making, Brinson showed that the tail is wagging the dog and has been for as long as people have been investing. He defined the first two decisions as the investment policy and the third as the investment strategy.

Brinson demonstrated that the third and final decision explains very little in terms of the average variability of returns. Almost all the average variability in returns was explained by the first two decisions. Yet, which of these three decisions does the media focus on almost exclusively? The third. Which of these three decisions do most of us (FSPs included) generally focus on? The third. The companies that manufacture these sorts of products do little, if anything, to set the record straight about causation. Here's what Brinson himself had to say about asset allocation services that use active management:

Most individual investors probably should not be paying an active management fee. They would be better off to use some passive-like, or low-fee instrument for their asset allocation. Furthermore, investors should be skeptical of anyone who cannot prove a long record of success when they imply they can enhance your returns by giving asset allocation advice.[2]

A number of years ago, I had an epiphany. A wrap program I was recommending to many of my clients had just undergone a fairly significant product enhancement. New RRSP-eligible investment pools were being introduced to allow clients the opportunity to legally skirt the foreign content restrictions in RRSPs, which had just been increased to 30% of the book value of the amount invested. The higher foreign content limit for registered plans combined with new RRSP-eligible funds meant a lot of clients went from just under 20% foreign content to over 50% foreign content in their registered portfolios. By adding these new funds, clients were able to *enhance their expected returns without changing their risk tolerance.*

Over the months that followed the introduction of these new investment options, clients were sent revisions to their investment policy statements that showed how their expected return (the "managed account premium") would increase, while the expected standard deviation (i.e. variance) of their portfolios would remain unchanged. In effect, these funds had extended the so-called "efficient frontier" of how well investors could do on a risk-adjusted basis. They allowed the program to develop an entirely new frontier that was superior to the old one at all levels of risk tolerance. Expected returns increased, while expected risk remained unchanged.

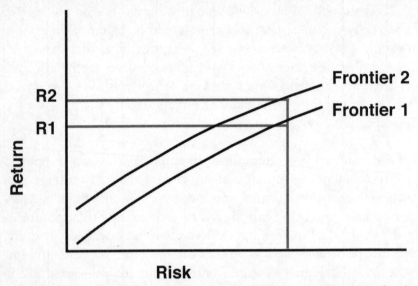

Best of all, the changes were entirely consistent with the responses given to the questionnaire used to design the original IPS. My epiphany, therefore, was a direct result of the validity and importance of decision number two. The same asset classes that had always been used were now being used *in different proportions than had previously been the case* and had improved the universe of possible client portfolios as a result. This all came about through the intrepid skirting of Canada Revenue Agency's foreign content limits for RRSPs, which have since been scrapped altogether.

Anyone who believes that asset allocation dominates portfolio return considerations should refrain from timing the market or engaging in either stock picking or fund picking. That's almost never what happens in practice. As a result, there are many observers who believe that instead of being the knowledgeable experts that the marketing machine portrays them to be, thousands of "professionals" don't even understand the products the industry is selling. Industry veterans such as John Bogle have long lamented that a marketing culture has overtaken the culture of stewardship within financial services.

There has been an industry-wide dogma expounding the primacy of strategic asset allocation where most people adhering to the dogma have likely never even read the Brinson research, much less understood it. The Brinson research shows that security selection accounts for less than 5% of any given portfolio's variance in performance on average—and the effect was often negative. People in general, and FSPs and the media in particular, have simply been focusing on all the wrong things in their reading, writing, and investing.

Decision One: Choose the Asset Classes

The choice of asset classes matters greatly and the concept of how much one investment moves in relation to another is called correlation. Correlation is vital when contemplating which asset classes will be used in constructing a portfolio. Just as combinations of risky stocks exhibit less risk than individual securities themselves, combinations of asset classes can have less risk than individual asset classes. Two investments that move in lockstep have a correlation coefficient of 1.0. Those that move in exactly opposite directions have a correlation coefficient of –1.0. Those that move randomly, where movement in one asset class has no bearing on the movement of another, have a correlation coefficient of 0. These are said to be non-correlated. Asset classes that move similarly are said to be highly correlated, while those that move somewhat similarly are said to be weakly correlated, and those that move in opposite directions (even if only modestly) are said to be negatively correlated. Most asset classes are at least somewhat positively correlated.

In general, the less asset classes are correlated, the more portfolio risk is lowered. It is also important that these asset classes are not particularly volatile of and by themselves. Research done by Ibbotson Associates in Chicago shows that risk decreases as the number of randomly selected asset classes increases. Diversification improves the risk/return trade-off and the best form of diversification is to add more asset classes.

In most instances, any twelve-month period would see some asset classes go up and others go down. It is rare indeed to have all asset classes move in the same direction over even a relatively short time frame. Risk can be thought of as the range of possible outcomes for any given asset class over any given period of time.

The more asset classes available in the universe of investment options, the better. Therefore, the old view of asset classes being narrowly defined as domestic stocks, bonds, and cash is a limiting factor. What amazes me is that marketing people talk about how having five or six asset classes is far superior to having three or four. This may be true, but wouldn't having eleven or twelve asset classes be better still? That doesn't mean all these asset classes have to be used, just that they should be available in case you choose to use them.

Decision Two: Choose the Normal Weightings

The second decision that Brinson says investors need to make relates to the proportions of the asset classes used by investors. As we saw earlier, changing the mix can go a long way to enhancing return and risk needn't necessarily increase as a result. The discipline of decision number two should be enforced through an IPS.

Any strategic asset allocation needs to be formally written down so that it can be purposefully adhered to. Whatever number is chosen, there should be a written discipline to rebalance back to that target. It might be done automatically or manually. It might be done when there's a significant market movement or at a prescribed point in time. How and when it is done is secondary. The important point is that once an asset allocation is set, there should be a system in place to keep it within those parameters and to evaluate whether those parameters continue to be appropriate.

Be extra careful when using actively managed mutual funds. One of the major drawbacks of the mutual fund industry today is that virtually none of the funds are pure; they all have multiple asset classes (including cash) within them, making precise control of one's asset allocation nearly impossible.

Decision Three: Select the Securities

The third decision is where virtually the entire industry lives: picking stocks and funds and timing the market. This is next to useless. To begin, active management is not a precondition of strategic asset allocation; in fact, it can be a significant hindrance. Actively managed pools of capital are less pure than asset class indices. In other words, the tendency to pursue decision three using mutual funds almost certainly compromises control over decision two to some extent. Since decision two is more important, why would a rational person skip over it just to get to decision number three? The degree of compromise depends on how pure the pools of capital in question are.

As soon as an FSP recommends one manager over another, it automatically raises the question: "Why did you recommend this manager?" If security selection is so minor an explanatory variable as to be nearly insignificant, one wonders why any serious thought should be given to manager selection at all. How professional is it to make a big deal out of something that explains very little? Why not just buy the asset class? At least this way, the FSP doesn't have to be bogged down in counterproductive debates about funds being in the third or fourth quartile when they were in the first quartile for three consecutive years before the recommendation was made.

Obviously, FSPs have to recommend something. Since they could be indifferent to both active and passive management, why not let the consumer decide? *Is there any better and more compelling way to communicate the relative unimportance of security selection?* If it was a big deal, surely the FSP would have a strong opinion. Since it's not, why should an FSP care either way?

People who look at the research and then put the interests of the client first would likely be hard-pressed to give a compelling answer. Anyone who is truly committed to the primacy of strategic asset allocation should be comfortable with using investment options that seek to replicate the index they are benchmarked against in the purest, simplest, cheapest, and most tax efficient form available. Professional FSPs could simply spell out the pros and cons, risks and limitations of each and then let clients decide based on their own comfort levels and preferences.

Virtually every firm in the industry today goes out of its way to downplay the fact that the fees they are charging for portfolio management through security selection within an asset class usually do more to benefit themselves than their clients. They are deliberately telling less than the whole story. Although these firms and the FSPs who work there also do a number of very good things and are quite concerned about the welfare of their clients, when all the cards are not on the table, there is still a need to clean up the system. We need to put an end to the misinformation that has been allowed to take root by financial advisory firms, their employees, and most of the media.

The surest ways to improve risk-adjusted returns are to either alter the mix of existing investment options or to add new asset classes that have favourable risk/return characteristics.

The logic involved with progress is often perverse. Before we become too self-satisfied with how previous generations resisted change, let's take a step back. We all need to understand that people often do things a certain way simply because "they were always done that way." Business schools have been teaching technical analysis for about as long as they've been around.

How many people go through life saying things like, "I don't believe in insurance," even though they never take the time to assess how the proper use of insurance might assist them in meeting their retirement objectives, estate planning needs, and deal with latent tax problems? Old biases die hard and although we hate to admit it, everyone has biases of one kind or another, often based on actual life experiences.

The 90% Solution

Few things in life are certain. However, most reasonable people would likely agree that if something could be proven to hold true 90% of the time, then that's about as good as one could expect in light of inherent uncertainty. As fate would have it, the number 90% comes up frequently as a threshold that explains a number of important but disparate things in the field of capital market research.

First, research done in the 1980s by a team of researchers led by Gary Brinson showed that strategic asset allocation explains over 90% of a portfolio's variance over time in a diversified portfolio. Although there were other factors, it was clear to Brinson that most of any given portfolio's volatility could be explained by the extent to which it deviated from the prescribed mix of stocks, bonds, and cash.

Second, research done by Fama and French shows that over 90% of a portfolio's return can be explained by looking at three factors. The so-called "three factor model" shows that market (stocks vs. bonds), size (small vs. large), and valuation (value vs. growth) are the primary drivers of returns. Tilting a portfolio toward stocks in general and small, cheap companies in particular can enhance long-term performance.

Finally, there are dozens of research papers done around the world that demonstrate that about 90% of all actively managed funds lag their benchmarks over long time frames (usually ten or twenty years) and that the 10% or so that do better can't be reliably identified at the time of purchase.

Taken together, these three bits of information paint a clear picture of what a rational and prudent investor should do given the uncertainty of capital markets. That investor should buy a wide variety of cheap investments that track broad asset classes and tilt them toward value stocks and small company stocks to maximize long-term, client-specific, risk-adjusted returns. That's also exactly what professional FSPs should recommend.

It bears repeating that nothing is for sure and that there are 10% exceptions to the three bits of research noted above. Still, it is rather disingenuous to point to exceptions in an attempt to disprove something that is generally true. For instance, lottery tickets are generally a bad investment. While it is true that there are sometimes people who win and win big, the reality for the majority of ticket holders is rather less fulfilling. As such, the decision to buy lottery tickets in the first place is not a particularly rational one.

Most FSPs, advisory firms, and financial product manufacturers agree with the notion of diversification. Some talk about risk preferences as demonstrated by tilting toward stocks in general and stocks of small, cheap companies in particular, but virtually no one advises clients to consider forgoing active management and buying broad asset classes rather than spending money on management fees that will likely lead to a lag in performance.

If FSPs are going to be viewed as professionals, then surely they should be required to make full and clear disclosure of the most likely outcomes given the balance of probabilities associated with any recommended course of action. Fiduciary responsibility requires that the clients' interests come first. Although the ultimate outcome of any decision can never be totally certain, investors deserve to know their odds of success before an FSP counsels them to act in a manner that is contrary to research.

Getting a formal IPS in place allows FSPs to act as the "portfolio police" for their clients. It allows them to construct purposeful portfolios that consider the clients' unique perceptions of risk and reward by setting allocation limits on pre-agreed asset classes by focusing on those factors that have been shown to be of most importance.

Scientific Testing

The reasonable man adapts himself to the world; the unreasonable one persists in trying to adapt the world to himself. Therefore, all progress depends on the unreasonable man.

—George Bernard Shaw

What would you think if you met someone who wrote a book on how to pick winning lottery tickets? Seriously. I'd wonder why anyone smart enough to devise a system to do something so potentially lucrative would do something so stupid as to share it with the world. Think about it. If you could come up a with a way to reliably win even 5% of all lotteries you bought tickets for, you'd be fabulously wealthy if you entered often enough. If you tell everyone else how you do it, they'll go out and do it too... and your winnings would evaporate. Everyone who reads your book will win at the expense of virtually everyone who didn't read the book.

The only rational behaviour for people who are devious enough to come up with a scheme to win lotteries consistently is to hoard that information for their own personal and exclusive use. What's a couple thousand dollars in book royalties compared to many millions in lottery winnings every second Thursday?

Built-In Obsolescence

In the 1990s, it seemed everyone had a take on how to identify top-performing mutual funds. At the time, it seemed no one could get enough information about what mutual funds were, how they worked, and how to build portfolios using them. Annual fund-ranking books presumably helped consumers make smart, time-less investment decisions. Today, no one publishes books that rank funds. Why did people lose their appetite for fund picking?

Why did most books disagree on what the best funds actually were? If the research was indeed empirical and predictive, shouldn't they have all identified the same funds? And if the books were so committed to a long-term perspective, why did so many of the recommended funds change from one year to the next—even from the same authors?

My view today is that those authors weren't selling timeless and useful information at all, they were simply selling books. And books that need to be updated annually have the handy attribute of built-in obsolescence, meaning they could be tweaked, repackaged, and sold anew twelve months later. From the authors' perspectives, the best thing about these books was their imminent disposability. The second best thing was likely the lack of accountability that the books entailed.

Why would any consumer bother to check the long-term track record of a book from, say, 1996 to see how the recommended funds actually performed by 2006? After all, the thinking goes, whatever was recommended back in 1996 must surely no longer be relevant given all that has happened since. In those days, consumers were always on the lookout for the latest investment idea and could always be counted on to run out and buy the latest version of their favourite rating book the next year.

The whole exercise legitimized the notion of stock picking as a valuable pursuit. None of the books made mention of the fact that there was zero research indicating that this had been done reliably in the past; they simply implied that it could be done—and people believed them.

Whether performed at the micro level (by a hotshot broker in red suspenders) or at the macro level (by a superstar "money manager" in charge of billions of dollars), the books lent credence to the notion of security selection as an activity that can be reliably used to outperform "the markets." The problem is that past performance is not to be used as an indicator of future performance. In other words, between the ubiquitous prospectus disclaimers and the self-professed fund-picking gurus, one group had to be right and the other group had to be wrong.

I took on the challenge of sifting through the most prominent fund-picking books from 1996 (with rankings based on June 30,

1995 results) to see how the ten-year numbers stacked up as of June 30, 2005 and published my findings in the *Globe and Mail*. Just how insightful were these books, really?

The results were stunning. In all four books, the majority of recommended funds lagged their benchmarks over the ten-year time period. A large proportion of the funds weren't even good enough to merely survive the ten-year period. Many studies have shown that "survivorship bias" causes current performance numbers to look considerably better than they really are. It's easy to have a respectable class average if you don't have to take a massive dropout rate into account. *Nonetheless, the funds recommended had a collective performance record that could only be described as awful.*

Perhaps even more disconcerting was that the authors generally used only three years' worth of data to make a pronouncement on a fund's relative merit. In their minds, thirty-six monthly data points were the minimum required to make an informed decision regarding performance. Imagine if your favourite polling company used similar methodology.

What if someone ran a poll revealing that fifteen out of thirty-six voters intend to vote Liberal in the next federal election? Based on this finding, the polling firm might announce that, since over 41% of Canadians polled intend to vote Liberal, we're in for a Liberal majority government. What they won't say is that a sample size of thirty-six is far too small to be relied upon in any way when seeking real insight into the minds of the electorate. The range of possible outcomes with such a small sample means the Liberals could be in for anything from total annihilation to the largest landslide in Canadian history. In short, any poll with a sample size that small is effectively useless.

Of course, having most funds lag their benchmarks would make little difference if people could reliably identify the handful that would ultimately outperform. But can this be done? Once again, contrary to what these books implied, earlier independent research showed that superior funds could not be reliably identified beforehand. I guess there's a first time for everything. I should also add that near the fronts of these books, some authors even included passages saying that they believe good managers can be reliably identified. However, no rationale was ever given as to why they held this opinion.

Then, near the backs of the books, they sometimes wrote things like "research puts the contribution of security selection—that is, choice of specific investments—at only 2%" when discussing performance. In other words, "We think superior managers can be reliably identified, but we've seen no evidence to that effect and it is of no consequence anyway." That is the gist of their logic anyway.

What exactly was the objective of these books? Was it to help readers select funds that would outperform their benchmarks? Was it to help them pick funds that would merely outperform other funds? What if through the illusion of scientific rigour these books managed to promote mutual funds in general and book sales in particular but offered no real fund-picking value at all? Furthermore, fund companies, fund managers, and FSPs who recommend funds are constantly telling their clients to take a long-term perspective, so why were these books being updated annually?

I'll tell you who loved these books: the companies that had funds ranked as top performers. It was great for business. Corporate Canada has always loved the legitimacy that comes from third-party endorsements—no matter how questionable the research behind it.

But if a high percentage of guru-endorsed funds end up lagging their benchmark by a wide margin, the only truly rational way to justify picking funds at all is if one could have a high degree of confidence that the funds that are chosen had a high probability of outperforming. That's not going to happen. It's the same reason most people should never set foot in a casino.

Let's look at this from an advisory perspective. It has been suggested by some commentators that the primary role of FSPs is to assist clients in avoiding "The Big Mistake." If this is indeed a fair job description, then one could argue that helping consumers avoid funds that lag could be reasonably depicted as a value-adding activity. People could then write books called *Heavy Missers* or *Dumb Funds*. Their mandate would be simple: help consumers avoid underperforming funds. If increasing the likelihood of beating a benchmark could be achieved by weeding out losers, wouldn't it be just as useful to identify those funds that are laggards? Since it's tough to position yourself as an expert if you only help people avoid dogs, that attempt was never made.

Ironically, all this doesn't necessarily mean the gurus were up to no good. I suspect these people honestly believed what they were writing, just as many FSPs (myself included, once upon a time) honestly thought these guys could do what they said they could. But they were plain wrong, and yet so many people believed them.

We're left with two possible explanations: either the authors knew their recommendations were a load of hooey or they didn't. If they didn't, then they were merely guilty of trying to make a few bucks by preying on society's seemingly insatiable quest for disposable information and professing to be able to do something they could not. On the other hand, if any author actually knew in advance that their books were hogwash, then that author would be wilfully misleading people. So which is it? And which is worse? Were these "gurus" unwitting alchemist wannabes or wily snake oil salesmen? Hopefully, it should be clear by now that I believe it is the former. Nonetheless, the "conspiracy of ignorance" that remains rampant to this day got a huge shot in the arm when these books first came out.

Since my article appeared in the *Globe and Mail*, I've had conversations with two of the four gurus. They insisted that their intentions were good. Again, I want to stress that I have always believed them. In my view, these are basically decent, well-intentioned, hard-working people who were trying to perform a legitimate service for fund companies, consumers, and FSPs. They helped the companies and FSPs—two out of three ain't bad. Here's a quick Q&A that came from a couple of those conversations in which the guru asked questions and I responded to them:

Q. Why not compare recommended funds to the average fund in its class?
A. I could do this but is that really appropriate (especially going forward)? I believe STANDUP FSPs should be willing to make comparisons between the entire universe of alternative products with similar mandates.

Q. Did you have your research rigorously tested in an academic setting?

A. No. But neither did any of the authors, so what's your point? Besides, there was considerable prior opinion supporting efficiency/equilibrium thesis when the books were published. The lack of disclosure regarding evidence that contradicts the implicit value proposition of the book could have been noted. It seems to me that theories ought to be tested at least as rigorously as outcomes since outcomes are unambiguous.

Q. Why ten years? It is not the most appropriate time frame.
A. Says who? If the time is too short, it's likely just momentum. If the time frame is longer and managers/mandates change, then that is used as an excuse. Just what time frame will you guys be accountable for anyway? Besides, so much of the industry refuses to acknowledge the mountainous evidence pointing to the skewness of survivorship bias.

Q. Did you account for other factors that need to be considered (suitability, manager changes, mandate changes, fund mergers, etc.)?
A. Again, no. But this line of questioning supports my theory of built-in obsolescence too. It sure is "convenient" to always have an excuse for why what was supposed to happen didn't happen. Totally unbiased ways of testing are extremely hard to devise.

Q. Lower return with lower risk is a viable objective. Some funds were recommended on that basis.
A. Agreed. But if a fund delivers a substantially lower return with only modestly lower risk, did it still deliver on value proposition? If no, I'm still right. If yes, then why not just invest in T-bills? T-bills would offer lower risk and lower return too. Was that option put forward? Was there a discussion about asset allocation? If authors were serious about discussing risk and reward, shouldn't they have funds explained by low risk/low reward, market risk/market reward and high risk/high reward parameters?

Furthermore, since the authors said they believed that fund picking can be done reliably, shouldn't they have cited a reason for their opinion? Had anyone ever done this convincingly in the past? If yes, they should have referenced it. If no, then why wasn't the "pioneering" nature of "we think this should work, but we can't be totally sure about it" more explicitly disclosed? Even then, shouldn't they have at least cited the work done by world-renowned economists like Fama, French, Samuelson, Merton, Miller, Sharpe, and others who dispute their fundamental thesis?

Why do so many FSPs depict themselves as being superior fund pickers? Fund picking is a discredited value proposition in today's financial services industry. Unfortunately, the majority of consumers fail to see it that way, having been bamboozled by all the books, magazines, newsletters, and websites dedicated to identifying top performers. These "resources" are really just perpetuating the myth of fund picking as a reliable activity.

In sales parlance, this is called a "presumptive close." The presumptiveness of mutual fund sales is more like this: "We have looked at both your circumstances and the funds available to meet your objectives. Having done so, which would you prefer, this Mackenzie Fund or that AGF Fund?" This kind of proposition, while seemingly innocuous, is full of presumptions, including:

- investing is the logical next step
- the client needs a mutual fund as opposed to another product
- the funds noted are the best alternatives available
- the decision at hand is primarily one of fund picking rather than asset allocation, tax minimization or some other objective
- superior funds can be dependably identified
- the FSP is uniquely qualified to identify superior funds

The other element of benchmarks is the comparison of funds to one another as opposed to a relevant benchmark. The industry is sneaky that way. Since the vast majority of funds lag their benchmark in the long run, the industry has chosen to score itself against itself. Mutual funds are rated according to their performance relative to other mutual funds rather then in relation to a suitable benchmark.

For instance, if there are one hundred funds in an asset class and sixty lag their benchmark over a five-year period, one might get a false impression when looking at quartile rankings. There would be twenty-five funds in each performance quartile, yet approximately ten funds in the second quartile would have lagged the benchmark. It gets worse. In the very long run, fewer than 25% of all funds beat their benchmark. One could go to a ranking book to find a fund with a ten-year track record that is ranked in the first quartile and, as a result, buy that fund even though it may have lagged its benchmark!

By comparing one product with another, the financial services industry has created the impression of a balanced, apples-to-apples comparison. This comparison is fair in a relative sense (i.e. we can see which funds have been *better than the others in the past*), but that's as far as it goes. The industry is establishing a kind of kangaroo court where no comparison is being made to the real challenger: the asset class that the portfolio is benchmarked against. That would be far more meaningful to consumers and far more damaging to the mutual fund industry.

Continuum of Available Products

For years now, FSPs have had a wide array of diversified investment products to choose from in constructing portfolios for their clients. New products are constantly introduced into the marketplace, so it is often difficult for laypeople to keep track of the options out there. One thing that everyone needs to remember is that there is no such thing as a silver bullet, off the shelf product that is demonstrably superior in all circumstances. That being said, people want assistance in sifting through the wide array of available options to get a handle on the relative merits of each.

It stands to reason that most STANDUP FSPs prefer products that are cheap, tax efficient, pure, and transparent. Performance generally flows out of these more predictable traits. As time marches on, more and more products are being released that offer precisely those characteristics. Here's an assessment of what's out there, from the products most closely associated with SPANDEX Advisors all the way to those associated most closely with STANDUP Advisors. Obviously, individual securities cannot be placed on this continuum.

Traditional back-end load (DSC) mutual funds

Virtually everyone working as a planner and many people working as brokers today got their start by selling back-end load mutual funds. This is probably still the most popular way for advisors to receive compensation for financial advice when working with retail clients. They cost far more than they are worth, they are almost always impure, they hide advisor compensation in embedded commissions and trailing commissions, and they even lock the client into a seven-year redemption schedule that can compromise flexibility down the road.

Traditional front-end load mutual funds

This is just the same product as the one above, but at least the client isn't locked in to a redemption schedule and the advisor might be a little more inclined to offer better service precisely because of the flexibility afforded by the lack of a lock-in.

Low cost, actively managed no-load mutual funds

Moving right along, we can accomplish the same thing as with the previous option, but with funds that cost considerably less. This is true even if you compare the true no-load funds to the "F Class" versions of the traditional third-party funds. The no-loads don't advertise and so keep their costs down. They also offer no or virtually no trailing commissions to advisors, so anyone using them in a retail situation would have to send the client a separate transparent bill (either based on the quantum of assets being managed or the number of hours spent working on the account) as a means of receiving payment. Some fund companies have the added bonus of offering totally pure funds too.

Index mutual funds and ETFs

Index products are completely pure, extremely tax efficient, totally transparent, and cheap, cheap, cheap. Cost is perhaps the most important determinant of investment performance, so anything that you can do to limit your expenses in gaining access to a diversified and balanced portfolio is an extremely good thing.

Asset class funds

Research going back about forty years shows that capital markets can be best explained using a three factor model. The "enhanced" index funds are actually slightly more expensive than the products listed previously, but they take an intelligent approach to indexing by adding value through trading strategies and tilting holdings toward value stocks and small company stocks. This makes a wonderful complement to conventional index and, if desired, actively managed options.

Three Investment Product Value Propositions

If one accepts that risk and return are related and that any informed investment decision requires a clear consideration of both, then there are essentially three alternatives: market type risk with market type return, less than market risk with less than market return, and above market risk with above market return. The extent to which one mixes and matches these is primarily a question of risk preference.

Similarly, there are three primary product types available for investors who want to use diversified investment products as portfolio building blocks: actively managed funds, exchange traded funds (ETFs), and "enhanced" index funds. Actively managed funds involve technical and fundamental analysis where the stock-picking managers buy those securities they believe will outperform the market as a whole. Exchange traded funds aim to replicate the market, both its risks and rewards. However, since these products have a cost (albeit a small one), they are certain to lag their benchmarks over time. Enhanced index funds are like ETFs in that they believe in market efficiency, but differ because they are not concerned about tracking error. Enhanced indexers believe risk and return are related (i.e. that markets are not only "efficient" but that they are also in "equilibrium"). The enhancement, therefore, is to willingly take on more risk in the expectation of increasing returns by an equal or greater amount.

To many, these three product lines offer a logical continuum of choice. Depending on one's views, any or all could be used in portfolio construction—at least in theory. In practice, active funds typically (but not always) achieve below-market returns in the long run with risk levels that can be more than, less than, or approximately equal to the associated risk. It is certainly true that some active managers have performance records that look better than the benchmark. However, two points remain crucial:

1. Outperformers over statistically significant time periods are rare.
2. No one has figured out how to reliably identify outperformers in advance.

If people could identify outperforming managers in advance, those managers would most certainly be worth hiring. Of course, that's sort of like saying if people could identify winning lottery numbers in advance, those numbers would certainly be worth playing. Sadly, outperformers are like lottery numbers—they cannot be reliably identified in advance. Every mutual fund prospectus on the planet says so.

In contrast, ETFs get market returns minus costs while taking on market levels of risk. Since they are concerned with tracking error as a primary definition of risk, ETFs are required to buy and sell stocks when they are added to or removed from the index in question. If you define risk as "the extent to which my investments deviate from the market as a whole," then ETFs are for you.

Finally, enhanced index funds typically (but not always) offer above-market returns in the long run precisely because they seek out securities with above market risk. It is noteworthy that the enhancement strategy does not involve a one-to-one relationship. In other words, enhanced index products typically involve modest increases in risk relative to a market level while simultaneously aiming for moderate to strong improvements in long-term returns. While this is generally the case, it sometimes takes decades for this risk/return attribute to play out. A simple summary would be that enhanced indexers buy the index, but are smart about it.

Here's a simple and fairly current illustration regarding these concepts. In early 2006, the *Globe and Mail*'s personal finance columnist Rob Carrick ran a story called "The financial industry by the numbers" in which he offered a few tidbits about 2005, including the revelation that the S&P TSX composite returned 24.4% on the year (with dividends reinvested), while the Ivy Canadian Fund (the biggest Canadian equity fund) returned only 7.1% over the same time period. Perhaps even more telling (since one fund is hardly representative) is that only 26 out of 266 Canadian equity funds beat the index over that one-year time period.[1]

Another consideration is how one might define risk: is it standard deviation or tracking error? Again, actively managed funds have all manner of standard deviations relative to the asset classes they invest in. Some are higher and some are lower. There is no way to summarize them other than to say standard deviation can vary considerably and on a case-by-case basis. The easiest products to understand are ETFs. They view risk as tracking error. To ETF investors (and product manufacturers, presumably), risk is defined by how much the investment deviates from the index it is set up to track. Enhanced indexers are more concerned with standard deviation than tracking error. As such, it might also be said that enhanced indexers view risk in absolute terms while traditional indexers view risk in relative terms, that is, relative to a benchmark. Neither is clearly right or wrong, but FSPs should try very hard to ensure that their clients understand the difference so that they use products that reflect their own views.

Investors should consider their own views regarding risk, reward, and the probability of outperformance when making investment decisions, and advisors should offer dispassionate guidance to assist them. True professionals offer dependable evidence for all possible explanations and choices and let the clients make the final decision. Their primary objective should be to offer accurate advice based on empirical research while addressing all material facts. Deliberately remaining silent on these material facts is a form of manipulation and has no place in a professional environment.

Are Markets Efficient or Not?

One of the great debates in the financial services industry surrounds the notion of market efficiency. The debate has raged since Eugene Fama wrote his doctoral thesis positing that markets are sufficiently efficient and that it is improbable that a manager can reliably add value over a long time frame (i.e. stock picking is unlikely to yield better-than-market results). Perhaps "raged" is a bit too strong, but the question has festered and simmered and existed as a sidebar within the industry for a long time. Most FSPs, however, never discuss it with their clients. Thoughtful, client-centred STANDUP FSPs have been struggling with this for years. Sales-oriented, product-centred SPANDEX FSPs have been either blissfully unaware of this, or totally unwilling to bring it to their clients' attention.

If markets are efficient, then fundamental and technical analysis is essentially useless, since market prices would reflect all relevant information instantaneously—with exceptions for insiders. If the analysis that underpins security selection yields no additional useful information, then we're left with making stock picks based on hunches and trends. As such, security selection based on empirical analysis is not likely to add any value over time.

A moment ago, I suggested that the question of market efficiency leads to a clear choice between two mutually exclusive responses—either markets are efficient or they are not. Could there be a middle ground in the form of a more nuanced position? That's a challenge for many FSPs. The problem that comes about when you think about it logically is how do FSPs make meaningful recommendations to clients in light of this? Does it have to be an all-or-nothing proposition? What about degree? For instance, what if markets are somewhat efficient or mostly efficient, but there were still some opportunities to exploit mispricings that crop up every now and again?

When approached from this perspective, the question then becomes, just how efficient do you think markets are? And just how inefficient do markets need to be in order to try to beat them? For instance, two people could actually agree that markets are 80% efficient (accepting that a percentage of efficiency cannot actually be measured). One person could conclude that active management should be used to try to "beat the market," while the other could conclude that an 80% degree of efficiency is too high a hurdle to clear and so recommends that clients just "buy the market." Therefore, even if reasonable people could agree on quantification (which latter is actually impossible), they could still differ on what to do about it. The problem remains, as mentioned previously, a matter of opinion.

Here's a sample letter that might at least allow for some latitude:

Disclosure of Investment Philosophy

This is to acknowledge that my FSP, Joe Brilliant, has advised me that he believes capital markets are sufficiently efficient to justify the use of passive and/or asset class products most of (and possibly even all of) the time. He believes this approach features relative predictability and tax efficiency and has advised that I consider building my portfolio using these investment options predominantly.

Joe has further advised me that by using actively managed investment products, I may be compromising the asset allocation set out in my investment policy statement and that I may incur higher tax liabilities as a result of higher portfolio turnover. Moreover, these potential shortcomings do not offer any evident or reliably predictable quid pro quo as there is no evidence to indicate that one can determine in advance that those actively managed investment products will reliably outperform passive or asset class alternatives. As such, Joe's view is that neither fund picking nor stock picking should be attempted. That being said, Joe affirms a willingness to work using those approaches (up to 100% of the portfolio) where it is my desire to do so.

In essence, Joe believes that the role of professional FSPs involves identifying tax-minimization strategies, ensuring that clients have the right amount and right kind of insurance, set and maintain suitable asset mixes, and maintain discipline. The one thing that he does not believe FSPs should attempt is to identify either securities or securities pickers that will outperform after fees over meaningful time periods.

While there can be no assurances that a passive approach will outperform an active alternative, Joe has advised me that in the very long run (twenty years or more), he believes it is probable that a passive or asset class approach will offer superior long-term, client-specific, risk-adjusted, after-tax returns.

_____   _____   _____
Client   Joe Brilliant   Date

Perhaps this is an area where reasonable people can agree to disagree. At least this kind of disclosure recognizes that there's an issue, tries to depict the problem, allows the FSP to offer a personal opinion (an obvious component of giving advice), while still allowing for client choice—it is the client's money, after all. The issue here is not whether people are allowed to have an opinion. Of course they are. The issue is whether they are manipulating a process in order to effectively (perhaps even unwittingly) impose their opinions on others who are coming to them for independent advice. Compare this with what many FSPs do today: they offer to work with people *provided that those people accept their views about active management.*

We've already looked at how an IPS (along with documents like the one above) can offer structure to a client-FSP relationship. What about the "softer" side of advice? Specifically, there are many people who now think advising is at least as much about understanding behaviour quirks as it is about understanding efficiency and inefficiency. Is there anything going on that would make it difficult for a STANDUP FSP to keep her clients focused on the really important things?

Investment Pornography

Sex Sells. —Anonymous

There are many people who feel that the media, far from being the sentinels of consumer interests, are really just unwitting lackeys for corporate interests. After all, who pays for newspaper and television advertising? And what would the media write about if they clearly acknowledged that outperformance is random and therefore unreliable?

Given that so many people in the media perpetuate what some observers feel amounts to a giant hoax, is it any wonder that STANDUP FSPs have their work cut out for them in keeping consumers focused on the things that are truly important? Far from being particularly critical of Corporate Canada, the national media are essentially unwitting accomplices that aid and abet the presumption that stock picking as a value-adding pursuit. It may be argued that if markets truly are reasonably inefficient, they might be giving people vital information they need to make informed day-to-day decisions. You be the judge. Since no one can be certain, all we know is that they provide daily quotes and sound bites about market moves, trends, forecasts, and "what it all means"— for better or worse.

There's another way that the media causes people to alter their views. More often than not, the media portray misdemeanours and malfeasance as being perpetrated by FSPs rather than corporate interests. Again, although FSPs are by no means uniformly lily white in their conduct, the same is true of corporate interests. Still, the media are fond of playing "pin the blame on the FSP" by disproportionately accepting the industry's view when things go awry.

Although the value proposition of security selection might be tenuous, it is constantly legitimized by the circular logic of the national media. The cycle goes like this:

Reader: "This issue must be important because it hit the headlines today. Did you see today's headlines? I've got something important to ask you..."

Some STANDUP FSPs might say:

"Yes, I saw the headlines, but so what? Do these headlines have anything to do with your retirement plan, really?"

The challenge for all FSPs is to cut through the clutter and to get consumers to focus on the things that are:

a) important, and
b) within the consumer's personal control.

The chapter on behavioural finance will go over this in more detail, but for now let's just work on the premise that the vast majority of headlines should not cause anyone to pick up the phone and call the FSP or log on to a computer terminal and start trading. Besides, even if it were important, it would be too late for virtually everyone by the time they read about it in the paper or saw the feature on television anyway. If markets are indeed sufficiently efficient such that outperformance is improbable, it means that by the time the information has been made available, the implication will have been felt. If there's news that interest rates have gone up unexpectedly, the bond market will reflect that new reality in mere minutes, if not seconds. Calling your FSP the next morning to "sell all bonds in excess of five years' duration" in response to the "news" is like locking the barn door after the horse has left the stable.

The industry has a term to describe those economic and political events that get people interested, even excited, but have virtually no real value: "investment pornography."

Background Noise

One thing that people need to sort out for themselves is whether various elements of "the news" really are just investment pornography. Ironically, unimportant but interesting tidbits of information grab financial headlines on most days. The information is usually nothing more than background noise in the busy hubbub of life for a person seeking financial independence. Part of the job of a good FSP is to act as a filter and to ensure that clients are not unduly swayed by these seemingly important sound bites that rarely add up to anything. Investment pornography can include the following items:

• changes in interest rates, employment, inflation, and GDP
• fluctuation in currencies
• the price of oil, gold, and other commodities
• where the TSX, Dow, S&P 500, Nasdaq, Nikkei, and FTSE closed
• yield curves
• housing starts
• consumer confidence
• news about mutual fund sales or redemptions
• hot stocks, funds, and sectors
• new highs and cyclical lows for the markets

Anyone focusing on a time frame of twenty years or longer isn't going to care much about the day-to-day, week-to-week, or month-to-month gyrations of any of these items. But people read about them nonetheless (newspapers have to print something!) and people watch the business news daily (CNBC has advertisers to satisfy). As the saying goes, "In the short run, returns are virtually unknowable; but in the long run, they are virtually inevitable." Truly professional FSPs won't make predictions about what any of the gyrations mean or will lead to because these fluctuations don't genuinely matter. Professional FSPs focus not only on things that matter but also on those that are within their control.

Not surprisingly, virtually every bit of financial news is portrayed (at least implicitly) as something that demonstrates market inefficiency and that could lead to disproporationate profit. It should be obvious by now that any focus on decisions about investment strategy is counterproductive. But since that's where the media and the world outside would have consumers look if left to their own devices, STANDUP FSPs have a daunting task ahead of them, yet not for reasons that you might intuitively think. It's not that the media is unduly hard on FSPs (although they generally are), it's that they are unduly sycophantic toward corporate interests. The media blathers on about all the unimportant things we just looked at. Who can blame consumers for thinking they're important?

Unfortunately, as soon as someone is seduced by the hoopla of earnings, forecasts, trends and the like, they become far more likely to do something stupid with their money. Focusing on the wrong things can lead to making the wrong decisions. If FSPs can just get their clients to keep their eyes on the things that matter, they will have likely earned their fees.

Of course, journalists are just as subject to the "tyranny of the mortgage payment" as the typical FSP. I've spoken with a fairly wide variety of journalists in my day. My sense is that most are actually quite similar to the typical FSP. They're decent, hardworking, and reasonable people who have been co-opted by a large, profit-driven, and self-interested industry that has a clear and unfair advantage in portraying itself as the protector of all that is good and right.

In essence, many journalists even joust with a number of FSPs in a never-ending game of "blame reversal" where each side ends up sniping at the other while the real culprits (manufacturers, distributors, and the regulators that do more to protect them than to sanction them) get away virtually unscathed. The conspiracy of ignorance has an accomplice here. The strategy of divide and conquer has also served corporate interests very well through the years.

As with active managers and SPANDEX FSPs, there's a certain degree of self-preservation going on here too. I was once at a conference where a delegate asked a money manager if he thought markets were efficent. "Of course there are inefficiencies!" the manager replied, "I wouldn't be here if that weren't the case!" That was the questioner's point all along. Whether markets were efficient or inefficient, the only way stock pickers (including SPANDEX FSPs) or media people get paid is if they can convince enough people that there are inefficiencies. Imagine if you tried this line of thinking on your local clergy:

> Parishioner: "How can you be sure that God exists?"
> Clergy: "Of course God exists. You wouldn't need me if God didn't exist, would you?"
> Parishioner: "Exactly. Now please answer my question."
> Clergy: "I thought I did."
> Parishioner: "No you didn't, you simply proved my point."

Once again, we're getting ourselves into a religious debate that simply cannot be proved or disproved. The media are every bit as guilty of tautology as anyone else might be. Note that I'm not suggesting that the parishioner is either right or wrong on the matter under consideration, but I'm simply pointing out that there's ample room for skepticism given the line of reasoning being used by the clergy. When self-interest is allowed to creep into the advice being given, it is only natural to suspect the motive of the person giving the advice.

None of this proves a thing about efficiency or inefficiency. The existence of investment pornography merely complicates the questions surrounding good advice. If good financial advice isn't about understanding trends and making forecasts, then what is it about?

Behavioural Finance

I can calculate the motion of heavenly bodies, but not the madness of people.
—Sir Isaac Newton

The phrase "you're only human" is used almost daily in describing the foibles of life. Plenty of people routinely make mistakes, but most people don't get too upset because, hey, you're only human. It is human nature to sometimes do things we know we shouldn't. We persist because of entrenched habits or the feeling we get when we treat ourselves. In some instances, we procrastinate because we don't want to deal with certain responsibilities or obligations that we've been putting off.

One of the most interesting aspects of being human is that we sometimes focus on things that are fun while ignoring other things that are more purposeful. For consumers and FSPs alike, this can manifest itself in some perverse ways. For instance, even though there is a mountain of research that seems to justify economics' reputation as "the dismal science," since it is so often thrown off course by human behaviour, there are generations of people who have gone through our school systems to get formal training in "classical" economics. Markets don't always behave the way they're supposed to because markets are just the sum total of a large number of people and sometimes people make weird decisions.

Since people are only human, many observable "macro" trends don't always play out neatly in a "micro" sense. This quirk of human nature certainly has applications in the field of financial advice. From a planning perspective, there are just too many things that people don't focus on because they seem like the sorts of things that "would never happen to me." Human nature is a major deterrent to life insurance purchases, for instance. It also explains why so many of us still don't have Wills and Powers of Attorney in place.

What FSPs Shouldn't Be Doing

FSPs often focus on attributes like style diversification rather than on asset class diversification, even though the Brinson research clearly shows that considerations such as style diversification are also nearly useless since they're investment strategy decisions. For instance, an FSP might recommend adding a growth manager to complement a pre-existing value manager rather than looking for entirely new asset classes that, when added prudently to the investments already in place, would serve to improve risk-adjusted returns much further than style diversification ever could.

Professional STANDUP FSPs don't engage in anything other than abstract discussions about the direction or timing of the market or market performance. Everyone who has even implied an ability to make reliable predictions should offer a massive mea culpa *and move immediately to rectify the misconceptions that they themselves have perpetrated as a result. Consumers and FSPs alike should spend most of their time reviewing and adhering to investment policy statements and looking for planning opportunities. Beyond that, most of what FSPs do might be referred to as "constructive behaviour modification."*

Instead of focusing on things that are controllable (cost, asset class purity, tax efficiency), the majority of FSPs focus on the most random and uncontrollable element of portfolio design: performance as gained or lost through security selection and market timing decisions.

Perhaps it's just more fun to focus on security selection and market timing decisions. Most consumers are generally unwilling to pay more than a few basis points for services that optimize portfolios with a wide range of asset classes and regularly rebalance those portfolios back to those targets. There's not much profit margin available in promoting investment policy, even though they are highly important. On the other hand, there's a whole lot of money to be made in the monolithic industry focusing on security selection and market timing.

Any professional who is serious about putting the interests of the client first should acknowledge that the employment of active management is, to some extent at least, an exercise in corporate profit maximization. The industry has shot itself in the foot. Having convinced all of society (and especially the media) that security selection is actually worth something, it can't kick the habit and come clean with the whole truth because profitability would plummet.

The Big Mistake

The main duty of the FSP is to ensure that clients avoid "The Big Mistake." Of all the advances in the field of personal finance, there may be none more important than the fairly recent discoveries in behavioural finance. Even the ongoing dispute between active and passive products predicated on differing views of market efficiciency may pale in comparison.

Behavioural finance is the study of how emotional decisions caused by human factors often lead to poor investment choices and reduced investment returns. A growing body of research demonstrates how this "human side" of investment decision-making has a major impact on actual performance outcomes. In spite of this, there's no reference in any textbook for FSPs to teach them how to stay the course and deal with the roadblocks associated with their clients' emotions.

Daniel Kahneman and Amos Tversky are likely two of the most influential social scientists of the twentieth century. Relatively few people have heard of them. Their research into decision-making has precipitated a sea change in finance. These psychologists have conducted extensive research on how people perceive and react to uncertainty. In 2002, Kahneman was awarded the Nobel Prize in Economics together with experimental economist Vernon Smith. In essence, they demonstrated that people don't always think rationally or behave optimally regarding their decisions, especially when it pertains to their own money. Furthermore, people seldom understand risk in terms of both the likelihood of something happening and the degree of damage that might be inflicted if it does happen. This is likely one of the reasons so few people carry the right kind and right amount of life insurance.

These findings are particularly interesting when combined

with the Nobel Prize in Economics from the previous year. In 2001, the Nobel went to George A. Akerlof, A. Michael Spence, and Joseph Stiglitz for their work on markets with asymmetric information (where agents on one side of a transaction have more and/or better information than agents on the other side). It is sometimes called "the economics of information" and has applications in comparing relatively uninformed FSPs to relatively well-informed academics regarding market efficiency and in comparing relatively uninformed consumers to relatively well-informed FSPs when it comes to retail investment products and strategies.

It seems many consumers come to FSPs for insight, only to get well-informed opinions. Informed opinions ought to be superior to uninformed opinions, but should not be confused with facts. Many FSPs would be well advised to consider the three possible ways of processing information: you could know something and know that you know it; you could not know something and know that you don't know it; and finally, you could not know something and be totally unaware of your own ignorance. This last situation is arguably the most dangerous. I suspect many FSPs don't recommend that consumers consider passive options because they are simply unaware of the evidence in support of it. They are ignorant of the evidence because they simply assumed they "already had it all figured out" and so moved on to other things.

Returning to behavioural finance, while some experts believe there are investors out there who can exploit human foibles for personal gain, Kahneman doesn't think it can be done. He is of the strong opinion that markets are efficient. He says: "People see skill in performance where there is no skill...People are overly impressed by the performance of money managers, who sell what they've been doing for the past few years. It is difficult to realize that you would get very similar patterns if there were no skill at all in picking stocks or running funds." He goes on to say that: "...the idea that any single individual without extra information or extra market power can beat the market is extraordinarily unlikely. Yet the market is full of people who think they can do it and full of people who believe them. This is one of the great mysteries of finance: why do people believe they can do the impossible? And why do others believe them?"

Qualified FSPs can be useful in offering reasonable counsel that comes from a perspective that should mitigate potentially self-destructive tendencies. STANDUP FSPs understand this intuitively. In spite of this, FSPs receive *no formal training* in the field of behavioural finance before they start in the business. That's beginning to change, but there are many who believe that it's taking too long.

There are thousands of FSPs working today who had to demonstrate the ability to calculate intrinsic values of special warrants and the price of a security trading ex-dividend and cum-dividend. In reality, most never use these sorts of skills after writing their licencing exam. That same course material did nothing to explain behavioural concepts like anchoring or loss aversion, even though these and other emotional and intellectual blind spots go a long way to explaining investment experience.

Once again, it seems the financial services industry has trained an army of representatives to be salespeople, not true advisors. Any FSP should understand that advice needs to be offered from the client's perspective and that the client is going to feel overwhelmed by some of the complexity and uncertainty of capital markets. University courses leading to an advanced degree in financial planning, therefore, also need to add an entire body of work to their course material dealing with tangible case study approaches on how to assist consumers in staying the course and avoiding "The Big Mistake." Imagine the good that qualified FSPs could do if educators actually taught them how to apply solutions to these problems.

Ironically, Kahneman and Tversky are also two of the biggest allies that stock and fund pickers have. People engaged in the business of security selection argue that if people make repeated mistakes regarding risk and reward, then clearly capital markets must not be altogether efficient. The behavioural finance research deals with individual decisions made by particular investors, whereas "the market" is actually the sum total of all investors (private and institutional, large and small) that reacts to information as it becomes available. Therefore, even though individual investors might make inappropriate investment decisions, the market as a whole might not.

This is the essence of the problem. On the surface, many consumers have sufficient knowledge of capital markets to make adequate financial decisions. In spite of this, there is evidence that shows massive net redemptions when mutual fund values are dropping and massive net sales when markets are on fire. If the phrase "buy low, sell high" is such a trite little truism that any fool can understand, why do so many people ignore it and do just the opposite? Similarly, if the principle of diversification is so basic that it is seen as a "motherhood" issue that everyone understands and agrees with, why were so many portfolios wildly overweight in technology when the bubble burst?

If left to their own devices, consumers will frequently make emotional decisions during market swings and manias, even if they later acknowledge (usually with the benefit of 20/20 hindsight) that they were not making logical decisions at the time. But people can make irrational decisions even when markets are behaving "normally," if such a description can be applied to markets at all. Professional FSPs should be able to save well-intentioned consumers from themselves in these times of weakness.

Dr. Meir Statman of Santa Clara University is a leading authority on behavioural finance. He offers a number of examples of how our outlook on anything is really just a function of our vantage point relative to the thing we are observing.

At its origin in 1896, the Dow Jones Industrial Average stood at 41 (that's not a typo). By the end of 1998, it stood at 9,181. Here's the question: what number would the DJIA have stood at in 1998 if all the dividends paid were reinvested? Can you guess? It turns out that most people guess somewhere between 30,000 and 80,000, which seems plausible enough. The actual answer is 652,230. The simple reason most people guess far too low is a concept called anchoring. People use the figure of 9,181 as an "anchor" to their guess and make a significant cognitive error in the process. Most people never expect it to be possible for the actual number to be that much higher.

We all make cognitive errors because the brain is designed to deal with the important problems in life, but the perspective the brain uses to deal with more complex problems isn't always accurate. Being mindful of behavioural finance, we can see how FSPs can be useful in helping people to see newer, more accurate realities.

This might explain how an FSP might use the principles of behavioural finance to give a client a better sense of perspective, which in turn would hopefully lead to better decision-making. Let's say an FSP is talking to a client who wants to impulsively buy or sell an investment. The FSP could point out that there are two parties to every transaction and that (since investing is a zero sum game before costs), only one of them can "win" in the assessment of the purchase or sale in question. Who's the buyer and who's the seller and why are you so certain you know more than that person? There's an old poker saying that if you can't spot the patsy in the first half hour at the table, then it's probably you.

All things considered, the professional FSP can play many vital roles. As an educator, they can teach clients how to frame their expectations. As a coach, they can help them retain a proper focus. As a financial physician, they can work to find the best treatment available *based on investment science*. Along with these important roles come a number of important challenges, such as convincing clients that their own brain often misleads them and keeping investors calm when markets are choppy.

When I talk to friends who move up the corporate ladder and into management, many say their biggest challenge is managing people. I think to myself that they don't know how easy they have it. *Professional FSPs have to manage people who are often irrational, emotional, and unaware of their own biases in dealing with their life savings! They do this in a context of the popular media constantly acting as though unimportant things are actually extremely important.*

A 2001 Dalbar study came up with interesting results regarding behaviour and performance. It showed that during the seventeen years from 1984 to 2000, the average U.S. stock fund investor earned returns of only 5.32% a year, even though the S&P 500 returned 16.29% over that same time period—a stunning testament to the importance of behaviour in investing.

Attempted market timing is a classic portfolio strategy error. Throughout history, market timers have come and gone with no meaningful evidence of any capacity to predict things in a manner that is statistically significant. Market timing is simply the manifestation of a major cognitive error called "hindsight bias." After all, we all know that hindsight is always 20/20. There are now commercially available funds that attempt to time markets. Perhaps investors who want to engage in this practice could consider giving their money over to stock pickers rather than trying to time markets themselves. I doubt there would be a materially differnt outcome.

The world is full of stories about people who got into technology stocks because there was a sense that "this time was different." Books that talked about "new paradigms of security valuations" seduced people. Greed, one of the two primary drivers of human activity in capital markets, had taken over in the late 1990s. Sadly, the third millennium brought a different storyline. In retrospect, many of the people who got in too late (and held on too long) admitted that they "should have seen it coming all along." That's hindsight bias. The past is always clear when viewed from the perspective of the present.

Investors often behave badly due to any of a number of other behaviourally motivated biases: fear of regret, myopic loss aversion, cognitive dissonance, representativeness, and overconfidence being the most likely remaining culprits. Research shows that *even those who do understand risk often act irrationally in spite of their comprehension of these concepts.* If the primary role of FSPs is to help their clients earn adequate returns while employing additional related wealth management services, then anything that assists in performing that role should be taught from the outset.

The New Keynesians

The emerging role of the professional FSP is both an interesting and unique one. On the one hand, we're talking about people who know minute details about things that most people never think of. Most FSPs bombard clients with hard data, graphs, research reports, and numerous more "serious" and quantifiable metrics explaining investment performance. Many can ramble on about fixed income investments and the comparative merits of rate anticipation and relative value swaps the way most people talk about Saturday's hockey game. On the other hand, FSPs have to stay tuned into their clients' deepest emotions if they ever hope to gain the necessary trust to get people to act in ways that may be contrary to their potentially dangerous natural instincts.

In short, a good FSP can be a valuable resource in understanding a number of concepts. Being a trusted financial professional will go well beyond managing money in the future. Although FSPs know all about money, they have a particularly important role to play in educating their clients about themselves. Interestingly, the word *educate* comes from the latin *educo*, which literally means to "draw out." Good FSPs will ultimately draw out the best in their clients.

It is becoming increasingly clear in the context of financial advice that most FSPs are left-brained people offering left-brained (i.e. logical and empirical) explanations for why things might happen and what to do in response. The trouble is, most people make financial decisions with the right side of their brain, the one that deals with the emotional aspects of decision-making. How much training do FSPs have these days to assist them in guiding their clients emotionally? The answer is usually none. In spite of this, behavioural finance is something most FSPs need to grapple with on a daily basis.

Let's use the ideas of another well-known economist to illustrate the coming together of both conventional economics and behavioural economics when explaining the role of a new-age professional FSP. John Maynard Keynes was an extremely influential economist who felt that the primary role of governments was to mitigate the vagaries of the business cycle—to have highs that were less high and lows that were less low, while still growing the economy. His idea was sort of like portfolio design in seeking adequate returns with acceptable levels of risk.

One of Keynes' most notable contributions to economics was in the field of fiscal policy. He believed governments should spend more money (perhaps incurring a deficit) in order to stimulate the economy when things were slow and then spend less (or tax more) when times were good to make up for any previously incurred shortfalls. One of the primary shortfalls of Keynesian economics was modern politics. Voters would be sure to throw out any politician who taxed more or spent less. In this context, no one should be surprised by debt levels in many developed nations.

Still, Keynesian economics is a funny thing and more universal than you might think. Instead of looking at the financial stability of a nation, why not draw an analogy with an individual household? The most basic truism of investing is "buy low, sell high." Conceptually, FSPs have a role with their clients much like governments had in implementing Keynes' ideas: they have to get their clients to do things they might not otherwise be inclined to do. Human nature being what it is, clients are inclined to buy when things are going up and to sell in a panic when the markets are heading south. Put another way, the role of a good Keynesian public policy administrator is to constructively temper the amplitude of the business cycle for the benefit of the greater public good. One might say that the parallel role of a good FSP is to temper the amplitude of client emotions. There's a distinct need to help people resist the temptation to buy just because the investment has been going up or to sell just because it has been going down.

To most people, money is an impenetrable topic that they wish someone could explain using plain language and simple concepts. There is still a large number of FSPs who consider it beneath them to employ techniques rooted in behavioural research, even if they were properly taught. Many FSPs who resist or happen to remain ignorant of the findings of the behaviouralists are probably also ignorant of or still resisting the findings of Sharpe, Miller, and Markowitz.

It is generally accepted (although there is little *reliable* empirical evidence) that good FSPs are often useful in dealing with the concerns of behavioural finance. Pioneers in behavioural finance like Richard Thaler at the University of Chicago have done further academic research demonstrating that when people are confused and anxious, they do irrational things like selling low and buying high, even as they profess to be sensible long-term investors.

If FSPs came to understand how most consumers of financial information think *before* being allowed to go out and assist in planning their clients' financial futures, the world would be a richer place. In a business that's all about connecting and relating, we train our FSPs to be technically proficient in analyzing data that defies meaningful short-term analysis, yet we do a horrible job of training them to empower the people they serve to take control of their lives by ignoring the investment pornography all around them.

People too often focus on things that are out of their control. Chasing a hot stock or a hot fund has another negative consequence: tax liabilities. A recent study showed that taxes eat up as much as one-sixth of the average mutual fund return, which is only 9% to begin with. Since approximately 54% of all mutual funds in Canada are held outside registered plans, this is a significant concern. Amin Mawani, Moshe Milevsky, and Kamphol Panyagometh of the Schulich School of Business at York University in Toronto have researched the effects of taxation on mutual fund portfolios. In a recent study published in the *Canadian Tax Journal*, they conclude that "taxes exceed management fees and brokerage commissions in their ability to erode long-term investment returns."[2] A responsible FSP can help consumers to resist making questionable trades.

In the United States, new legislation compels mutual funds to disclose after-tax returns. The York research turned up some interesting results, including the fact that when funds are ranked for their after-tax returns, the order generally differs from pure fund performance rankings. On average, funds moved up or down twenty-eight spots in the rankings compared to their peers as a result of their tax efficiency (or lack thereof).

Research done by John Bowen of CEG Worldwide reinforces these ideas. He demonstrates that "client-centred" FSPs are more financially successful on a personal level than "market-centred" FSPs. This is largely because the work being done is more meaningful to the client, who generally appreciates the more purposeful and customized approach that is invariably used by client-centred FSPs.

As old-school numbers and salespeople within the industry become more and more in touch with the emotional side of investment and financial planning, there will be an ever-increasing need to gravitate toward the new paradigm.

Examined from a behavioural perspective, it seems FSPs generally do add value over time, but this has virtually nothing to do with the products they recommend. Instead, it has more to do with the implementation of planning opportunities and constructive behaviour modification. I should acknowledge that the term "constructive behaviour modification" sounds awful to many people. Many think it sounds downright manipulative. To my mind, the emphasis needs to be on "constructive" rather than on "behaviour modification." One might want to contrast this with the way the financial services industry works today, which one could refer to as the "unwitting complicity in profit-maximizing and client-harming behaviour modification."

What needs to be remembered is that the real manipulation occurs in the culture of security selection and market timing discussions. When people talk about what the Bank of Canada is going to do at its next meeting, they are manipulating themselves into thinking the decision will have a material impact on their portfolios. It won't. When people read a magazine that discusses how reforms to corporate governance laws are too ham-fisted or proceeding too slowly, they are being manipulated. In the grand scheme, those things simply don't matter very much. In most cases, they won't matter at all. The role of the FSP is to get clients retired and to keep them retired in a lifestyle they have come to expect. Beating or predicting the market's short-term movements (or even understanding them) is simply not in the job description.

Among many experienced and successful FSPs, the best clearly understand that there is a far greater need for an emotional connection than for a logical connection when dealing with clients. They pay thousands of dollars out of their own pockets to take courses that teach them how to draw out personal information about their clients that would be helpful in working with them. The psychology of capital markets is a difficult subject and one that few are prepared to address directly.

One person who is actively engaged in the alignment of life goals with planning objectives is Bill Bachrach. Bachrach has built a consulting and training empire by catering to and teaching FSPs how to peel back the layers of the onion that are the human emotions associated with personal finance. He teaches courses and has written a number of books predicated on the simple "Values-Based" question: "What's important about money...to you?"[3] The ensuing process allows FSPs to more deeply understand and respond to the values and dreams of their client base. Aspiring FSPs are not taught to do this kind of open-ended information gathering unless they pay the freight themselves *after* they start in the business.

On top of ensuring that our financial professionals need a comprehensive academic training in a wide variety of interdisciplinary fields associated with wealth management, there is obviously more reform needed. True professionals should certainly be able to understand the "soft," right-brained mechanics of personal finance as well.

Remember that only the most recent generations of MBA graduates have been taking mandatory courses in ethics. Similarly, new university graduates with a degree conferring the right to practice as professional and holistic financial advisors will need to address the very real gap in the education system as it presently stands. Our number-cruncher FSPs are going to have to write some essays, role-play with their classmates, and do some interactive learning in diagnosing both the financial *and the emotional* distresses facing prospective clients.

FSPs have never been taught the importance of behaviour in investing, so they have come to the conclusion that behaviour must not be very important since it isn't being taught. We need to set the record straight right away and to teach our FSPs that investor psychology is a very, very big deal.

It should also be noted that one needn't be an investment neophyte to have one's behaviour modified in a constructive manner. A 2006 study done with students from the Wharton and Harvard Business Schools asked students to allocate a hypothetical $10,000 between four competing index funds.[4] The funds all had identical mandates and structures—they differed only in the fees they charged. In this instance, the lowest cost fund ought to be the preferred fund—if a person was to invest rationally. Fewer than 20% of all students did this. The jury is still out on why this might have happened, but one theory is that the brainiac students were diverted by extraneous material in the prospectuses and as such, did not focus on the really important information, namely, the funds' respective fee structures.

A Behavioural Bias toward Inaction

Biases don't only exist in terms of what one buys. They also exist in questions like when one might sell. You've probably read a number of promotional pieces about people or organizations that have a "bias toward action." These are the people and companies that don't just stand around and watch the world turn, these are the doers of the world. Many people are comforted and perhaps even inspired by this kind of attitude, but personal finance is one field where they shouldn't be.

Extremes are dangerous in many endeavours, but when it comes to managing your finances, dormancy almost always beats hyperactivity. Nearly every major study on the subject has shown that portfolio turnover correlates negatively to performance. In layperson's terms: the more you trade, the worse you do. Every trade involves costs, including trading costs, bid/ask spreads, and possible tax liabilities. The more you trade, the more these costs eat into your returns.

It's one of the great ironies about wealth management. Many people assume that in order to stay on top of your finances, you need to monitor them unflinchingly and to make swift, sure, and informed decisions when circumstances change. Nothing could be further from the truth. As it turns out, the most successful investors are usually strategic thinkers who are prepared to wait years for the rest of the world to clue in.

If left to their own devices, most people would likely trade too often, and excessive trading hurts overall performance. This happens primarily because people believe they can discern trends when random events cause prices to display trendlike attributes. Behavioural economists would consider this a clear example of investor overconfidence. Many people look at short-term results and extrapolate the outcomes into a longer time frame. These people are likely to use the phrase "the trend is your friend" in their approach to portfolio management. Lottery corporations have been known to run ads that explain there is no "strategy" to playing slot machines and that irrespective of which machines have paid off recently, each individual pull produces a random outcome that is independent of the previous pull. Financial services companies ought to run similar ads regarding the movement of security prices.

This is another area where FSPs can add value. They can act to encourage their clients to trade less by insisting that perceived trends are actually nothing more than coincidental and random outcomes and not the sorts of things that one should consider "useful information" when trading securities. Unfortunately, a large portion of the industry does nothing to clarify this misconception and even goes so far as to imply causation where none exists. Newspapers that run contests where thousands of contestants pick a basket of stocks to see which will outperform over a short time frame merely legitimizes security selection as a socially acceptable form of gambling that masquerades as an intellectual undertaking.

Until ten or twenty years ago, investment management was largely transactional, meaning FSPs only got paid when clients completed trades. In the recent past, as the paradigm of FSPs as value-adding, advice-giving professionals has become more prevalent, the financial services industry has moved from giving away advice and charging for transactions to giving away the transactions and charging for advice. Discount brokers and technology have played a major role in this shift. Today, do-it-yourself (DIY) investors can trade online for virtually no transaction costs. Of course, just because transactions charges are modest, that doesn't mean the trades are "cheap," since the other factors mentioned above should also be considered.

This is why the financial services industry in general—and investing in particular—is so perverse. Things that are generally true elsewhere in life are patently false there. When investing, activity correlates negatively to results and the most expensive products are generally the worst performers precisely because cost reduces returns. Marketing people are constantly trying to get people to trade more and/or add bells and whistles to their investment products. The implication of their ad campaigns is that these pursuits add value. The reality is that these pursuits usually subtract. Most consumers are none the wiser. Why would they ever catch on? The fundamental propositions used by the financial services industry are essentially sound when applied to other fields.

Research done at the University of Michigan and published in 2003 showed that purchase decisions made by mutual fund investors are influenced by salient, attention-grabbing information and that investors are typically more sensitive to salient, in-your-face fees like front-end loads and commissions than they are to operating expenses. As a result, they are more likely to buy funds based on performance, marketing, or advertising. The research showed a consistent negative relationship between flows and front-end load fees. In contrast, they found no relation between operating expenses and fund flows. Out of sight, out of mind. Their research showed that marketing and advertising (things that are generally embedded in fund operating expenses) accounted for this. The findings lend credence to the notion that mutual funds are sold, not bought, and that behavioural factors normally associated with poor consumer decision-making (such as being fairly oblivious to price) caused people to make some perverse decisions.

The financial services industry grew out of a sales culture that made money when engaging in trading activity. Therefore, people giving financial advice less than a generation ago had a clear personal financial incentive to get clients to trade more even though increased trading activity was repeatedly shown to do more for the FSP than for the client. Unfortunately, there was no way for consumers to determine whether advice to transact a trade was genuinely in their best interests or simply dreamt up by the FSP to increase revenue. Over time, individual securities were replaced by mutual funds as the investment vehicles of choice for most consumers.

Irrespective of the products used, it should be noted that SPANDEX FSPs think and act like salespeople, while STANDUP FSPs think and act like value-adding professionals. Unfortunately, when the system was set up, it was done in such a way that every transaction carried the potential for FSP bias.

Eliminate the Bias

It is a truth very certain that when it is not in your power to determine what is true we ought to follow what is most probable.
—René Descartes

There are two primary types of bias in financial services: a bias for active products in favour of passive ones, and a bias in favour of embedded compensation products over unbundled products. In many instances, this is the same problem, since many active products are available primarily with embedded compensation and virtually all passive products are available without embedded compensation. This is why many FSPs profess to favour active management but still refuse to recommend some of the most highly respected funds available like those from PH&N, Mawer, Chou, and Beutel Goodman. Active or not, no embedded compensation usually means no shelf space with most FSPs.

Our challenge in converting a mere industry into a bona fide profession is to eliminate all forms of bias so that FSPs motives can never be called into question. The obvious solution is to create a level playing field, and there is an equally obvious way of doing that: simply have all products pay FSPs the same.

There are two possible ways of meeting this objective: 1) increase the compensation on passive products by bringing it up to the level paid by active ones, or 2) reduce the compensation paid by active products, bringing it down to the level paid by passive ones. From an elimination of bias perspective, either would work, but from a "do what's right for the consumer" perspective, the second option is clearly more appropriate. This is because of DIY investors.

Anyone who wishes to work without the input of an FSP should be allowed to do so without having to pay for that decision. Many observers believe that most people would be better off working with an FSP. That being said, though, what might be right for *most people* may not be right for *all people*, and it would be arrogant to suggest that someone's services are so vital that people should be forced to pay for them whether they use them or not. Earlier this decade, the OSC, under the guidance of Julia Dublin, tried to establish a new framework for offering financial advice—one where self-serving outcomes could be avoided. Known as the Fair Dealing Model, the approach was strenuously opposed by the majority of corporate stakeholders for a variety of reasons. Recently rechristened the "Client Relationship Model," the objective of the reform is to elminate product recommendations that lead to self-serving outcomes.

Compensation considerations can cause clear biases and steps should be taken to eliminate them. Many FSPs the world over have repeatedly acknowledged this bias in opinion polls and studies of advisor attitudes and behaviour. In all the discussion about consumer protection, how can the majority of advisors continue to insist that they are putting clients' interests first while simultaneously insisting on non-disclosure of compensation?

The Final Frontier

Over the past several years, I've spoken to representatives at a number of advisory firms about their philosophies in order to get a sense of their values and corporate culture. One of the things that struck me was the consistency with which virtually all companies preach the notion of FSP independence and how few actually adhere to it when it comes to the question of market efficiency.

Companies will say FSPs can work using either transactional or buy-and-hold philosophies. Either way, there's room. They say you can be a comprehensive planner or a simple investment specialist. Either way, there's room for that too. The FSPs can be commission based or fee based. Either way, they would be welcomed. In short, companies talk a good game about giving FSPs a suitable platform and then leaving them alone to run their practice however they see fit, provided that the FSP remains compliant.

When I ask companies to demonstrate their tolerance of both active and passive philosophies, the troubles start. Suddenly, the firms that champion independence aren't so independent anymore. I'm not suggesting that anyone needs to agree with the perspective taken by EMH adherents. My only request has been that companies show the same degree of tolerance for differing views as society shows for minorities in general. Think of how minority voices throughout the years were treated at first and how they have come to be treated when society came to realize that minority perspectives are to be celebrated, not marginalized. Surely there should be no room for intolerance merely because some people are different or see things differently.

In a society where intelligent and reasonable people might differ, those differences should be explored and discussed rationally. Is it anyone's place to tell people whether they should agree with or be opposed to same-sex marriage? What about capital punishment, abortion, euthanasia, or other moral dilemmas? The gay rights issue has been described as the human rights issue of our generation. I would go so far as to venture that the debate between market efficiency and market inefficiency is the financial services industry's practice management issue of our generation. As with all other questions that cannot be answered definitively, surely there is no place for discrimination just because someone happens to disagree with another's opinion.

Even more reprehensible is the way many advisory firms portray STANDUP FSPs who believe in market efficiency as bad apples, as if independent thought were a vice of some sort. They say a belief in market efficiency is contrary to corporate values, even if those values include explicit references to the firm not interfering with the FSP-client relationship. The distribution companies that are tied to companies which manufacture actively managed products seem to be particularly zealous in their intolerance of efficient market adherents.

Perhaps it is time the politicians were alerted to this shameful and self-serving conduct. The Charter of Rights and Freedoms enshrines explicit equality rights for all Canadians. It protects individuals against all sorts of systemic inequality and, to a degree, intolerance. Meanwhile, some FSPs are being discriminated against because they see things differently, act accordingly, and steadfastly put their clients' interests first. Regulatory bodies and self-regulatory organizations (SROs) do nothing to stop this abominable practice. The industry is unfit to police itself and the time has come for political intervention.

Do FSPs Recommend Going to Las Vegas?

Consistency is an important part of any endeavour and people constantly look to professionals to offer consistent, impartial advice tailored to their circumstances. Someone with certain symptoms could visit three or four physicians and presumably get the same diagnosis with each. Qualified physicians take a dispassionate approach to medical advice.

Increasingly, FSPs are talking as though they are professionals—but are they? More to the point, are the recommendations of FSPs consistent, impartial, and rational? Surgeons are required to explain the pros and cons of various procedures to patients in terms that patients can understand, but the final decision rests with the patient, who will decide based on personal values, preferences, and the facts involved.

There is considerable evidence that the majority of actively managed mutual funds lag their benchmark and that the handful that outperform cannot be reliably identified before the fact. So, would a professional financial advisor recommend to a client that they should take a trip to Las Vegas and gamble with their life savings as a retirement strategy?

Actively managed mutual fund companies are like casinos: you can play any number of games (pick from a dizzying array of funds) and you might win some money if you're one of the lucky ones. What is certain is that the house will always make money (the fund company will always collects its share of the MER). Just as most people are often better off financially if they never set foot in a casino, they are about equally likely to be better off if they never use actively managed funds. Most mutual fund managers are like croupiers in disguise.

As with casinos, active mutual fund companies always make money and that money is always made from the people playing the game. A handful of participants make money and a handful essentially break even, but most participants lose.

Let's assume that 90% of people going to casinos lose money and 10% make money. As with casinos, the 10% who outperform are probably just luckier than the others, but no more skilled, since no one has devised a way to reliably identify the superior performers before the fact.

But if most people who go to Las Vegas lose, why do so many people make the pilgrimage anyway? Many observers think people gamble because gambling is something that's fun to do, but having fun and making money are very different things. People go to Las Vegas to be entertained, but they invest to maintain a secure retirement, and we know that there are a number of people who find it "entertaining" to check the financial pages regularly.

The distinction, as it pertains to giving financial advice, boils down to that which is possible and that which is probable, as well as meaningful disclosure. No one doubts that is it possible to win lots of money at Vegas. However, these positive outcomes are also improbable. Given that this is so, is it professional to counsel people to try to outperform when the most likely outcome of making that attempt is to underperform? Aren't FSPs supposed to help consumers make smart decisions with their money? Aren't there risks and limitations that need to be disclosed? Even if consumers were prepared to take that chance, shouldn't they at least be advised that the odds were long before setting out?

If we all agree that it would be irresponsible to bring your entire life savings on a trip to Las Vegas, why do so many "professional" FSPs recommend that people invest all their money actively? Whether the topic is a trip to Las Vegas or the use of active management, the risk exceeds the reward. Better to stay out of the casino and simply buy the index or some facsimile thereof. But that's not what most FSPs recommend. Why the "do as I say, not as I do" attitude?

We all know that FSPs will tell their clients it's unwise to be so cavalier with their money as to risk blowing it at a casino, but that's the point. If the analogy holds, then FSPs would have to acknowledge that it's similarly unwise to pursue active management—and for exactly the same reason. Both offer the possibility of winning in exchange for the probability of losing. People can't have it both ways. A major concern here is disclosure. When someone deliberately fails to tell the whole story in an attempt to manipulate an outcome, motive can certainly be called into question.

In the future, FSPs will need to stop hiding behind exceptions as an excuse for making blanket recommendations. Everyone knows that there are people who have smoked two packs a day for seventy years and never had cancer. Everyone also knows that there are people who died of cancer before age forty even though they never took a single drag. While there are exceptions in both cases, there is clearly an established and clinically proven link between cigarette smoking and cancer, just as there is a clear link between actively managed products lagging passive ones. The costs of portfolios are the carcinogens of the investment world and active strategies cost more than passive ones.

Doctors don't actively recommend that patients take up smoking, do they? They might acquiesce, but that's about as far as it goes. I'm okay with acquiescence. Far be it from me to deny someone of their right to be wrong. That's why we need better disclosure on product packaging. I'm not suggesting people shouldn't be allowed to "try their luck" if that's their choice. Casinos, cigarettes, and actively managed mutual funds are all legal in Canada, but only two of the three are widely seen as socially questionable. It is simply hypocritical to encourage people to engage in irrational behaviour and then suggest that your advice is professional, unbiased, and in clients' best interests.

What Would You Do with More Free Time?

Wrap accounts have been gaining market share for about a decade now. Commentators have offered many reasons for this trend: enhanced reporting, purposeful and disciplined investment decision-making, automatic rebalancing, and tax optimization among others. My sense is that it's a lot more basic than that. After all, you don't really need a wrap account to do any of those things.

While all of the above attributes are true, it doesn't necessarily mean these attributes explain the reason behind the rapid ascendancy of wraps. Like all investment products, wrap accounts are popular essentially because advisors recommend them. The reasons for their popularity typically focus on why consumers like wraps. Basically, advisors and the companies they work for like wraps a lot more than consumers do. Wrap accounts generally cost more money for consumers and, correspondingly, they usually pay more too.

While the reasons above are often used to get clients to sign on for wraps, wholesalers and inside sales representatives typically pitch them to eager advisors in an entirely different manner. Promoters tell advisors they can "free up their time to do more important things" by using wrap accounts. Advisors in turn go to their clients and say they can now spend more time doing tax planning, retirement planning, and insurance and estate planning as a result of the time saved. If wrap accounts are true to their word, then indeed the time could be spent on those noble pursuits—or anything else, for that matter.

Look at it this way. If you had a job that required forty hours a week to fulfill your duties and new products or technologies came along that would allow you to be 20% more productive or efficient, what would you do with those eight freed-up hours? There are essentially three options:

1. Have fun (e.g. go golfing etc.).
2. Acquire new clients (i.e. be more profitable).
3. Offer more and better services to existing clients.

Which would you choose? Having worked with many FSPs who recommend wrap accounts, my experience has been that the majority choose the first option, a few choose the second option, and fewer still choose the third. What concerns me is that I have never seen a reputable study regarding either how much time the use of wrap accounts actually frees up or how that time is spent if and when it is actually freed up. Without reliable empirical evidence, isn't it a little disingenuous to suggest there's only one possible way to deploy the newfound hours in your day? Isn't this especially true if anecdotal evidence suggests that most of that free time is being spent on something else?

Don't get me wrong; there's nothing inherently bad about recreation or acquiring new clients. It's just that so far, most of what I see in wrap account time savings is FSPs making more money while doing less work and clients footing the bill through higher costs.

Balanced Compensation

Speaking of wrap accounts and portfolio balance, many FSPs experienced in strategic asset allocation often refuse to use balanced or asset allocation mutual funds because they allow fund managers to make tactical decisions that might be at odds with a long-term strategic plan. Other FSPs like these sorts of funds precisely because it allows them to build balanced portfolios while simultaneously attempting to tactically shift between assets classes based on shifting circumstances.

Coincidentally, using balanced funds instead of a combination of stock and bond funds maximize advisor revenues. This is a real concern. Given the recent focus on fund costs and the value of advice, the time has come to deal with this issue of compensation. Balanced funds pay advisors the same as equity funds. Many observers have long been concerned about how recommendations might be compromised through differing payment structures. Equity funds pay 5% up front with a 50 basis points (bps) trailing commission (DSC) or 0% up front and a 100 bps trailing commission (front end). Income funds pay 4% up front with a 25 bps trailing commission (DSC) or 0% up front with a 50 bps trailing commission (front end).

It's bad enough that different mutual fund asset classes pay FSPs differently, but balanced funds really muddy the waters. In my view, there are two possible solutions to this problem:

Option #1:

Working on the assumption that balanced funds are simply hybrids of equity funds and fixed income funds and that a typical balanced fund is 60% stocks and 40% bonds, then the compensation ought to be a hybrid as well. Perhaps the trailing commission ought to be 80 bps when it is normally 100 bps on a front-end basis at present. Similarly, the most appropriate DSC compensation would likely be somewhere in the middle—perhaps 4.5% at the point-of-sale and 40 bps annually. The current format allows advisors to make more money by either fudging their strategic asset mix or by ignoring the subject altogether. If equity advice really is worth twice as much as fixed income advice, then compensation for a blended product option should reflect that. If this were true, this means that balanced fund MERs should be reduced by about 20 bps and that FSP compensation should go down by that amount too.

Option #2:

Working on the assumption that advice is advice and that there should be no disparity in cost, all embedded compensation products would offer the same advisor remuneration. Since equity funds and balanced funds already pay the same, it seems logical that income funds should pay the same as well. This means trailing commissions for income funds would pay just as much as equity and balanced funds so that advisors would no longer be tempted to recommend balanced funds as a means of artificially boosting their income. Income fund MERs would go up by about 50 bps as a result. I suspect sales of income funds would mysteriously increase if this were adopted. I also suspect that most FSPs want to do the right thing provided they don't have to accept less money in the process.

If you believe advice for stock funds is genuinely worth twice as much as advice for bond funds, then you would presumably think Option #1 makes the most sense. If, on the other hand, you think FSPs should receive the same compensation irrespective of the asset classes recommended, then Option #2 is probably what appeals to you. What is obvious is that there is an inconsistency that the industry needs to come to terms with. A case can be made for either approach, but the status quo seems to be flawed one way or another.

Reconciliation Time

All this raises the question of why, after all this time, has the industry still not formulated a consistent, logical, and rational perspective on the value of qualified financial advice? The financial services industry is inconsistent because it can be and remaining so maximizes profitablility. I've asked these same questions in articles published in national magazines targeted toward FSPs. I request that readers write back to explain it all to me. No one can, however, because there is no adequate explanation. In short, the status quo drives STANDUP FSPs crazy because they want to do sensible things, but the industry has become so dysfunctional in its quest for profit and its pandering to SPANDEX FSPs that it doesn't even bother pretending to be sensible.

To make matters much worse, consumers are still being made

to pay trailing commissions to discount brokerage firms where advice is neither requested nor received. This suits SPANDEX FSPs very well of course, because they can tell their clients that it costs no more to buy (A Class) mutual fund products from them than from a discount broker.

The SPANDEX Advisors like this because it forces consumers to (grudgingly) do business with them. In contrast, STANDUP Advisors look forward to separating their compensation from the cost of their products because they are confident that they have a compelling value proposition and that they can defend their fee easily. It's just another example of the industry pandering to the lowest common denominator and professing to "put the client first" while remaining thoroughly committed to the advice channel. This last piece of rhetoric really drives STANDUP Advisors batty. By paying firms that offer no advice (discount brokerages) the same as those who offer advice (advisory firms), firms basically send an implicit message that the advice being offered is worthless. The STANDUP Advisors in the advice channel are of the opinion that with friends like that, who needs enemies? That fee is supposed to be for the FSP's advice, wisdom, specialized knowledge, and guidance. At a discount brokerage, there is no FSP to offer any of this, but the embedded compensation to the firm persists.

The "value proposition" of qualified advice would be appreciated far more if it were put out in the open where people could see what they are paying and have discussions around the value of what they are getting in return. Unbundling would accomplish this quite nicely.

Parts and Labour Sold Separately

The essence of a genuine professional man is that he cannot be bought.
—H.L. Mencken

One of the great conundrums of the business of offering financial advice for a living is that some products offer more embedded compensation than others, while some offer none at all. This can cause a huge bias in the product recommendations made by FSPs and casts doubt on whether they can be considered true professionals under current circumstances.

Many believe that the only way to be sure about the appropriateness of advice and suitability of recommended products is if the link between products and compensation is broken once and for all. Otherwise, the motive of the FSP can and will always be called into question. The principle of the primacy of consumer interests is so entrenched that it applies to all walks of life. Let's look at auto mechanics.

Pretend that we have a simple matrix regarding parts and labour. You can use quality replacement parts or cheap knock-offs as one decision and you can install them yourself or hire a mechanic as another. Now let's pretend these variables are linked. What if your actual options were only twofold? What if you need to choose between quality parts installed at home by yourself or knock-off parts you install by the mechanic at the garage? Which would you choose? The choice invites some implicit trade-offs between cost, quality, and convenience. Both options have benefits, both have drawbacks.

Right away, you might think this is a silly comparison. After all, parts are readily available and the person who installs them should not influence the decision of which are used. This is the point. A small but growing number of FSPs believe that asset class funds and ETFs are manifestly superior investment products than conventional actively managed mutual funds. Many FSPs avoid ETFs and asset class products because they don't pay any embedded compensation. Instead, many of these "professionals" continue to perpetuate the myth that financial advice is "free" since clients aren't handed a bill with FSP compensation as a distinct line item. As a result, most consumers are unaware of how they're paying or how much they're paying.

Think about this from a consumer's perspective, especially if that consumer is like me around a garage. I don't know a carburetor from a caliper. I need help. Imagine if a mechanic told customers that if they want the work done at his garage, they would have to agree to using inferior, knock-off parts. You can use quality parts if you do the work yourself, but you have to use knock-offs if you get someone else to do it for you. How would you feel if your mechanic gave you this option? Wouldn't the first question be: "Why can't I get the good parts and still pay you your hourly wage to install them, Mr. Mechanic?" Indeed.

As a consumer, how would you feel about a system in which embedded compensation encourages the people offering advice to offer a potentially inferior product? Shouldn't consumers be encouraged to choose products based on merit alone?

Auto mechanics are on to something. Say what you will about the price and quality of their work or the training required to perform it, at least there are no surprises when you come to pick up your vehicle. When the expectations are set out clearly and in writing before the fact, it is difficult to challenge what they've done if it accords with those expectations.

The cardinal rule of the financial services industry is that the client comes first, and FSPs are expected to subordinate their own interests to those of their clients. Part of this rule involves a "no surprises" commitment to professionalism. This is a noble objective, but one that is open to wide interpretation. If a prospective client sees two different FSPs on a matter and receives different advice—either about planning concepts or products to be used—does this mean one or the other is being negligent? Provided they are reasonable, each set of recommendations should be considered. But there is a problem with most investment recommendations: embedded compensation.

The introduction of F Class mutual funds is a step in the right direction, but the industry still panders to the lowest common denominator since newspapers typically only publish numbers for A Class funds. Essentially, Corporate Canada will happily throw STANDUP Advisors a bone by manufacutring unbundled products, only to pretend that those products don't exist after having done so.

To recap, F Class funds strip out FSP compensation, effectively offering the same investment products at a reduced cost. The cost is reduced by the exact amount of embedded compensation, allowing consumers to make a clear distinction between mutual fund management fees and expenses and FSP compensation. Now that virtually all mutual fund companies have released F Class funds (the "F" is for fee), it is time to take a closer look at what consumers are really getting. Most embedded compensation equity mutual funds in Canada have a management expense ratio (MER) of about 2.65%, made up of trading and administrative costs of about 0.5%, a 1% fee for the mutual fund company, a 1% embedded advisory fee, and tax. There are often additional trading costs that don't even show up in a fund's MER.

The aforementioned advisory fee is called a "trailing commission" if you are an FSP running an ad in a local newspaper and a "trailer fee" if you are a fund company executive doing an interview with the same newspaper. Every FSP advertisement I have ever seen *requires* the FSP to refer to trailers as "commissions." Every interview I've ever read of an executive from a manufacturing or distribution firm refers to trailers as "fees."

It never ceases to amaze me how corporate interests conveniently break their own rules of conduct when it suits them. Terminology is perhaps a small point, but whether trailers are commissions or fees clearly cannot depend on who is doing the talking. Most people wouldn't care much how they are described, but we should have one set of rules for everyone. In a desire to offer certitude, I would add that the CRA views trailers as commissions

Even if consumers go to a discount broker, do all their own research, and execute their own trades (paying a transaction charge to do so), they will still have to pay the same MER because DIY consumers are not generally allowed to buy F Class funds at a discount brokerage.

The embedded compensation side of the mutual fund industry is so convinced people need FSPs that they set up the system so that consumers have to pay for FSPs whether they use them or not. These same companies then tell FSPs with a completely straight face that they are firmly committed to the advisory channel. If this were true, they would either prohibit discount brokers from selling their products or, at the very least, insist that if discount brokers want their products on the shelf, they should use the F Class versions.

Embedded compensation mutual fund companies won't do either because they are interested in distributing their products as widely as possible. Profitability and maintaining market share supersede any loyalty to their primary distribution channel. It would be refreshing if just one embedded compensation company stood up and walked the talk by removing its products from the shelves of discount brokerages as a gesture of solidarity with and commitment to qualified advice.

Discount brokers are getting a great deal in this arrangement: the same compensation as qualified FSPs with none of the work or liability! Truly professional FSPs don't back down from the notion that qualified professional advice costs money. The fact that most FSPs don't stand up for this concept illustrates that many of them doubt whether or not they really add value.

An exception to this practice is the Toronto-based company ASL Direct. Until recently, the company only used to rebate A Class trailers to their clients, since product manufacturers (you know, the people committed to the "advice channel") wouldn't sign off on the F Class agreements necessary to make the unbundled versions of their products available to DIY investors, so ASL Direct simply rebates them; other firms are following suit.

This merely exposes the oligopolistic competition between other discount brokerages for all the world to see. Until now, they have used red herrings like the restriction of trade to keep F Class versions off their approved lists. There are no valid legal restrictions that demand this. Their policies are a profit-motivated ruse that unfairly gauges DIY investors and ASL has effectivly outed them.

And ASL has even gone one better. The firm also offers institutional class funds and rebates the trailing commissions on those too, passing the savings onto unitholders. For those people who wish to buy hedge funds, ASL Direct also rebates all performance bonuses on top of all existing trailers.

The options available to DIY investors are a lot more equitable because of companies like ASL Direct. Not surprisingly, there are a number of FSPs who have their accounts at ASL Direct too. This is only natural, since their employers seem intent on forcing them to bill themselves if they keep their accounts at the firm they work at.

At a time when people desperately need guidance in their increasingly complex financial affairs, advisors should resent the fact that their suppliers are talking about how their services are invaluable while simultaneously paying other distributors—who do not offer advice—an identical level of compensation. It seems, however, that many SPANDEX FSPs are not resentful. If embedded compensation companies can create a demand for their products, a large portion of the population will want to buy them. If it costs no more to buy them through an FSP than it does to buy them from a discount broker (i.e. the MER is identical), people might as well buy the products from an FSP. It becomes obvious that these FSPs are thinking strictly about themselves if you follow their logic. Even if the advice rendered is worth only a fraction of what consumers are paying, it will be worth it since the price is identical even if they get no advice. Since some advice is worth more than no advice and since consumers are free to disregard the advice if it is inappropriate anyway, why not have a second set of eyes looking over the situation?

Imagine if your auto mechanic used this line of thinking. Let's say you need a new part that costs $140. You call the mechanic and say you will need it by the weekend and that you understand it will cost $140. You agree to come over on Saturday to pick it up, but when you do, the mechanic says it will cost $240 plus tax. You look puzzled and say, "What do you mean? When I called on Tuesday, you said it was only $140 for the part." At this point, the mechanic, full of self-righteous smugness says, "Well, yes, the part does cost $140, but it will cost $100 to install it."

You respond by pointing out that you were simply looking for the part and that it was your intention to take the part home and install it yourself in your driveway and on your own time. The mechanic says that is immaterial. The cost is $140 for parts and $100 for labour and that is what you will have to pay, whether it is installed at the garage by a mechanic or in your driveway by you personally.

He is so confident that he and his staff will do a bang-up job and that you will mess it up somehow, that you'll need to pay for the service whether you use it or not. Any mechanic who tried this stunt would have consumers reporting his little operation to the Better Business Bureau in no time flat, and for good reason! With mutual funds at discount brokerages, this stunt is common practice.

The status quo suits both the advice and the DIY distribution channels. The advice channel, with its inferiority complex due to the dominance of SPANDEX FSPs, doesn't seem to care about whether it can actually deliver what it purports to deliver. That element of the industry likes the fact that it costs no more to use "the very best" in positioning its services. Meanwhile, the DIY channel loves the fat profit margins that come with charging for services that are never delivered. Again, if you ran a garage and could consistently and legally charge for services that you proudly *didn't* provide, wouldn't you love it? That's exactly what discount brokers are doing and the embedded compensation mutual fund companies are letting them get away with it! And governments and regulators are guilty of complicity because they're well aware of the situation but do nothing to shut it down.

But what would happen if discount brokers couldn't sell embedded compensation (A Class) funds? For starters, discount brokers would be a lot less profitable than they are now. They would likely have to raise transaction charges or new account fees just to remain marginally profitable. The pricing gap between the advice and DIY channels would close but it would never go away. Repeat after me: *qualified financial advice costs money.*

Direct fees are charged for tax preparation. You can do your own taxes and save yourself some accounting fees or you can delegate the task to a qualified professional. This professional will simplify your life, do a responsible job, and charge you a predictable fee for services rendered. In the future, consumers are simply going to have to decide whether they are going to act as their own advisor or pay for advice and, if so, what a fair price might be.

With most FSPs, the level of gross compensation earned for product placement is identical regardless of credentials, experience, or service. The wrinkle is that firms allow FSPs to keep different percentages of their income depending on the firm's "payout grid" and the volume of sales done by the FSP. A higher sales volume means a higher payout. Note that FSPs don't get bonuses or pay increases by making more money for clients in good markets, losing less money in bad markets, or saving an inordinate amount of tax—they get paid by volume of sales.

Some professionals cost more than others in the same field, so the notion of identical pay for identical product placement regardless of FSP seniority and sophistication will also change. In a transparent fee-based environment, everyone knows instinctively that it costs more to get a partner at a specialized Bay Street law firm to do legal work than it costs to get a small-town generalist lawyer with a storefront office at the corner of Main and Elm. It stands to reason that FSPs with more experience, credentials, profile, and aptitude will command a higher fee than raw rookies out of the chute once fees become the prevailing compensation model for FSPs.

Some consumers who are currently on the fence and use an FSP only grudgingly might move to discount brokers; the advice channel obviously doesn't want this, but the market segments itself pretty clearly. In general, people either want to work with an FSP or they don't, just as people choose whether to do their own tax preparation. There should be an opportunity for consumers to engage in a meaningful self-selection process.

If advice costs money, it logically follows that it will cost more to work with an FSP than to do the work yourself. Under present circumstances, there is no real reason why people disposed to investing in traditional embedded compensation mutual funds wouldn't want to use an FSP. Any value added is worth the inescapable fee that is being paid anyway. This is not the case if portfolios are constructed with individual securities and ETFs.

Also bear in mind that a lot more goes into financial planning than just portfolio management.

The system obviously needs to change. There are billions of dollars invested in mutual funds at discount brokerages that are paying these firms embedded fees while no value-added services are being rendered. That's tens of millions of dollars that discount brokers are earning annually that rightfully belongs in consumers' pockets. As it stands today, you can file your own tax return, hope you don't miss anything, and save yourself a few bucks in the process. You can defend yourself in court, take your chances with the judge, and save yourself some legal fees. What you cannot do is invest by yourself using embedded compensation funds without paying full advisory fees. The same holds for insurance. These pricing biases simply have to end.

As an FSP, I obviously believe FSPs add value. I also believe most consumers are better off using an FSP. However, I do not believe the system should condone pricing structures in which consumers have to pay for professional advisory services even if those services are neither requested nor rendered. The most obvious solution is to abolish embedded compensation products altogether. The myth perpetuated by some FSPs that advice is "free" would be exploded. Those who want advice would pay advisory fees and those who do not want advice would be able to forgo them.

What Do Most FSPs Recommend and Why?

Most consumers have taken the view that if the cost is not visible, it doesn't exist. Studies show that the majority of consumers have no idea what a typical mutual fund costs on an ongoing basis (its MER). As a result, FSPs are unlikely to voluntarily put compensation out in the open because it reminds their clients about something they would never think about otherwise: FSPs have to earn a living and that the money is ultimately coming out of clients' pockets.

The incontrovertible fact no one seems to grasp is that it is always the client who pays the FSP for services rendered. So many FSPs say they recommend embedded compensation funds because only embedded compensation funds pay them. That's hogwash. *No funds pay FSPs. Only consumers pay FSPs. The difference is that embedded compensation funds have devised a seemingly benign way of collecting FSP compensation from the client and distributing it to the FSP. Make no mistake: in one way or another, FSPs are paid exclusively by their clients.*

Most SPANDEX FSPs fear the elimination of embedded compensation because the status quo protects their personal financial well-being. Making a voluntary transition from commissions to fees involves a painful restructuring of their business model—certain short-term pain for presumed long-term gain. In spite of how FSPs blather on about taking a long-term view, FSPs are human and there is still the matter of short-term pain that has to be endured. If the transition is to occur with even a modicum of integrity, there will be a significant drop in income while it is being made. People instinctively move away from pain, so it should come as no surprise that FSPs aren't dealing with the disconnect between their positioning and their compensation method of choice.

Pain or no pain, the need for reform is clear. Consumers rely heavily on advice from intermediaries, although many have almost no understanding of the costs of obtaining this and are unable to gauge its quality. The advice itself is often compromised by the incentive effects of embedded commissions paid by product providers. The commission-driven sale of these products remains the norm, leading to persistent concerns about consumer detriment. Research has shown statistically significant evidence of FSPs recommending one provider's offering over another because it paid a higher commission.

Many FSPs earning commissions genuinely want to become true professionals, but given their past history, they don't know how to make the leap. How do you tell a client who has been with you for twenty years and never paid you a direct fee in his life that you now believe he will be better served by paying a direct fee? To make matters worse, it is difficult for many FSPs to "do the right thing" and become STANDUP Advisors when competitors are making more money by picking the low-hanging fruit, preying on consumers who are insufficiently sophisticated to know there are other business models out there. Perhaps more than anything else, the general lack of consumer awareness has allowed the sales-oriented FSP business model to flourish longer than it rightfully should have.

Where Does FSP Loyalty Lie?

The choice comes down to the FSP making a decision about whose interests will come first: the client's, the FSP's, or those of the corporations. Anyone looking at this rationally would agree that corporate intersts ought to finish third in this little contest, but that's not the way it usually goes. The client is always supposed to come first and, with a few caveats (e.g. fees to clients cannot be so low that FSPs go out of business), most FSPs would suggest that the preferred order of priority should be:

1. Clients
2. FSPs
3. Corporations

Nonetheless, in many instances (especially with SPANDEX FSPs), the order is reversed. Consumers could confront FSPs with the question of "who's your daddy?" Unbundling allows for the truth to be spoken and for appropriate actions to follow. Putting the client first is part of every FSP's fundamental fiduciary responsibility. Sadly, the industry is set up to make that exceedingly difficult and the people being hurt the most (consumers) remain indifferent.

Proponents of the embedded compensation model argue that consumers are not demanding a fee-based arrangement from their FSPs and often don't understand important differences if and when they are presented to them. If a vast majority of consumers are essentially indifferent, why should anyone, including regulators and legislators, care? This indifference is largely due to consumers being blissfully unaware of how embedded compensation can cloud the judgement of FSPs. You can't be outraged by something you don't understand.

Embedded vs. Unbundled

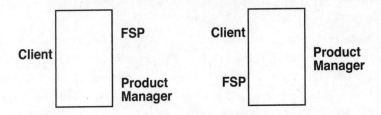

Whose side are you on? By moving to an unbundled format, FSPs can demonstrate that they are aligning their practice with their clients' best interests. Without bundling, FSPs are perceived as sales agents for product manufacturers.

Since the industry allows FSPs to select their own business model, there is considerable resistance toward the complete unbundling of parts (investment products) and labour (FSP fees) because the short-term pain is certain, while the long-term gain is anything but. Not only do FSPs have an emotional bridge to cross, there's also the matter of having to pay mortgages along the way. Remember that there are also some FSPs, notably at banks, who receive a salary for their work. Part of the problem is that many advisory firms have been slow to put platforms in place that would allow FSPs to serve their clients in an unbundled manner. There are a number of FSPs who want to move to a more professional business model but are being thwarted by their employers.

Ultimately, FSPs will need to choose between moving swiftly, but willingly, to transparent fees or being pushed into that same arrangement regardless. Assuming FSPs want to move to a fee-based arrangement as soon as is practically possible (i.e. jump before being pushed), what would advisors and their clients need to know before starting?

On the client side, the most compelling reason to move to a fee-based arrangement is that it closely aligns client interests with FSP interests. Since clients are paying fees based on the size of their portfolio, FSPs have a clear incentive to make portfolios grow and to mitigate portfolio declines. The more the account grows, the more the FSP makes; the more the account declines, the less the FSP makes. The fee-based model might also allow for fee deductibility for non-registered accounts that would not otherwise be possible. Unfortunately, no model is perfect. As with other arrangements, there is no incentive for an FSP to counsel a client to pay down non-deductible debt.

It should be stressed that even if FSPs firmly believe it is in their clients' best interests to switch, they cannot force any client to share that view. *Both FSPs and consumers naturally resist change. If you're a consumer who is working with an FSP you trust, ask yourself one question: "Would I be prepared to take a considerable voluntary risk in my own career, knowing that it could take perhaps six full years for me and my family to be as well off as a result?"* Since people tend to avoid pain if possible, I suspect most would honestly answer no, even though six years is a reasonable time frame for FSPs to expect when running the gauntlet.

Eradicating embedded compensation should mean total product flexibility and independence. Any FSPs reading this and considering the switch should know that those who have already done so believe it generally takes about three years to accomplish this switch and three more years to regain the revenues that were forgone in doing so. In other words, if you begin in 2007, you'll be financially worse off until about 2013, at which point you will more or less break even and then do better afterwards. Any FSP contemplating retirement before 2013 probably wouldn't be inclined to work toward this transition, although it might still be worth it in terms of practice value upon retirement.

In essence, the more an investment product costs, the more leakage there will be in its expected long-term return. This is counterintuitive to the way most other products are sold. People generally expect expensive cars to be better than cars that cost less and this is generally true when considering other types of products. There's an old saying in the sales industry that suggests you are what you sell, so people don't want to be seen to be selling "cheap" products. Furthermore, FSPs want to make as much money as possible for themselves and their families, so they generally don't talk about price.

Automobiles are depreciating assets and will one day be worthless due to normal wear and tear. Better made cars cost more, but generally depreciate at a slower rate, so spending relatively more may be a sensible consumer decision. Investment assets, on the other hand, generally appreciate over time, so the best value is often secured by using products that cost the least, allowing for maximum appreciation of value over time. This is an important distinction. Virtually all other consumer products add value by minimizing depreciation, while investment products add value by maximizing appreciation.

The SPANDEX FSPs most resistant to change are the ones who would be the most exposed as not having anything appreciable to bring to the table on behalf of their clients.

Compensation Logic

Have you ever met an accountant who sends himself an invoice after preparing his own tax return? It would be a bit silly, wouldn't it? In fact, the concept is entrenched in law. For instance, you can hire a maid or a gardener to do work around the house, but you can't legally pay yourself (or your spouse) for doing the same work.

Accountants bill their clients for services rendered, but there are millions of Canadians who file their own returns and forgo paying professional fees in the process. Whether it is wise to use a tax professional depends on the complexity of one's situation and their ability to implement appropriate tax strategies. Nonetheless, it is a personal decision that is made on a household-by-household basis. People generally do what they believe is in their own best interests.

No one in their right mind would bill themselves and then add the bill payment to their personal income. If an accountant was making $100,000 a year, would he bill himself an additional $1,000 to prepare his own return? He would have to pay about $450 in tax that would otherwise not be due if he did.

In spite of the ridiculousness of sending yourself a bill for services rendered to yourself, this is what virtually every FSP does today. This is because most FSPs buy mutual funds with embedded compensation for their own accounts, even though the fund companies would allow them to buy funds without embedded compensation instead. Even those FSPs that work at a conventional brokerage firm bill themselves for their own accounts. Does this sound like FSPs might be compromised in some way?

180 — John J. De Goey

I wrote a column in *Advisor's Edge Report*, an industry magazine, where I pointed this out to my colleagues. I asked if any of them could shed any light on the matter and many chose to do so. It seems most FSPs licenced to sell only mutual funds did so because their firms still didn't have platforms for fee-based accounts. In contrast, FSPs at traditional brokerage houses certainly had fee-based platforms, but their employers steadfastly refused to allow them to transact business without billing themselves. Either way, we ended up with FSPs who were bright and conscientious but forced to do something against their will.

Remember that A Class mutual funds include commissions and/or trailing commissions included in the fund's MER. The FSP pays the full MER, then has the embedded compensation added to her taxable income. For instance, a $100,000 mutual fund portfolio invested entirely in equities, means the FSP is effectively paying herself $1,000 a year for her services due to a 1% trailing commission paid to her by the fund companies. This payment is added to her taxable income and taxes are due on it. The firm gets its pound of flesh, then the FSP pays other personal costs associated with her own practice (things such as rent and staff salaries) and then gets to keep what's left over after the taxman takes his cut.

Many consumers don't realize that FSPs don't get to keep 100% of their commissions and fees. That's because some of that income is paid to the firm to cover the costs of staff, administration, compliance, licencing, marketing, and so forth. For those FSPs who work at traditional brokerage firms, they might be allowed to keep 40% of their gross earnings as revenue. For those FSPs who recommend primarily mutual funds to their clients, the payout rate is usually much higher—they might be allowed to keep 70% of their income, paying the remainder to the firm in overhead costs. This difference exists because brokers have a lot more services provided to them by their firms, which pay for these services by charging the brokers more to work for them. In reality, both types of companies pay their FSPs on an increasing scale based on their revenues to the company.

Let's assume that FSPs in both environments are in the top marginal tax bracket. In using an A Class mutual fund instead of an F Class fund, the FSP is adding 1.06% to the annual MER, 1% in an embedded trailing commission, and 6% GST on that trailer. For example, a fund that has a combined MER of 2.65% in an A Class format should cost about 1.59% in an F Class format. Let's say the FSP invests $100,000 in an A Class equity fund that pays her a 1% annual trailing commission. If the top marginal rate is assumed to be 45%, just look at the *annual* leakage involved:

FSP Environment	Cost	–GST	–Payout Loss	–Tax Loss	=Total Income
Financial Planner	$1,060	($60)	($300)	($315)	$385
Stock Broker	$1,060	($60)	($600)	($180)	$220

Assuming that planners are paid at a 70% payout rate and brokers at a 40% payout rate, the planner only gets to keep $385 of the $1,000 that she is effectively charging herself. She is $615 worse off *each year* as a result of her using A Class funds…and that's not as bad as our broker friend. The broker only gets to keep $220 of his additional $1,000 cost to himself—a massive leakage of nearly 80%!

Would you entrust your life savings to someone who acts in such a dysfunctional manner? What credibility do FSPs have when they seem more interested in boosting their gross income through increased sales volume than in making sensible financial decisions with *their own money*? The culture and predisposition toward sales, to the point where damage might be done to the financial well-being of FSPs themselves, needs to change. This is a culture that has been deliberately fostered by product manufacturers and distributors. Would you expect your accountant, doctor, or lawyer to act in such an illogical manner? Would you have faith in their "professional" services if they did?

Embedded-compensation mutual fund companies have had F Class mutual funds available to Canadians for over half a decade now and they insist that brokerage and planning firms have agreements and systems in place with all clients where F Class funds are being purchased. The rationale is that they wouldn't want clients getting advice without paying for it. Of course, paying for advice and then not getting it (as with A Class funds offered through discount brokerages, for example) is perfectly fine.

No FSP in their right mind would offer F Class funds to their clients without charging a separate fee because personal bankruptcy would surely follow. Mutual fund companies acknowledge that FSPs should not be made to charge for effectively advising themselves, so the requirement to charge is waived for FSPs. Curiously, the vast majority of FSPs who recommend mutual funds to their clients use A Class funds for their own accounts as well.

Lobbying efforts to force discount brokerages to use F Class funds have proven fruitless. It seems that in the mutual fund world, "discount brokerage" can be just as much an oxymoron as "commission-based professional." In addition, there are no insurance-based equivalents to discount brokerage. With insurance, you get the equivalent of A Class mutual funds at a discount brokerage—you pay for advice whether you get it or not and whether you need it or not.

The industry recognizes that it is unfair for FSPs to have to bill themselves for doing their own research and planning (even though most FSPs continue to do so) but does not recognize that an embedded fee for "advice" where no advice is given is a rip-off for consumers. If you're getting professional advice, you should expect to pay for it. It follows that if you're not getting advice, you shouldn't *have to* pay for it.

As for FSPs, the fact that so few take advantage of this option demonstrates that the prevailing mentality is predominantly rooted in sales rather than advice. This, plus the fear that their clients and/or spouses won't understand them and their firms and/or spouses won't support them. Eliminating embedded compensation will force FSPs to act in a more consistent, client-centred, advice-oriented manner.

What Do Parts Cost?

The simple continuum we looked at earlier gives you a sense of what parts might cost. Most ETFs generally cost anywhere from 0.18% to 0.55%, asset class F Class mutual funds generally cost between 0.55% and 0.80%, and actively managed F Class mutual funds generally cost anywhere from 0.53% to 1.90%, so there's considerable room for variability depending on the products you use. In order to make a more meaningful disclosure to consumers, FSPs could offer a listing of actual costs associated with each unbundled product. This way, consumers could see for themselves what the products cost and could simply add the FSP's fee on top. The total cost of the portfolio is simply the weighted average of the sum of the parts.

It should be noted that many FSPs will be justifiably worried that if they cannot earn commissions, they will have to make this type of disclosure. These transactional FSPs understand that they may well be forced out of business by more professional FSPs who are able to work in an unbundled environment. They will also likely resist the implementation of professional standards for the same reason. It's time the industry smoked out the salespeople—these FSPs will fight financial services reform as though their lives depended on it. Many advisory firms make the matter even worse, while some SPANDEX FSPs add considerably to the corporate bottom line.

In a very real sense, the lives of sales-oriented SPANDEX FSPs depend on commissions. They will speak of the nobility and honour of earning commissions and of the many decent people who have done so for generations. They will say that they themselves are beyond reproach in their personal business practices and will resent any inference to the contrary. These people miss the one inescapable fact that virtually all consumers understand intuitively that the term "professional salesperson" is an oxymoron.

What Does Labour Cost?

Even when clients know what the MER of a product is, they are often hard pressed to explain what portion of that goes to their FSP. They deserve to know. Consumers should be told how much an FSP is being compensated. Some products pay more than others and as long as the compensation is at least partially hidden and lacking in uniformity, how can consumers be assured that what is being recommended is truly in their best interests?

There are plenty of FSPs who make recommendations that are motivated at least somewhat by compensation issues. The first rule in the financial advice industry is that the interests of the client come first. But how is this monitored? At present, as long as the FSP can rationalize an investment as being consistent with client objectives, the investment choice goes unchallenged. Many believe that the petroleum industry has done a good job of educating consumers about the constituent parts of the costs of their products. Big Oil has chosen to put pie charts on many of its pumps in order to demonstrate how the price of gas is carved out. Big financial companies could easily follow suit if they were genuinely committed to more and better disclosure. Here's an example:

100% A Class Mutual Fund MER=265 bps (2.65%)

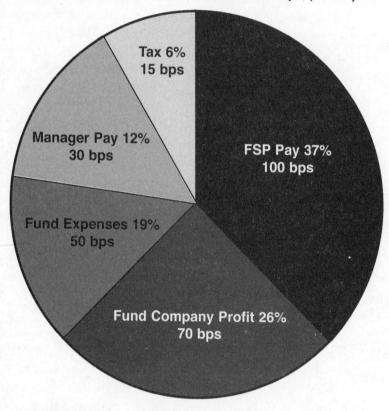

In an unbundled environment, a total advisory fee of somewhere between 1.5% (small accounts) and 0.5% (very large accounts) likely represents reasonable value. The trend is moving toward comprehensive advice charged as a sliding percentage of the assets managed. For example:

All Assets under $250,000	1.40%
Additional Assets up to $2,000,000	0.70%
Additional Assets over $2,000,000	0.35%

Here's a sample disclosure letter that a STANDUP FSP might use in providing greater transparency regarding services:

Explanation of Compensation

Remuneration is always tied to one of three factors: invested assets, fee-based deliverables, and unavoidable commissions.

Option 1: Direct fees based on the household assets invested
• Investment products have no embedded compensation. Fees are paid directly and transparently by the client.
• No acquisition or disposition costs, provided the policy of eight trades per person per year is adhered to.
• Superior flexibility due to lack of restriction on future trading activity.
• Where embedded compensation exists (previous purchases), the advisor's fee is reduced accordingly as an offset.

Fees are in accordance with the amount of assets in portfolio(s) of the client(s). Fees are 1.4% on the first $250,000, 0.7% on all additional assets up to $2 million, and 0.35% on all assets over $2 million.

Option 2: Fee for services (not related to products at all)
• Written recommendations regarding planning objectives.
• Written financial independence calculations (perhaps including a sensitivity analysis).
• Any ad hoc projects involving reviewing, analyzing, and recommending planning objectives.

Where this option is chosen, the total fee depends entirely on the time involved. The advisor's time is charged at $300 per hour and his assistant at $50 per hour.

Option 3: Unavoidable commissions
Some products such as life insurance and oil and gas flow through limited partnerships pay a commission to both the FSP and the advisory firm. These products are not available as a component of the standardized fee-based format. These products are recommended only when applicable to the circumstances of the client(s) and investments in these products are not used in the calculation of fees in Option 1. For example, if a client invests $500,000 initially and an additional $100,000 into a limited partnership, the fee calculation would be made using only the $500,000 invested (i.e. there is no offset provision). Please ask about specific

compensation amounts if purchasing one of these products, since actual formats and amounts can vary significantly.

By signing below, you acknowledge that you have read and understood these three compensation formats.

Signature _____   Date:_____
      Client

Signature _____   _____
      Client   Joe Brilliant

Once accounts are over $250,000, the annual fee becomes a blend of the differing marginal rates. This blended fee drops as accounts get bigger. Think of it as a volume discount. The 1% benchmark that many media people seem to think is reasonable is reached at $583,333. Accounts below this amount would cost more than 1% per year and accounts above this amount would cost less.

A fee-based format recognizes three concepts: the alignment of FSP and client interests, the economies of scale implicit in the rendering of qualified advice, and the need to weed out inefficiencies at various thresholds (price points). Since FSP compensation is now linked to the size of the portfolio and not the placement of any product in particular, there is a clear consistency of purpose. If the account goes up, the FSP makes relatively more. If the account drops, the FSP makes relatively less.

Note that FSPs get paid even if accounts go down. This is entirely appropriate. Consumers need to be reminded from time to time that FSPs are not clairvoyant and cannot predict market movements.

Many FSPs make the point that they need more than 1% as compensation for taking on smaller clients since these clients involve nearly as much work as larger ones. The problem is that the logic cuts both ways. If small accounts should command a premium, large accounts should be accepted at a discount. The marginal fee rate format takes economies of scale into account.

Under this scenario, the marginal fee model could involve charging a small processing fee (e.g. $50 per trade) on securities trades where the FSP receives no compensation. This wrinkle can more closely align the interests of the client, the FSP, and the advisory firm. Better still, clients could be given a certain number of free trades annually. Trading costs money and should only be used to improve the portfolio. Increased activity beyond a prescribed limit can be charged to the client.

Beyond purposeful rebalancing, trading activities should be kept to a minimum. The FSP of the future will work in concert with clients to ensure all aspects of their financial affairs are attended to. This partnership with the client should be aimed at attaining financial independence in a suitable time frame and then maintaining a consistent quality of life beyond that point.

Beyond that, the most important elements of the relationship should be put in writing so that there can be no doubt about who is doing what.

Part Three
Necessary Disclosure

Necessary Disclosure

One can resist the invasion of armies, but not the invasion of ideas whose time has come.

—Victor Hugo

Why are so many FSPs afraid to have a discussion about how and how much they are paid? It's ironic, given that their clients have already "gone first" in this personal disclosure. Even though most FSPs have a pretty good sense of how much all their clients make, many continue to balk at reciprocating—and then go on and on about how the financial advice business is all about openness and trust.

The simple reason for this is that there's a fear of the unknown. Even though most people want to work with others in an upfront manner, there's a feeling among a significant number of FSPs that consumers will recoil in horror once they find out how much financial advice costs. FSPs would rather not have that discussion than have it—only to confirm their darkest fears.

In fairness, it's human nature. I was with my wife in California a couple of years ago and we were doing some sightseeing around Los Angeles. We considered going to a Sony studio, but they informed the public beforehand that there had been an "unspecified but credible threat" against American cultural institutions in keeping with the aftermath of 9/11. We chose to stay away. The next day, we went to Universal Studios. It wasn't until we got home that I reflected on our decision more fully. If the threat was indeed general (terrorists don't generally tip their hands regarding future attacks), then what could possibly make Sony more of a target than Universal? They were equally likely to be targets. We stayed away from Sony precisely because they had the decency to disclose that a threat had been made. It wasn't until I got home that I realized we had effectively punished Sony for its candour. I suspect many FSPs are afraid that something similar would happen if they were to disclose their compensation to their clients.

Who Wants Transparency?

Many observers are both amused and confused by some FSP's inconsistencies. For instance, some FSPs lament about the costs of running a practice to their peers but go on to dismiss the high cost of the products they recommend to their clients. As with so many things in life, one's priorities are revealed through the choices one makes. If FSPs really want to reconcile rhetoric and reality, they should seize the opportunity to be consistent in their thinking. Doing so would allow them to demonstrate that they "get it" when it comes to ethics, transparency, the alignment of interests, and the importance of cost. To put it mildly, they're now feeling the heat.

But FSPs are a resilient lot. These days, they have taken to watching their expenses more closely than ever before. Having a strong entrepreneurial streak in them, many clearly understand that costs matter. Whether it's rent, computer software and hardware, photocopying costs, online access, you name it, FSPs are certainly minding their Ps and Qs. This is a good thing. Anyone who believes in market forces generally does so because of the inherent belief that if you give individuals the power to make micro-level decisions in their own enlightened self-interest, those decisions will likely be better than if imposed from above.

As a result of all this, a trend in the industry is the transparency of cost recoveries. It used to be that FSPs accepted a lower payout rate and had their firms cover a number of variable costs on their behalf. Now many FSPs are asking their firms to offer the most competitive payout rate possible so they can outsource the variable costs of running their practices. Essentially, FSPs want their firms to give them the latitude to get their own product suppliers in order to control costs. They also want their firms to provide statements showing exactly how much each line item expense actually costs so that they can better monitor things. These FSPs are acting the way any other responsible small business owner would.

However, this is not what some FSPs do when making invest-ment recommendations. For some, their conduct is virtually the exact opposite. Although cheap and high quality products that don't involve embedded compensation have existed for years, some FSPs who go to their managers asking for unbundled, item-ized billing withhold that option from their clients.

There are FSPs out there that simply don't want to have a con-versation with their clients about how they're getting paid, how much they're getting paid, and how much their advice is worth. Many are scared to death because most consumers have come to think that financial advice is free since they never get a bill for it. Get many of those same FSPs in a room with their operations man-agers and sparks fly over discussions of cost recoveries.

Many FSPs say they resist unbundling because they would make the same amount of money and the client would pay the same amount of money either way. This is not necessarily true. With unbundling, clients could easily substitute expensive prod-ucts with cheaper ones and pocket the difference. If this were to happen, the FSP's compensation wouldn't change, but client costs certainly would!

Furthermore, how many FSPs have a letter of engagement (LOE) that sets out the obligations of both parties once they begin to work together? We've already looked at the cost of parts and labour. Although FSPs need and deserve to be paid, consumers deserve to know what they're paying and what services they should reasonably expect in return. In this regard, it's like any-thing else: an informed consumer is a good consumer. Just as with cars, cribs, and carbohydrate-reduced diets, the more consumers know about products, the better their decisions.

One reason some FSPs give regarding their resistance to item-ized unbundling is that some firms don't have the capacity to do the bookkeeping to track their "accounts payable" (i.e. tracking how much their clients pay them). This strikes me as being hard to believe because companies have had the capacity to extract month-ly amounts via pre-authorized savings programs for many years now. Still, to the extent that it is true, we can thank our friendly broker and dealers (the companies that FSPs work for) for this gap in the system. Virtually all firms should be able to do fee payments similar to an automatic monthly debit. Alternatively, giving out an invoice once a year is hardly onerous, especially if the FSP is already meeting with clients regularly.

Before looking at what STANDUP FSPs are doing in their own practices in outlining the scope and nature of an engagement, it might be useful to refer back to the compensation disclosure document used in the previous chapter. You'll note that the sample document contemplates three ways an FSP might get paid. This presumes three possible business arrangements:

1. A traditional "advisory" arrangement with transparent, asset-based fees.
2. A "professional" arrangement where there are hourly fees for deliverables.
3. A "customer" arrangement where the FSP merely facilitates product placement.

It should also be noted that all Certified Financial Planners (CFPs) and Registered Financial Planners (RFPs) have been required to use LOEs for some time now. Having a CFP or RFP designation isn't the be all and end all, but FSPs with one of these designations who aren't using LOEs are contravening their obligations as charterholders of these designations. There's a strong sense that even some of the best FSPs are not doing all they can (or must) to fulfill their obligations as professionals.

On one hand, this might not be too surprising since the industry doesn't want to come down too hard on those FSPs who at least have their heart in the right place. Attempts are being made to assist FSPs (most of whom genuinely want to do the right thing) to actually go out and do the right thing. There are both STANDUP FSPs and SPANDEX FSPs out there. Without being too judgemental, the industry is trying to use carrots as opposed to sticks to get SPANDEX FSPs to make the leap that they have resisted until now and become legitimate professionals.

Good disclosure leads to better consumer decision-making. As such, the group that should want this kind of disclosure more than any other are the consumers who continue to insist that finance is too complex and full of jargon. Having a series of simple one- or two-page disclosures and engagements that have been stripped of legal wording is a great way to improve consumer understanding, which in turn should lead to better FSP-client relationships.

The following three sample LOEs offer examples of how a STANDUP FSP might go about formalizing client relationship through such a document. Although the obligations for both parties are clearly different in all three letters, it is useful to note that letters can be devised that reasonably depict whatever arrangement is deemed to be most appropriate. One can mix and match any number of LOEs, compensation disclosure documents, and product cost disclosures. The three letters are written as accompanying documents to the compensation disclosure document we looked at a moment ago. Each letter corresponds to one of the compensation models offered. As the business of offering financial advice becomes increasingly transparent and increasingly professionalized, this sort of discloure is bound to occur. It should be a welcome development in the ongoing evolution of professional financial advice.

Letter of Engagement (1)

The financial planning process is an important step toward achieving your personal financial goals. This letter highlights the activities involved in developing, implementing, and maintaining your ongoing financial affairs and confirms our engagement. Throughout our working relationship, we will make regular use of the Professional Financial Advisor Organizer (PFAO) binder, as well as the contents therein, including your written investment policy statement (IPS).

Highlights of Activities

Given that you have been a client for some time already, this letter re-affirms the nature of our engagement in working together. When you became a client, the initial phase of work involved accumulating and organizing facts about your current and desired financial status and identifying your specific goals and objectives. All information has been held and will continue to be held in strict confidence. A series of recommendations was made using the six-step process itemized in my "Information Summary." (A copy should be kept in your PFAO binder.)

This affirms that we should meet at least once (but preferably twice) a year to review your personal circumstances using the templates set out in the PFAO binder. The mandatory annual meeting will be used primarily to review your IPS and general circumstances. The optional (no extra cost) semi-annual meeting will be used to review other elements of your financial circumstances including risk management, debt management, tax planning, and independence calculations. In conducting these meetings, you should always bring your PFAO binder with you to ensure all information is current. You should also keep meeting minutes in your PFAO binder.

It should be understood that:
• The engagement is only between the signatories identified below.
• The engagement will extend indefinitely.
• Any actual or perceived conflicts will be disclosed before actions are taken.
• Assumptions will continue to be identical to those in the Information Summary.

Remember that future events may cause material differences between the prospective and actual results. By mutual agreement, this financial information will be used solely to assist you and your advisors in guiding your financial decisions and will not be shown to a third party for any purpose without your consent. The advisor assumes that the client will actively participate in the entire process. As such, the appropriateness of advisor recommendations depends on the reliability of the data provided by the client. The client will be free to follow or to disregard, in whole or in part, any recommendations made and will be responsible for any and all decisions regarding implementation of any recommendations.

Objective

The primary objective of this engagement is to assist the client in managing his or her personal financial situation. This will emphasize personal financial and life goals and will include strategies to attain them. Any subsequent projections or planning activity will be prepared from information provided by the client. By signing below, both parties indicate their understanding of this engagement and agree to abide by the responsibilities and expectations set out in it.

_____   _____

Client   Joe Brilliant

_____

Date

Letter of Engagement (2)

The financial planning process, though sometimes complex, is an important step toward achieving your personal financial goals. This letter confirms the terms of our engagement.

Highlights of Activities
• The FSP is acting solely as a planner for a specific project as listed in Option 2 of the Explanation of Compensation form.
• The engagement is only between the signatories identified below.
• The engagement will not extend to include any formal product recommendations. Once the planning recommendations have been delivered, the engagement will have been fulfilled unless subsequent planning requests are made later.

Should you choose to go on to become a full client, the items listed in the last bullet point (and disclosed in Option 1 of the Explanation of Compensation form) will be performed in accordance with the generally accepted six-step financial planning process. Any actual or perceived conflicts will be disclosed before actions are taken. You will be given an analysis of the data accumulated and the values expressed, and after reviewing this analysis with you, there will be an opportunity to transfer your investment account(s) to my management and to complete a fee-based agreement that is renewed annually on or about the anniversary date and based on your most current portfolio value. You will also be given a complimentary copy of my "Professional Financial Advisor Organizer" binder to assist in monitoring and coordinating your financial affairs.

We will then begin implementing the written recommendations. Future events may cause material differences between the prospective and actual results. By mutual agreement, this financial information will be used solely to assist you and your advisors in guiding your financial decisions and will not be shown to a third party for any purpose without your consent. My fees contemplate your active participation in the process, and the appropriateness of my recommendations depends on the reliability of the data that you provide. You will, of course, be free to follow or to disregard, in whole or in part, any recommendations I may make and will be responsible for any and all decisions regarding implementation of these recommendations.

Objective

The primary objective of our engagement is to offer written recommendations that would assist you in arranging your financial affairs. I do not express any assurance on the achievability of the recommended strategies. By signing below, both parties indicate their understanding of this engagement and agree to abide by the responsibilities and expectations set out in it.

_____   _____

Client   Joe Brilliant

_____

Date

Letter of Engagement (3)

The financial planning process, though sometimes complex, is an important step toward achieving your personal financial goals. This letter confirms the terms of our engagement.

Highlights of Activities
• The FSP is acting solely as a broker for a specific product as listed in Option 3 of the Explanation of Compensation form.
• The engagement is only between the signatories identified below.
• The engagement will not extend to include a written financial strategy or formal planning-based recommendations. Once the purchase is complete, the engagement will have been fulfilled unless subsequent purchases of the identical product or a similar product are made later.

Should you choose to go on to become a full client, the items listed in the last bullet point (and Disclosed in Option 1 of the Explanation of Compensation form) will be performed in accordance with the generally accepted six-step financial planning process. Any actual or perceived conflicts will be disclosed before actions are taken. You will be given an analysis of the data accumulated and the values expressed, and after reviewing this analysis with you, there will be an opportunity to transfer your investment account(s) to my management and to complete a fee-based agreement that is renewed annually on or about the anniversary date and based on your most current portfolio value. You will also be given a complimentary copy of my "Professional Financial Advisor Organizer" binder to assist in monitoring and coordinating your financial affairs.

We will then begin implementing the written recommendations. Future events may cause material differences between the prospective and actual results. By mutual agreement, this financial information will be used solely to assist you and your advisors in guiding your financial decisions and will not be shown to a third party for any purpose without your consent. My fees contemplate your active participation in the process, and the appropriateness of my recommendations depends on the reliability of the data that you provide. You will, of course, be free to follow or to disregard, in whole or in part, any recommendations I may make and will be responsible for any and all decisions regarding implementation of these recommendations.

Objective

The primary objective of our engagement is to offer a product that would assist you, given your personal financial situation. I do not express any assurance on the achievability of the product's objectives. By signing below, both parties indicate their understanding of this engagement and agree to abide by the responsibilities and expectations set out in it.

_____   _____

Client   Joe Brilliant

_____

Date

What's an Appropriate Level of Disclosure?

Think of the countless studies pointing to the fact that cigarettes cause cancer. Although this causality is generally accepted today, it was not always the case. When the evidence linking cigarette smoke to cancer began to show up in research papers, there were significant members of the medical community whose first reactions were denial. Suppose you were a physician in the 1950s who did not discourage cigarette smoking. Suppose you actively encouraged it (as some did) as a benign means of relaxation. As time goes on, evidence mounts that your opinion is incorrect and your view shifts from being in the majority to being in the minority. Would you continue to cling to your position?

The dilemma that professional physicians faced was one of grave consequence. As the primary advisors regarding their patients' health and welfare, there was an obligation to alert patients of any material risks associated with consumption of the product. On the other hand, the evidence (in the early days at least) was not definitive and there was a professional reputation to protect. What should a professional, client-centred physician do? What would a patient whose health is on the line want the physician to do? Should concerns be raised when the evidence started to come out or only once a sufficient body of evidence had been developed?

The idea of being a STANDUP FSP hinges on the twin pillars of research, which should be dispassionate and rigorous, and disclosure, which many feel should be compulsory. One pillar is never enough. Physicians learned this first hand a generation or two ago. Those who tried to deny the evidence were ultimately seen, with the benefit of hindsight, as being less than professional. But some things are less clear even today. For instance, there is no definitive cut-and-dried evidence regarding the active/passive discussion. However, there are many who feel that that, too, is worthy of disclosure. If neither party can muster definitive evidence in favour of its position, can either party professionally promote a position without at least acknowledging the other side? Many people believe disclosure is likely the best way to combat wilfull ignorance.

Regarding the carcinogenic effects of cigarettes, everyone knows of someone who has been a chain smoker for over half a century, yet who has never had even the slightest hint of cancer in their system. Winston Churchill was supposedly one such person. Alternatively, everyone knows of someone who has encountered cancer at an early age in spite of a generally healthy (and possibly exemplary) lifestyle. Mario Lemieux springs quickly to mind.

In short, there are always exceptions. There are instances where one might expect something to occur where it does not and others where one would normally anticipate no consequences, yet consequences crop up nonetheless. The main point, however, is that these exceptions do not disprove the general rule. Just because it is possible to smoke ceaselessly and not get cancer doesn't mean smoking is advisable. Similarly, just because it is possible to contract cancer even without smoking does not mean that one should feel certain that it couldn't happen to them. Given that the linkage is compelling but not absolutely definitive, is the statement "cigarettes cause cancer" a matter of fact or a matter of opinion? Once again, accepting that the social sciences always allow for at least a modest amount of uncertainty, most reasonable people would be comfortable saying that the carcinogenic impact of cigarettes is now a generally accepted fact. Looking back on the past half-century, it should be obvious that the medical profession could have been and should have been more forthcoming about the harmful effects of cigarettes. Have we learned as a society?

Given that most people agree that more should have been done to alert the general population sooner, what has society decided regarding the proper role of professional intermediaries such as physicians? Specifically, should they have simply disclosed risks once they became aware of them, or, given that cigarettes are not only carcinogenic but also highly addictive, should they have played an active role in encouraging and helping their patients kick the habit? In other words, is mere disclosure even enough, or were physicians, through their adherence to the Hippocratic Oath, expected to actively engage in the constructive modification of their patients' habits? It might come down to what one considers to be material.

How exactly might a person define the word *material*—as in "FSPs must always disclose all material facts"—when making recommendations? Dictionaries suggest synonyms including *relevant*, *substantial*, and *pertinent*. To my mind, any information that causes a person to change their opinion or behaviour is material. For example, if you were a smoker and I was the first to inform you that cigaretttes cause cancer, I would say that this information would be material if it caused you to change your habits. One could quite properly add that this information could be relevant, substantial, and pertinent whether one gives up smoking or not. But to me, changing one's behaviour is a pretty reliable sign of genuine materiality.

For a number of years now, I've been disclosing to my clients in writing that most actively managed mutual funds lag their benchmarks and that the few that seem to outperform cannot be reliably identified in advance. Not surprisingly, most of my clients resist using actively managed funds once they've been presented with this information. There is nothing in the industry that requires that this disclosure be made.

It has become clear to me that disclosure is a significant contributor to consumer decision-making and can be used to manipulate choices. What an FSP, product manufacturer, or advisory firm discloses often has an impact on what a consumer chooses, but where, then, does one draw the line?

Most FSPs don't make disclosures about the relative merits of active and passive management approaches and most clients don't change the way they invest or what they invest in. It seems that one has a direct impact on the other. The sales culture holds sway over the professional culture largely because material disclosure, which is a primary attribute of professionalism, is "bad for business." If FSPs and the firms they work for were genuinely concerned about their clients' welfare, not only would they give good and comprehensive advice but full disclosures would be commonplace.

FSPs and the companies they work for simply cannot have it both ways. Markets are either efficient or not. A "third option"— one that suggests that markets are *somewhat* efficient but doesn't pretend to be able to quantify the degree—might also be useful. Regardless of where an FSP might come down personally on a matter of opinion, the most current and reliable evidence for both positions ought to be disclosed at the outset.

If market efficiency is merely a question of opinion, then sure-ly everyone is entitled to their own beliefs. All correspondence should carry a disclaimer that states that other FSPs in the organization do not necessarily share the same opinions.

For anyone to disagree with another by clinging to an "opinion" out of self-interest is no excuse for denying the most reputable evidence available. Just when does an opinion cross the line to become fact anyway? If 99% of the world's population continued to believe that the sun revolves around the earth, would that constitute *ipso facto* evidence of that being the case? Surely we have come far enough as a society to know that saying something is so doesn't make it so and that questions of empiricism should never be reduced to something as juvenile as a popularity contest.

According to many highly regarded experts in finance, there is now sufficient evidence to allow fair-minded observers to conclude that markets are sufficiently efficient that it is improbable that one could beat them through security selection or market timing. If this is true, one could argue that the failure to disclose this evidence is nearly as inappropriate as saying cigarettes are not in any way linked to cancer.

In fairness, "many highly regarded experts" is not the same as a mountain of scientific evidence. Similarly, losing about one percent in returns, while significant, pales in comparison to losing one's life. But this is the problem with disclosure: just how definitive does the evidence have to be and how dire do the consequences have to be before disclosure is required?

Most FSPs think, talk, and act like sales agents. A small but growing segment of the FSP population (STANDUP Advisors) wants the industry to transform itself into a profession. Long steeped in a culture of sales, the financial services industry is clearly uncomfortable with the minority that uses a professional paradigm and expresses its views based on minority rights. I know of some firms that even force EMH FSPs to use disclaimers that are more boldly worded than those used by other FSPs in the same firm. Here's what rights expert turned politician Michael Ignatieff says about this:

The whole difficulty about recognition turns on the question of whether it means acquiescence, acceptance, or approval. When a majority grants a minority rights, is it required to acquiesce, accept, or actively approve of the practices of this group?[1]

Making recommendations that are not based on research is bad enough. But surely one ought to be allowed to make recommendations that are based on academic research. If the recommendations that are made do not involve an alternative interpretation where one exists, the "advice" can quickly become a sales pitch. Similarly, if there is a level of disclosure regarding the pros and cons of one approach or product without a similar degree of disclosure about something that is in direct competition, then how is a consumer supposed to make an informed decision about which way to go?

Many believe that the weight of the evidence rests squarely in favour of markets being sufficiently efficient and that it is ill advised to try to beat them through security selection. Others see it differently and that is entirely their prerogative. Given that the evidence is not definitive, both views are defensible.

A critical aspect of real professionalism is that practitioners do not impose their personal views on others. Different people may look at the same information and come to totally different conclusions. However, any professional offering advice based on information that is either not fully understood or not fully agreeable should disclose those things in dispute in a manner that allows the consumer to make an informed choice.

It would be disingenuous of any professional FSP not to at least portray all possible interpretations and alternatives fairly. Advisors are allowed to and indeed expected to advocate for one position over another but should do so only after giving all viewpoints a fair hearing.

Many people believe that FSPs should be encouraged to advocate for either market efficiency or market inefficiency. However, they should also be required to disclose the evidence regarding both options before doing so. The final choice should rest with the consumer.

The media is full of stories about how certain products or strategies are somehow better than others, when the outcomes they are championing are nothing more than random occurrences. Even when evidence comes forward that shows a way of doing things as flawed or a dangerous threat to society, it's extremely difficult to get entrenched corporate interests to change their tune. There are powerful elements of industry that are making huge sums of money by doing things the old way. These interests will deny evidence and confuse the issue as much as possible and for as long as is possible in a desperate attempt to protect corporate profitability. This is nothing new. Throughout history, we have seen examples of corporate interests denying high-level empirical evidence out of brazen self-interest while simultaneously purporting to be working on behalf of the valued clients.

The usefulness of active management is only one example. Opposition from the tobacco industry to research conducted by independent health experts is another. These days, world leaders such as Al Gore have taken to saying that the scientific debate about global warming is over and that no one familiar with the evidence seriously doubts that it is a significant and severe challenge to humanity. Of course, Big Oil is still doing its own research and denying the overwhelming global consensus.

The Cigarettes of Our Generation

With the challenges within the financial services industry, the heart of the issue is giving responsible advice. What role should a qualified FSP play? Do FSPs have an obligation to force clients to at least consider the evidence supporting both market efficiency and market inefficiency?

It has been suggested that actively managed mutual funds are the cigarettes of our generation because they can harm those who use them, yet disclosure of this fact remains inadequate. When the class action suits started in the tobacco industry, it was the tobacco companies (i.e. the product manufacturers) that were targeted for making harmful products without disclosing the material risks associated with their consumption. The physicians of the day (i.e. the professional, advice-giving intermediaries) were typically spared lawsuits because they were seen as mere conduits and not the root of the problem. If this precedent holds regarding market efficiency and associated disclosure, then mutual fund companies had better start putting bold disclaimers on the fronts of their prospectuses lest they share the fate of Big Tobacco. Legislators ultimately came to conclude that the welfare of the citizenry trumped the right of corporations to make profits and forced the disclosure on them at any rate.

Of course, unwittingly eroding your life's savings is less harmful than unwittingly shortening your lifespan. Still, while many people would suggest that their physical health is paramount, financial health would likely run a close second. In April 2006, Ontario's Minister of Health Promotion Jim Watson was quoted as saying, "If I had my druthers, I would not want to see tobacco anywhere in Canada."[2] Those are strong and uncompromising words. No doubt many people would be offended by them.

But no matter what you feel about their activities, politicians have a responsibility to protect the welfare of their citizenry. Sometimes that kind of protection might require what to some might seem like draconian measures. If governmental protection is indeed what is required and actively managed mutual funds isn't far behind cigarettes in terms of potential harm, then one would think bolder mutual fund disclosures are right around the corner.

Politicans muse openly about banning tobacco because it would be a cheap and effective way of dealing with health care issues. Similarly, bolder mutual fund disclaimers would likely be an effective way of dealing with pension funding challenges (i.e. CPP, OAS, GIS) that are bound to arise in the future.

Let's put it this way: if a person could make money by recommending product "A" and having product "A" pay a commission through the cost of the product or make money by recommending product "B" by receiving no commission and sending the client a bill instead, which option would the person doing the recommending choose? Today, a very large proportion of the total FSP population uses option "A." Not surprisingly, research consistently shows that most consumers have no idea about how (or how much) these people are being paid. It seems the people doing the recommending like it that way.

The use of actively managed mutual funds and the hiring of a conventional stock broker both presuppose that it is possible to reliably outperform markets over long time frames through security selection, market timing, or both. By acknowledging that this is not a reliable value proposition, many financial advisors would find it nearly impossible to justify their own existence, having spent their entire lives being wedded to the notion of purposeful security selection.

Still, if we are to believe FSPs and their firms when they say, "The client comes first," then this shouldn't enter into the equation. Whether done at the micro level by a conventional broker or at the macro level by a mutual fund manager, security selection generally costs about 1% per year. Holding FSP compensation and other factors constant, this is an opportunity to increase client returns by 1% a year. Similarly, there's an opportunity to find a price point where both the FSP and the client are better off— at the expense of the people doing the stock picking.

Let's say a client is fully invested in a mutual fund portfolio with an average MER (annual cost) of 2.5%. The pre-tax cost could be broken down like this:

Product Overhead: 0.5%
Stock Picking: 1.0%
FSP Compensation: 1.0%
Total: 2.5%

Now let's have a look at a couple of possible alternatives, using the idea of parts and labour sold separately, where the overhead is the product "cost" and FSP compensation is the financial services equivalent of "labour":

Option 1: Pass Savings on to Client
Overhead: 0.5%
FSP Compensation: 1.0%
Total: 1.5%

Option 2: Divide the Savings
Overhead: 0.5%
FSP Compensation: 1.25%
Total: 1.75%

Option 3: Who Needs an FSP?
Total Cost (Overhead): 0.5%

When making comparisons to the status quo base case, it becomes clear that Option 1 passes on a 1% saving (alternatively depicted as a 1% increase in return) to the client. In Option 2, since many FSPs insist they are underpaid, they could increase their compensation by 25% annually (a 0.25% annual fee increase to the client) and still leave the client better off by 0.75% every year. And for those people who don't believe an FSP adds value, or those who don't believe they need the services of an FSP, they can save a truly massive amount of money by simply buying market-based products.

If you asked an FSP to rate where their loyalty lies—with the employer/suppliers, clients, or their own families—very few would place the employer/supplier relationship anywhere other than in third place. If the client comes first and any FSP loves their own family more than the company president, then either Option 1 or Option 2 would be preferred over the status quo. That's because the FSP and their clients are always as well off or better off under Options 1 and 2. Only the employer/suppliers are worse off. Let's say the portfolio in question would earn 9.5% annually before costs. What would that mean for an investor with $100,000 invested for the next thirty years? Here's what those portfolios would be worth once the thirty years were over:

Option A: $1,006,265.70
Option B: $938,681.73
Option C: $1,326,767.90

By the way, what would the client's portfolio be worth if the status quo format were used? Would you believe $761,225.50? In other words, Option 2 would not only increase advisor income by 25% annually forever, it would leave the client with almost $200,000 more to retire on. That's a clear win/win scenario! The only loser is the product manufacturer, which is sometimes, but not always, also the employer. However, since the manufacturer consistently finishes third out of three in the great quest for loyalty, neither FSPs nor their clients should be unduly concerned.

The other observation is that the 2% spread between the "cheapest" option (fire the FSP and use asset class investment products only at 0.5%) and the most expensive (maintain the status quo at a cost of 2.5% annually) results in the "cheap" portfolio growing to be nearly twice as large as the "expensive" status quo. Since Options 1 and 2 result in portfolio totals about $300,000 to $400,000 less than the DIY approach using asset class investments, you can see why FSPs that do little more than pick investment products might have a hard time justifying their fees.

Where Does Causality Lie?

This brings us to the debate about causality. The debate lies at the heart of the market efficiency conundrum. The issue is whether what happens does so for a reason. Just because a black cat crosses your path, it does not mean that you'll have something bad happen to you that day. And if something bad happens to you that day, it won't necessarily be because a black cat crossed your path. Having two sequential events does not mean one caused the other.

The industry is full of disclaimers that past performance is not necessarily indicative of future performance. Even if a manager has a long track record of consistently beating the market, it wouldn't necessarily be due to superior security selection. If the Fama/French three factor model is correct, then one could theoretically divide the market for any asset class into small and large cap "buckets" and into value and growth "buckets." Having done that, one could simply discard the large cap and growth buckets and throw darts at the small cap and value buckets. The expected outcome would likely be one of "outperforming" the market, but it would likely have everything to do with overweighting small cap and value stocks and nothing to do with the individual securities chosen by the intrepid dart thrower.

Calibrating Disclosure

The financial services industry is still looking for the "Goldilocks" level of disclosure: not too much, not too little. How much disclosure is required before making a product and advice based decision anyway?

There are a couple of things that are now coming to the forefront of the financial services industry. They are the "value proposition" of certain financial products and the price of the associated financial advice. Let's look at the products first. Throughout history, there have been stock pickers who have beaten their benchmarks. However, the number of these outperformers has never been appreciably different for the number one might expect through random chance. Perhaps chance was the only thing driving these "superior results," not causal, value-adding research, insight, and shrewdness.

For forty years, the debate has raged. Throughout that time, social scientists have been able to run more and better tests, with better controls for survivorship bias, mandate consistency, start and end date bias, and other material factors such as costs, bid-ask spreads, and taxes. Both sides of this debate have scored points over the years, but neither has scored a decisive victory.

Most consumers cannot do a reputable job of explaining what investment products cost or how much of that cost goes to the FSP. Many FSPs seem content to do nothing to correct any misconceptions that may have taken hold.

Meanwhile, FSPs who recommend asset class products need to make these disclosures all the time. When they sell the product, they have to make the disclosure because the products involve no embedded compensation. In other words, they're going to have to hand their clients a bill. There's no way for these FSPs to pretend that advice is free. What's particularly curious is when these FSPs write articles about these asset class investment products. These products are like the mufflers we considered earlier. They're products, pure and simple. Anyone who needs help with how to use these products would be expected to pay for it. Advice is not free.

Astonishingly, compliance departments around the country seem determined to force FSPs to mention that muffler installation costs money, even if they only write about the mufflers. Meanwhile, those recommending competing products sometimes pretend that advice is free. Consumers are often none the wiser. If both were forced to make the disclosure, it wouldn't be a big deal. If neither made the disclosure, it might not even be a big deal. Reasonable people can disagree on the appropriate level of "Goldilocks Disclosure," but surely there should be one standard that everyone adheres to.

What really gets STANDUP FSPs riled is that there seems to be a severe double standard. One set of FSPs is being forced to make disclosures, while the other is not. Until now, the FSPs who never pretended that financial advice was free are the ones being made to make additional, self-evident disclosures, while those that pretend that financial advice is free are allowed to perpetuate their little self-serving misconception with impunity.

Scalpel or Laser?

Corrective eye surgery is a dicey subject. Everyone has an opinion about which method is the best. The vast majority of surgeons recommend and use laser technology, but a few surgeons still use scalpels. So which is best and how on earth does this apply to financial advice?

It matters here because of professionalism. Specifically, it matters because of the professional liability associated with what might go wrong and who is responsible if it does. No matter which tool is used, what matters most of all is whether the job is done correctly and without unwanted complications. As one might expect, professionals have engagement letters and waivers to sign before they allow their patients to submit to surgery. I know this because I had minor cosmetic surgery around my eye recently—no signed waiver would have meant no procedure. Professionals would never subject themselves to that kind of liability without coverage.

There are a couple of lessons here. First, the industry has done nothing to preclude practitioners from doing things the old fashioned way. Anyone who wants to act as a surgeon using a scalpel is entirely open to do so. What are generally seen as better procedures is not the point. Any procedure that is "good enough" can be used. There's a direct analogy between actively managed investment products and passively managed investment products.

Real professionals make disclosures. Whether the thing at stake is eyesight or a lifestyle in retirement, they explain the risks and limitations of alternative courses of action so that the client can make a reasonably informed decision based on current clinical research, available evidence, and various other factors. In signing a disclosure document, the client assumes full responsibility for the decisions taken as well as the associated consequences.

So if true professionals make disclosures about material risks associated with alternative procedures and tools regarding eye surgery, then why don't they do it with investment products? One of the biggest issues in the industry today is errors and omissions insurance. Note that one of the reasons many people feel more meaningful change hasn't materialized regarding consumer protection in the financial services industry is because there haven't been enough successful lawsuits brought against advisors...yet. Imagine if consumers sued an advisor for not making material disclosures the same way a consumer could sue a physician or surgeon.

Always remember that disclosure is not about taking sides or imposing a view. It is about a layperson making an informed decision in their own self-interest based on dispassionate facts as they are understood to exist. Any professional who makes this decision unilaterally without spelling out the terms and conditions associated with the competing alternatives is left open to legal action.

Making It Mandatory

Until the world of unbundled advice arrives, FSPs will be expected to make meaningful disclosures about how and how much they are being paid for the services they provide. This is best accomplished by having a single point-of-sale document that can be reviewed and signed by the client, who would get a copy for their files once the account was established. Consumers of financial products often complain that they do not understand how the business of financial advice works. That's too bad because if they paid more attention, they might get FSPs to be more forthcoming.

There are a number of other very real problems in the way things work right now, and as long as there's compensation embedded in the product, there's potential for trouble, especially if that compensation pays a disproportionately high amount at the time of the original sale. No one is saying that FSPs working with embedded compensation are necessarily dangerous, it's just that embedded compensation creates opportunities for outcomes that are sometimes self-serving to the FSP and not always in the clients' best interests.

Embedded compensation doesn't necessarilly hurt clients, but FSPs who earn embedded compensation are routinely put into positions where they might hurt their clients if they have a momentary lapse of judgement or just plain bad luck. The vast majority of FSPs who use embedded compensation products do not do anything unsavoury, but the opportunity exists and can easily be removed. The surest way to eradicate these problems is to remove the circumstances that allow the problems to occur in the first place. If the only way an FSP gets paid is through fees paid directly from the client, based on a formal, written agreement, awkward situations like those listed above are far less likely to happen.

The goal of any professional is to eliminate whatever biases might exist when offering independent advice to consumers. Since embedded compensation creates certain biases, the most obvious way to eliminate these would be to simply eliminate embedded compensation. If offering financial advice is ever going to be viewed as a genuine professional calling, the financial motives of the person giving the advice must not be allowed to influence the recommendations begin given.

A number of mutual fund companies have taken to automatically converting units in deferred sales charges (DSC) funds to the front-end variety once the DSC schedule runs its course. Others have taken to offering "lower load" options, where the upfront commission to the FSP is reduced along with a reduction in the holding period required to avoid early exit charges. Taken together, these two trends demonstrate how this could be implemented right now. If only the will to do so existed.

Realistically speaking, the will to change does not exist, so it might have to be imposed by legislation if there was a consensus that it was in the national interest. Legislative impositions are not nearly as draconian as some people make them out to be. After all, governments have imposed limits on fuel emissions and implemented bans on indoor smoking. This is just another example of how public policy levers could be used. For example, fund companies could be required to eliminate all embedded compensation within a number of years (e.g. eight or nine). The federal government could pass legislation in 2007 to prohibit DSCs beyond the point where the year of purchase plus the years left to free redemption equals 2014. Then, some time prior to 2014, it could pass legislation that bans all DSCs as of January 1, 2014. Funds purchased in

2008 could only have six years before back-end load penalties expired. Funds purchased in 2009 could only have five years before expiry, and so on. By 2013, there could still be a commission and trailing commission, but the exit penalty would expire some time in 2014. Finally, some time before 2015, legislation could be passed that bans embedded trailing commissions too. We could wake up on the morning of January 1, 2015 to a world without trailing commissions.

Embedded compensation causes bias and must be totally eliminated. It would not be enough to merely eliminate upfront commissions. If that happened, it would likely mean that fund companies would continue to exercise undue influence throughout the payment of ever-higher trailing commissions. This variation would be virtually certain, in my opinion. We'd have to take the final step. In order to achieve true independence, all embedded compensation—both upfront commissions and ongoing trailing commissions—would have to go. Only then would FSPs be free from the trap cast by a commissions-based selling environment.

Understanding how most FSPs have been paid up until now will go a long way in finding an FSP who can help you do what is right for your money. There are few FSPs in Canada today who are truly independent and who offer the widest possible range of products and services to their clients.

The time has come to press the issue. If FSPs are going to emerge from all the change the financial services industry is going through and hold themselves out as bona fide professionals, they will have to do away with embedded compensation. Anything less and their credibility would be too open to attack. If this were to happen, however, there would be a considerable amount of pain borne by both FSPs and consumers. No matter how badly you want to get to heaven, you'll have to die first. No wonder so many people have resisted moving forward for so long.

The Consequence of No Change

The system needs to be reformed. The cost of doing nothing is very high indeed, since the integrity of the entire financial services industry could be called into question. Figuring out an honourable way to leave the world of embedded compensation is job one and everything else regarding the establishment of a true profession flows from it. The current situation cannot continue indefinitely because there are simply far too many dysfunctional investment decisions being made as a result of the bias of compensation considerations.

The Ramifications of Unbundling

The test of a first-rate intelligence is the ability to hold two opposed ideas in the mind at the same time, and still retain the ability to function. One should, for example, be able to see that things are hopeless and yet be determined to make them otherwise.

—F. Scott Fitzgerald

The majority of FSPs are decent people. This is true whether they are fee based or commission based. It is widely accepted that there is no meaningful correlation between FSP competence and the compensation model used by that FSP. Both models (fees and commissions) are generally thought to have equally thorough and creative practitioners. As with any line of work, there are some who are better than others, irrespective of compensation model.

That being said, *it is vital to distinguish between competence and professionalism, which are very different things*. Competence seems to be evenly distributed, as far as anyone can tell. Professionalism, on the other hand, is at least somewhat determined by the manner in which one works with consumers. One might even develop a "Continuum of Professionalism" regarding financial advice. There are three basic stages to be applied to financial services and advice:

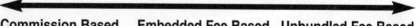

Commission Based   Embedded Fee Based   Unbundled Fee Based

On the left, we have the least professional (most sales-oriented) compensation model. It provides FSPs with a big paycheque up front and a little bit extra for ongoing services. This compensation method involves penalties that are to be incurred by clients if they redeem their products in anything less than the long term, effectively constraining their decision-making along the way.

Moving right, we come to embedded compensation, in which products offer ongoing commissions to FSPs for services rendered. These fees are collected by the company manufacturing the products and remitted to FSPs. They are recurring, offering no appreciable "up front" commission and no corresponding penalty to clients should they wish to use another product or FSP. Disclosure regarding the total cost to the client and the total compensation to the FSP remains largely piecemeal. Compensation may or may not be scalable and fees may or may not be deductible for non-registered accounts.

Finally, we come to unbundled compensation, the most professional compensation arrangement. It also involves a number of noteworthy differences. First, the FSP is paid *directly* by the client, so disclosure is never an issue. Second, fees are almost always scalable, meaning they taper downward as a percentage of total assets as accounts grow. Third, they are most likely tax deductible for non-registered plans. Finally, they may be paid from outside the portfolios themselves, leaving more money to compound inside the portfolios that use this format, but with a drain on other cash flows. Today, only a handful of STANDUP FSPs are confident enough in the services they offer to work using this format. One way to make decisions in life involves the question, "What would you do if you were not afraid?" That's a question most of today's FSPs need to answer by looking deeply into their souls.

MERs and Loads: What's the Difference?

No matter how much the industry likes to think progress has been made in explaining how mutual funds work, most consumers still don't get it. This struck me while speaking with a client. I wanted to make a clean break: clients were going to work on either an unbundled fee-basis or not at all, and the time had come to choose.

The client then surprised me. She said a friend had told her that it was cheaper to buy no-load funds. This is only true with a limited number of fund families. In most instances, clients who work with FSPs use traditional third-party funds (names like Mackenzie, AIM Trimark, AGF, AIC, and CI). In this case, the MER is usually identical whether the fund is purchased on a 0% front-end basis (with no load for early redemption) or a back-end load basis.

The cost of a mutual fund is its management expense ratio (MER). This is generally the sum of FSP compensation, fund company compensation, trading and regulatory costs, and GST. Newspapers report returns net of MERs, so if a fund shows a 7.5% rate of return with a 2.5% MER, it earned 10% on the year, deducted 2.5% through the MER, and passed the difference on to unitholders. The majority of consumers still don't understand that.

From a client's perspective, DSC funds retain the identical MER as no-load funds, but have a charge associated with them if they are redeemed early, generally within the first seven years after they are purchased. If the fund is held until the DSC charge expires, there is absolutely no difference between a DSC fund and a no-load fund, not in cost, content, tax treatment, or anything else. It should also be noted that while investors may always switch from one fund to another fund within the same family at no cost, there may be tax consequences in non-registered accounts.

However, if it turns out that for any reason the client wishes to sell the DSC fund early, there will be a charge. This drops over time. The friend of my client could potentially be right if DSC funds were used improperly. In this instance, the client would have paid the MER along the way, but would have also incurred a DSC charge upon disposition.

It should be clear that the real difference here is how the FSP chooses to be paid. This decision should always be made in consultation with the client. The A Class mutual fund options are either more money up front and less in future years (commission based) or some flat amount based on assets annually (embedded fee based). Neither is right nor wrong, it is simply a matter of personal preference. Client cost is identical.

The difference in the two structures is how the FSP's compensation is amortized. If an FSP is paid 5% up front and the fund only costs 2.5% a year, it should be obvious that the mutual fund company is out of pocket in the short term. As a result, the company would want to recoup its payment to the FSP should the fund be redeemed prior to the DSC schedule running its course. Since the FSP has already been paid and the client has presumably been told that this is a long-term proposition and that there are virtually always options within the fund family that would forgo these charges, the client is asked to foot the bill.

If the client chooses to liquidate less than 10% of that fund prior to the amortization period (DSC schedule) running its full course, these charges do not apply since this is considered a modest redemption made for liquidity/cash flow purposes and not a large-scale sell off. The 10% option can be exercised annually but is non-cumulative. In other words, a client cannot redeem 20% for free in year two if there was no redemption the previous year.

Assuming that clients understand this is a long-term proposition, they should be indifferent to the compensation model chosen. Of course, "no load" is not the same as "no embedded compensation to the FSP." Moving all the way to an unbundled environment would put an end to the misconception.

The GST of Financial Advice

The thing that keeps most people from working with a fee-based FSP is the fee itself. If consumers have worked with an FSP who didn't charge fees directly, the quantum of the bill was probably never openly discussed before. Sort of an "ask me no questions, I'll tell you no lies" kind of approach. Putting fees out in front changes that.

Perhaps the easiest way to understand the visceral hatred many people feel about paying fees (especially in years when markets are going down) is to consider how we reacted as a nation to the Goods and Services Tax (GST) when it was first introduced. I was working on Parliament Hill in the summer of 1990, doing a work term for my graduate studies program in public administration. There was a special committee that was set up to look into the effects of the GST on consumer prices. All manner of people and organizations came forward to express fear and loathing about the proposed changes to Canada's fiscal policy. People instinctively resist change.

Members of the government of the day went to great lengths to explain that the tax would now be "transparent"; it would now be out in the open, whereas previously it had been embedded in the price of the final product. (Does this sound familiar?) Government members insisted that the GST would be replacing an outdated tax system that charged large amounts for some things (manufactured goods) and nothing at all for others (services). Again, many consumers today believe they are paying a load to buy a product (a "good" called a mutual fund), while they feel they are entitled to free advice (a service) along the way.

The position of the government was that all things, both goods and services, should be taxed equally and that the tax should be out in the open, making it politically difficult to raise taxes in the future. Consumers weren't buying it. Putting a tax on sales receipts where none existed before created the distinct impression that taxes were going up, even though the GST proved to be revenue neutral. It was a measure that was tantamount to political suicide for the Mulroney government. More recently, the political decision to lower the GST from 7% to 6% garnered a lot of support for Stephen Harper.

It is widely accepted that the decision to promise GST cuts was bad public policy but excellent retail politics. Perhaps now readers can get a better sense of why so little has happened to unbundle products and advice in the past. Almost everyone in the financial services industry is scared of the backlash that is likely to follow.

By putting their fees right in the open, FSPs will be made to do business much like other professionals. There will be a constant assessment on the part of clients as to whether they are receiving true value for the services provided and advice rendered. This will be terrifying for many SPANDEX FSPs who do little to genuinely add value but will assist consumers greatly in determining who the true professionals are. Most consumers vaguely understand that they are paying their FSP indirectly, but have no real idea of how much money the FSP receives.

For now, if you want to be as assured as is reasonably possible that your FSP is looking out for your best interests, you should ask some pointed questions before making choices. Of course, the transition to unbundled fees requires a high degree of disclosure, discussion, and explanation about how this transition might reasonably be accomplished. The changeover must occur without undue damage to either the FSPs' welfare or clients' portfolio values. Both parties need to have their interests honourably represented if this transition is to move forward.

Rhetoric and Reality

Given the push toward consolidation within the financial services industry, there's been a sidebar debate raging for a number of years about the independence of FSPs in firms that offer proprietary products. This debate has missed the point entirely. So far, the media have focused on whether consumers are well served by moving from third-party products to in-house brands, even though most apples-to-apples comparisons show that the actively managed products are relatively homogeneous.

It's obvious why firms that offer in-house investment products want their clients to use them: profit margins. Many companies make only a few cents on the dollar when distributing products that someone else manufactures but perhaps eight to twelve times that amount when they distribute their own products. To use conventional business lingo, there's a much larger profit margin in manufacturing than there is in distribution.

Think of cookies: if a consumer switches from Keebler or Dare or Mr. Christie's cookies to President's Choice cookies, does that mean the consumer has been duped? Some companies have found ways to leverage their distribution network in order to compete with the third-party products already on their shelves. If clients want the new products, it means more profit for the vertically integrated provider. If clients don't want these products, distributors are no worse off. Consumers are free to use whichever products they want; they can make choices in their own enlightened self-interest.

Since there's a higher margin in proprietary products, there's a potential incentive for some FSPs to recommend a conversion into them if the FSP is a shareholder of the company that "manufactures" the product. Higher margins lead to larger profits, higher share prices, and personal enrichment. Motives could certainly be called into question, but no one should be an apologist for seeking profit. Every company in the industry has a business plan that involves some conversion of third-party products into the in-house brand, but the link should be made clear so that investors understand what they're getting before they sign on the dotted line. The current level of disclosure about "related and connected issuers" is understood by virtually no one. It was once permissible for companies to pay their employees more for in-house products—a flagrant transgression of the principle of independence. Before long, regulators stepped in and passed National Instrument 81-105, putting an end to this reprehensible practice.

The rhetoric coming from the financial services industry is that all products are essentially the same: companies have broadly similar products and they'll all get you to about the same place at the end of the day. The unspoken but clearly implied message is that it should not matter whether the products used are proprietary or independent, since they're all the same anyway. The problem is that independence is not revealed so much by what is put on the shelf for consumption as it is by what is effectively kept off.

Accepting that every FSP has to be affiliated with some firm in order to do business and ultimately will be expected to recommend some product or another to assist a client, the question really becomes one of undue direct influence. Sure, the house brand is being put on the shelf in order to offer more selection, which, in theory at least, should be better for consumers, but what about products that are effectively left off the shelf in the process?

This brings us back to the notion of embedded compensation. Nothing compromises independence and professionalism more. The majority of FSPs simply prefer to sell products that offer embedded compensation today. There's a game of half-truths going on that virtually no one is talking about. The game is that FSPs will recommend almost anyone's products (good or bad, third-party or proprietary) *provided that those companies pay them some form of embedded compensation.* Otherwise, FSPs will just pretend the other companies don't exist and continue to present themselves as independent professionals offering the widest possible range of investment choices for their clients. Most FSPs do everything they can to dissuade clients from buying products that offer no embedded compensation.

In making the transition, consumers will need to acknowledge that if FSPs say they need to be paid, there should be agreements to pay, provided the payments requested are fair. Most FSPs are simply too frightened to ask their clients to pay them directly and will go so far as to recommend inferior products in order to avoid having that conversation. These same FSPs still call themselves independent professionals.

Even if the companies that offer no embedded compensation had "best in class" products, those products would be tacitly blacklisted because FSPs are afraid to go to their clients and ask for direct payment. That's the saddest part of this situation. Everyone agrees that FSPs need to be paid for the important work they do. The need for payment misses the point just as much as the debate about proprietary funds versus third-party funds does. *The real point is that FSPs present themselves as true professionals, yet consistently act like the commission-based salespeople they were trained to be.*

The companies that employ FSPs play along. They approve products with no embedded compensation and point to that fact as evidence of independence but fail to establish a platform that would allow for unbundled billing. Can they help it if none of their FSPs actually recommend these products? After all, these companies will argue, the FSPs are not being denied access. Some companies drop all pretenses. If they don't have a proper platform for fee-based accounts, they simply won't approve F Class funds. What can STANDUP FSPs do to respond other than move their entire practice (at considerable cost and effort) to another firm?

Independence and Advice

There are many tricky situations tied to embedded compensation for people who offer financial advice. From a FSP's perspective, the primary issue has always been the need to earn a fair and reasonable living. Ironically, the question of real independence is often secondary.

For instance, many FSPs in the same firm, or even the same office, may use entirely different products when making recommendations to the public. Traditional third-party (embedded compensation) mutual funds, while diverse, are still quite similar in that the FSP gets paid simply and consistently, irrespective of which fund they recommend.

From a client's perspective, when working with an FSP, the issue is about getting unbiased advice. From where clients stand, it all comes down to "Can I trust this person to recommend what is truly appropriate for my circumstances?" No matter how ethical, empathetic, competent, and professional the FSP seems to be, clients instinctively wonder if the products and strategies being recommended are what's best—and for good reason.

That's the irony of the industry. On the one hand, there are literally thousands of embedded compensation mutual funds and principal-protected notes that offer a mind-numbing assortment of asset classes, sub-classes, and strategies for consumers. On the other hand, there are competing products—individual stocks and bonds, ETFs, true no-load mutual funds, royalty and income trusts—that pay the FSP nothing. The two types of investment products coexist as almost entirely mutually exclusive product lines.

How can consumers be absolutely certain that what is recommended from the universe of embedded compensation mutual fund products is what's most appropriate and that there's nothing else available that makes more sense for their circumstances? Specifically, how can the consumer be assured that there isn't a non-embedded product out there that suits them better? As long as one set of products offers FSPs a form of compensation for which they do not have to do what they desperately do not want to do—insist on direct payment from clients—there will always be an inherent bias toward those products.

As a simple matter of practice economics, many FSPs would not be in business if they could not earn commissions, so forcing FSPs out of a commission environment will force many FSPs out of the industry. Perhaps even more disconcerting is that those who have the biggest and most established client base are best positioned to weather this transition. For survival, size matters. Unfortunately, the size of a practice does not *necessarily* correlate with the professionalism of that practice.

Those FSPs who have fewer and smaller accounts but perhaps are more academically and professionally qualified may not make it. In the past, and probably in the short-term future, benefits accrue disproportionately to the big producer rather than the qualified professional. This is starting to change. As consumers become more discerning, the fulcrum will shift and there will be a tendency to move toward either working with a truly competent FSP or simply doing it themselves. With primary financial services stakeholder groups, consumers, and FSPs, we're looking at a scenario of short-term pain for long-term gain. Both FSPs and their clients will likely have to endure a period when they are temporarily worse off before things can become noticibly better. For both parties, there are definite risks and limitations associated with making the change away from embedded compensation.

What Adds Value?

All great truths begin as blasphemies.

—George Bernard Shaw

Some ideas have been around for so long that no one even knows where they came from. This chapter will discuss the benefits of a passive approach as compared to a valid active alternative. It will also extol the virtues of working with a qualified FSP as opposed to the valid approach of doing without.

One of the great assumptions of active management is that it makes sense. In other words, it is "sensible" to pay an expert a fee to try to do better than a market average. There's also a definition of insanity that suggests doing the same thing you've always done, yet expecting different results.

Since we've already seen that it makes no sense to pay someone else a fee to gamble with your money unless you are confident they can add value along the way, one should be fairly certain that the person one hires to add value is in fact doing just that. Traditional brokers have used the promise of superior security selection as their silver bullet for ages. More recently, many FSPs have come to the conclusion that the world is too complex and that they would rather hire "expert professionals" (i.e. money managers) to run specific mandates within their clients' portfolios. Here's what Chet Currier of Bloomberg News has to say about that:

> What mutual funds have always had to sell is diversification, convenience, liquidity, and something called "professional management." Well, the customers can get all the diversification, convenience, and liquidity they want from index funds that avoid the costs of security selection...

active managers deserve to be paid only for the amount by which they outperform the index, known by the shorthand term "alpha." Because active managers as a group stand little chance of beating the market (they are the market and they cannot hope to beat themselves), those active managers as a group deserve no pay at all.[1]

But if active managers do such a collectively poor job on the performance side as to not be deserving of any pay at all, why on earth would any professional, independent, client-centred FSP ever recommend using their services, much less making that kind of recommendation on virtually all occasions?

Credit Where Credit Is Due

People pay mutual fund managers a fee to manage a portfolio with a mandate to outperform a certain benchmark. If the manager is outperforming the benchmark after fees, consumers should say, "thank you very much" and not begrudge the fee. If, on the other hand, the manager lags the benchmark, either a new manager should be hired or the consumer should cut the losses by simply buying the benchmark or its nearest facsimile.

As long as the manager posts a return (net of fees) that exceeds the benchmark, they're adding value. The better the manager, the higher the fee that can be charged. Presumably, the manager could charge the same as competitors and still be handsomely rewarded, since investors would be pleased to give them a disproportionate percentage of total assets to manage. In other words, savvy consumers should not be opposed to high fees in and of themselves. However, they should be opposed to any fees that are worth less than what they cost.

Furthermore, the degree by which an actively managed mutual fund lags its benchmark is primarily determined by how much that actively managed fund costs. The more it costs, the more it lags, all else being equal. Lowering the cost merely increases the likelihood of better performance—it guarantees nothing. It should also be stressed that there are exceptions in both directions: cheap managers who lag their benchmarks and expensive managers who beat their benchmarks.

Remember that since most actively managed mutual funds feature embedded compensation and most index-type investments in Canada don't, there is an added performance burden for active management. Active management proponents argue that it is unfair to compare one strategy that generally pays FSPs (active management) to another that generally does not (indexing), since FSP payment further compounds the difficulties inherent in relative performance comparisons. Of course, they are right. Ironically, this is another reason to get on with unbundling. Without unbundling, a true apples-to-apples comparison is impossible for all funds with similar mandates but different compensation models.

In the end, FSPs could be ideologically indifferent to the debate between active and passive investing, because a case can be made for either (or both, in varying proportions). As long as the risks and limitations of each strategy are clearly spelled out from the outset, the integrity of the recommendation should never be called into question. It should also be noted that some asset classes can only be accessed through active management if one wants a diversified holding in that asset class.

Eugene Fama looked at twenty years of U.S. data from Morningstar for the period from 1976 to 1996. He split performance into two chronological halves, taking the top half of funds from 1976 to 1986 and then testing how they did from 1986 to 1996. The result was that exactly half were up and half were down over that second decade, after accounting for three primary explanatory variables: market risk, small vs. large cap, and value vs. growth.

If markets are reasonably efficient, then the only way to beat the market is to gain information that no one else has, analyze its significance (quantifying the impact on stock prices), and act on your hopefully accurate analysis *before anyone else can*. This last point is vital because there are thousands of pieces of information being thrown out daily (some more valuable and relevant than others) and millions of market participants receiving this information simultaneously. For one participant to be able to claim that they can reliably analyze and act on information more swiftly than *the broader market as a single entity* is rather unlikely.

Rex Sinquefield is the former co-chairman of Dimensional Fund Advisors in California. He says that in the social sciences, predictions are more general than specific because they involve people who might change their beliefs and objectives at any point in time. As such, Sinquefield says the burden of proof rests with active managers to demonstrate that they are regularly and predictably adding value.

Active managers try really hard to impress people with what they are doing. I was at a professional development conference hosted by a prominent mutual fund company recently where there were no fewer than twenty-one wholesalers (product specialists with a sales mandate) lined up—and that was only for the Toronto market. The intent was to show off the strength and solidarity of the company to FSPs before the session started. The clear message to the FSPs present was, "We've got a strong, dedicated army backing you up and helping you in your sales process." In looking at them, however, I couldn't help but think, "How much are they paying these guys and what is that doing to my clients' MERs?"

Embedded Compensation As Tied Selling

The concept of tied selling is well known in the financial services industry: access to a product or service is denied unless the purchaser also buys another related but different product or service. The latter becomes a precondition for access to the former in an all-or-nothing gambit. An example might be an RRSP loan. Banks used to be happy to lend you $5,000 to make an RRSP contribution, but only if the money was invested in their products. If you wanted to buy some other product, your loan was denied.

Regulators stopped this, but tied selling soon gave way to relationship pricing, in which that same bank would give you a loan, but it would be at prime if you used the bank's products and at prime + 1% if you used someone else's. While technically legal, many people still see such conduct as an unscrupulous abuse of position.

Here's the similarity: FSPs offer advice. If a consumer comes to an FSP and indicates an interest in using his services for some advice on the best index fund available, the FSP might politely ask that would-be client to leave and not come back. Advice is currently heavily predicated on embedded compensation. No embedded compensation to the FSP usually means no payment upon implementation, which means no advice in the first place. This is generally true unless the consumer goes to a discount brokerage, where the situation is often worse.

It is rather humourous how the industry has changed. In the middle of the last decade, popular industry motivator Nick Murray coined the phrase "no-load means no advice." This was never true in an absolute sense but true enough at the time since most FSPs were competing primarily against no-load providers such as banks. At the time, direct mutual fund seller Altamira had a large market share in Canada. It was a way of legitimizing the tied-selling aspects of mutual fund sales, since many consumers were focusing on the handicaps of back-end load (DSC) penalties rather than the benefits of qualified advice. It was a cute way of turning the tables on those companies that were gaining market share by trumpeting their no-load "value proposition."

Murray even had a little vaudeville routine that drove the point home. It was called the "no-load cardiologist," in which a "professional" cardiologist would be happy to do whatever you wanted and best of all there was never any load! People who visit cardiologists generally have no training in physiological matters and so are looking to a trusted medical professional for advice on problems that are vitally important to them. It didn't matter if they asked about CAT scans, EKGs, arrhythmia, or any other ailment or treatment, the advice was always the same: the no-load cardiologist would always do what *you* wanted and there would never be a load.

There have always been STANDUP FSPs out there who offer this kind of service, but they're still relatively rare. At present, people needing advice are left to choose between whether a fee or a commission (which establishes a load) is the best way to pay for that advice.

Why Work With an FSP?

Most consumers want to work with qualified FSPs. It is important to talk to someone face to face, and regular contact is important. There is also a sizable minority of consumers who feel using an FSP is redundant. These people choose to do their own financial planning and advising. They're known as the do-it-yourself (DIY) crowd.

Whichever camp one falls into, it is widely believed that consumers are becoming more sophisticated. The good news is that consumers *are* becoming more savvy; the bad news is, in my opinion, is that it isn't happening quickly enough.

One of the great ironies of the financial services industry is that financial service providers generally add value. They do it, for the most part, while using actively managed mutual funds that generally subtract value relative to passive products and strategies. Mutual fund companies know this and continually tell FSPs how great they are. Index providers only talk about cost because without an embedded payment mechanism for FSPs, that's all they have to go on. *It might be said that an often inferior product line has co-opted the complicit loyalty of those FSPs who recommend these products through what amounts to bribery!*

In case you think this is an unduly strident stance, let's look up the word *bribe*. The dictionary says a bribe is something (money or a favour) given or promised to a person *to influence conduct*.[2] FSPs function in an environment where it might fairly be said that de facto bribery could enter into the decision-making process regarding the products FSPs recommend.

It should be clear by now that most mutual fund managers fail to live up to their end of their value proposition of outperforming relevant benchmarks after fees. What about FSPs? For most people, mutual funds and FSPs are seen as two peas in a pod. What if we took the unbundling idea one step further and tried to determine whether FSPs are actually adding value equal to or in excess of the fees they charge?

Do FSPs Add Value?

This is a difficult thesis to test in a meaningful way. How does one quantify decisions that were *not* taken (e.g. buying Nortel at over $100 on the way up) when calculating FSP value? Although the question is a contentious one, there seems to be a strong consensus that FSPs do add value, just not the way most people think. For instance, working with an FSP does not increase the likelihood that an investor will beat an index, but it does reduce the risk of having that person substantially lag it. In essence, FSPs seem to reduce losses more than they maximize gains. This is actually a massive value-added attribute by itself, since behavioural finance research shows that people feel the pain of a loss more than twice as strongly as they feel the joy of a gain. Interestingly, the mathematics of capital markets means that a 49% market decline from a previous peak like the one that ended in October 2002 requires about a 98% rise just to get back to that previous level.

People sometimes think about ditching their FSPs and pocketing the difference in cost savings. In the opinion of essentially all FSPs, that would be penny-wise and pound foolish. By now, we all know that financial advice is not free and that FSPs cost real money, even if most do not give their clients invoices at the end of the year. But do FSPs add enough value to justify their fees?

If your FSP's only value proposition is stock or fund picking, then there is a case to be made for firing him. But before you do, make sure that that really is all that your FSP does. Many elements of financial advice never show up on a quarterly portfolio report.

The emerging field of behavioural finance shows that virtually everyone suffers from some quirks of human nature that cause them to do irrational things for some seemingly sensible reason. The problem is that people who rationalize often end up telling themselves rational lies. Good FSPs can help people who suffer from these quirks. Research has shown that well over half the population thinks they are above-average drivers. The same likely holds true for people (consumers and FSPs alike) regarding stock picking and fund picking. If that were true, then why is so much money invested in funds that have performed poorly? Where, exactly, does that little bit of constructive behaviour modification show up on a client statement? What about encouraging the client to take out insurance? What about setting up RESPs for young children at the first opportunity?

When discussing financial matters, it is generally accepted that fear and greed motivate people. Behavioural finance demonstrates that people are far more emotional than rational when it comes to their money, especially when they are living through wild swings in values. Most FSPs promote their services as offering return maximization (playing to people's collective greed), while the value of working with a professional FSP is usually gained through the peace of mind that comes with loss minimization. This is especially true as accounts grow.

Individual investors generally make decisions based on a multiplicity of inputs, including family, friends, popular media, coworkers, online research, and gut instinct. Other more personal factors like self-esteem and personal life experiences are also thought to be major contributors to decision-making.

Investors Behaving Badly

A landmark study conducted by CEG Worldwide examined investor behaviour for the period from January 1990 to March 2000. Aptly entitled "Investors Behaving Badly," it showed quite compellingly that FSPs have a positive impact on their clients' financial lives. It also showed that the traditional foundations of financial planning, such as setting financial goals, were often not in place for DIY investors, who were more inclined to be moved by short-term influences as a result. How many DIY investors do you suppose have an investment policy statement? In my lifetime, I've only heard of one.

Specifically, DIY investors were more likely to trade too frequently, which more often than not led to poor market timing. It is well documented that portfolio turnover correlates negatively to returns. These DIY investors often chase a hot stock, hot fund, or hot asset class, effectively buying near the top of the market when they do so. In forty-two of the forty-eight Morningstar mutual fund categories studied, higher net inflows occurred when performance was best. In doing this, DIY investors often focused unduly on immediate past performance and ignored the principles of diversification, something any qualified FSP would pay primary attention to when designing a portfolio. As a result, the study found that many DIY investors missed out on potentially better results through failed attempts at market timing. Investors are supposed to buy low and sell high, while it seems that most are naturally inclined to buy high.

What about DIY investors' sell discipline? Not only are DIY investors unduly confident in their own investment selections when they are dropping, they frequently delay in returning to the market after getting out. They reason that they need to be confident that the market is indeed moving upward again. Research shows that investors need to be right more than half the time when engaging in this kind of market timing (both when to get out and when to get in) in order to do as well as simply buying and holding. Most truly professional FSPs are sufficiently humble to know that predicting the future is a daunting task that should not be undertaken casually.

In 1996, 5.5 years was the average holding period for mutual funds. By 2000, with markets on a veritable tear, the typical long-term holding period had dropped to 2.9 years. Today, it is less than 1 year on average. How's that for discipline and a long-term perspective? In fairness, this is data for all fund investors, both those working with FSPs and those doing their own investing. I've spoken with dozens of FSPs over the years and they don't encourage their clients to trade nearly that often.

Furthermore, the CEG study showed that since DIY investors had consistently higher redemption rates and shorter holding periods, higher tax bills naturally followed. By not staying invested, they often missed those days when markets moved ahead strongly, something FSPs could have helped prevent. The average DIY mutual fund investor realized a return of 8.7% versus a market average of 10.9% over similar time frames.

The mathematics of this study implies that an FSP is worth 2.2% in fees. This may be a bit of a stretch, but the trend should be clear. Most DIY investors unwittingly take on more risk than those who work with an FSP, setting themselves up for self-destructive behaviour when things go sour.

This is an especially important consideration coming out of the bear market that began in 2000 and ended in 2002. FSPs add value by helping their clients to understand and cope with market fluctuation, putting movements into a historical context and keeping them focused on long-term objectives.

Again, the primary role of an FSP is to help clients achieve their financial objectives, whatever they may be and however they are defined. Beating a market index, or some composite of multiple indexes, is not how truly professional FSPs position their services. Rather, they should tell their clients that it is their role to get them retired and keep them retired with the least trouble by making smart financial decisions along the way.

There are three reasons why investors generally behaved as

badly as they did in the 1990s: the market, the marketers, and the media. The market at the turn of the twenty-first century was a seductive temptress. Everyone seemed to be making money and people who took a rear-view-mirror approach (expecting the near future to be much like the recent past) jumped in as the fear of loss was replaced by the fear of being left behind. Marketers capitalized on both disintermediation, the notion that information that was once only available from a controlled source (e.g. stock quotes in the 1970s) is now readily available to the general public, and the seemingly endless stream of good news. Investors took comfort in all the positive spin they were bombarded with. Finally, the media created a mania. People extrapolated the "good news" and believed the music might never stop.

Given the experience Canadians had with Nortel at the turn of the millennium, there might be another wrinkle that people hadn't necessarily contemplated. What if markets are essentially inefficient, but investors are essentially irrational? In other words, what if you believed the price of a security was already higher than it ought to be, but you bought it anyway because you were reasonably certain that on a balance of probabilities, someone would come along in the not too distant future and offer you even more money for it, thereby transforming an otherwise bad investment into a good one? If the price is wrong and you know its wrong, but you're reasonably certain there's a greater fool out there who will buy it at an even higher price, you might buy the stock anyway.

If you bought a stock simply because you were pretty sure the price was going to go up (due to human nature and in spite of your opinion that there was no rational reason for this to happen), that could be considered prudent, perhaps even shrewd. Is this investing or speculating? The case could be made either way.

While at odds as to which paradigm (efficient markets or irrational investor behaviour) best explains how markets function, the world's greatest minds in finance are united in their prescription. In other words, for all practical intents and purposes, it doesn't matter which viewpoint is correct. This is because both the efficient market and behavioural finance camps see the primary role of FSPs as maintaining discipline and setting and managing expectations. In short, they both offer the same advice:

- Buy and hold
- Diversify
- Put your money in index funds
- Pay attention to what you can control

What Else Might a Good FSP Do?

A whole raft of "value-added services" from yesteryear is now being given away as financial information becomes a disintermediated commodity. The middlemen (i.e. brokers) are being bypassed in this process and therefore need to do other things in order to truly add value for those who want to use their services.

Let's take a quick look at some of the things traditional brokers used to do and in some cases still do. These services include stock quotes, consolidated statements of holdings, asset allocation, proprietary securities research, and trade execution. Do you notice anything about this list? All these services can now be accessed by anyone who has a computer with an Internet connection. All of them are absolutely free, save for trade execution, which is almost free.

What does this mean in the context of "wisdom sold separately"? To many, it means that FSPs are required to assist their clients in maintaining a sense of focus and an even keel, particularly in uncertain times. Of course, FSPs are no more responsible for the events of September 11, 2001 or corporate malfeasance than anyone else. There was no way anyone could have foreseen these two events. Although FSPs were in no way responsible for these events, their clients still looked to them to "fix" the problems that the events caused. In a situation like this, the wisdom of perspective is crucial.

Consumers can have a perverse sense of perspective regarding what FSPs do. Many consumers resent paying their FSP if they have lost 10%, even if markets have lost 20%. Conversely, many don't mind paying if their portfolio has gone up by 10%, even if markets on the whole have risen by 20%. Neither is a particularly sensible or healthy approach. Consumers tend to look at portfolio performance in isolation, with a tendency to focus on loss aversion. A more appropriate approach would be to look at portfolio performance relative to life goals, accepting that some years will be better and some worse than others.

Some have suggested that there are only three attributes that are important for FSPs to have. They should be able to:

1. Spot problems and identify solutions.
2. Motivate people to act/change their behaviour.
3. Emotionally detach from investment markets.

This is a clear and simple synopsis of what FSPs can and probably should do. It should also be stressed that they probably should *not* be doing any of the other things that many consumers and the media pundits seem to think they should be doing. The role of the STANDUP FSP is to help consumers navigate the emotional minefield of financial decision-making and adding value has almost nothing to do with picking stocks or mutual funds.

Simplification and Perspective

There are a couple of FSP functions that on a good day might be worth a little more than investment pornography. If the attributes of any investment are the same now as what they were when the investor bought it, that investor should probably continue to hold the investment. Regression to the mean is a very real phenomenon. Professional FSPs wouldn't let their clients sell on emotions.

The main job of the FSP is to help consumers remain focused on their goals and to pursue them with determination and a sense of calm and context. Perhaps the easiest way to describe the function of an FSP is to *assist investors in overcoming their own irrationality.*

FSPs also add value through simplification. To the extent that an FSP can simplify and enhance your life by doing spade work, filtering data, developing shortlists, calculating adjusted cost bases, securing T3s and T5s, interacting with other professionals, or simply coaching you to top up that RRSP, there are benefits. Putting a price on it is virtually impossible, but it would be hard to deny that these activities are worth something.

Financial Planning

Everything in this chapter has been about investment design, discipline, and monitoring. This is not a book about financial planning, but rather a book about professional financial advice. The most significant aspect of this is the need to reform compensation structures for investment products. However, investment planning is just one part of financial advice and is often not even the most important part.

Most people reading this book will not have the tools to purposefully implement all the required aspects of a comprehensive financial plan, many of which require specialized knowledge that qualified FSPs (i.e. CFPs) themselves might not have. A comprehensive questionnaire should be required that goes into great depth on matters of tax and estate planning, business succession, proper use of insurance, and advanced financial planning solutions. The point is that in order to make the most of qualified financial advice, the person offering the advice needs to be completely thorough in practicing their craft. These other planning-oriented skills are often more specialized and therefore more valuable, although many people might not need that level of advice if their situation is relatively straightforward.

Most people expect long-term average returns of 3% to 7% above inflation, although FSPs have been known to use a wider range of assumptions. Planning is made more difficult if one considers the additional erosive effects of taxation.

Once people have been invested for ten years or more, returns should begin to approach their long-term real return targets. Remember that risk is not the variability of returns but the likelihood of losing money. Otherwise, months such as October 1998 and July 2002 would be depicted as risky months because of substantial market advances! Since people generally become slightly more conservative as they age, portfolios may be modified over time to be more conservative. For more about risk and time, please refer back to the diagram in Chapter 2: "Preparing FSPs."

There are three primary ways to increase investment returns:

1. Reduce fixed income exposure and increase equity exposure.
2. Increase value investment equity exposure.
3. Increase exposure to small and mid-sized companies.

There are three primary tax reduction strategies:

1. Deduct all allowable expenses.
2. Defer taxes until a later date when you might be in a lower marginal bracket.
3. Divide taxes so that family members in lower brackets can pay less tax.

Clients may also wish to consider the appropriateness of universal life insurance policies to meet tax obligations upon death and to provide tax-free growth while clients are alive and tax loss harvesting options if suitable alternatives are available.

Finally, consumers should remember that financial independence projections are made using assumptions only. If it turns out that someone falls short in their independence projections, there are only four possible assumptions that can be altered:

1. Savings rate: clients could save more on either a monthly or annual basis.
2. Rate of return: returns are fairly predictable provided one takes a longer view.
3. Retirement date: waiting longer increases savings and delays depletion.
4. Reducing lifestyle in retirement: this should only be considered as a last resort.

Clients have noted that they are not always aware of the various services offered by FSPs. That's likely because these things do not come up in regular conversations and communications with clients. Listed below are areas where expertise should be either directly or indirectly available through a qualified FSP.

	Advice	**DIY**
Active	1 Active Advice	3 Active DIY
Passive	2 Passive Advice	4 Passive DIY

The Four Quadrants of Financial Services

Although nothing is absolute, it seems that *most of the time, passive trumps active and people with FSPs trump DIY*. There are four combinations of active/passive and FSP/DIY. Let's explore the underlying assumptions that lead to each:

1. Active with an FSP

This is where most people are today. They work with a trusted FSP who will hopefully add value through insight, discipline, and planning opportunities and use actively managed investment products to do so. The presupposition is that both active security selection/portfolio management and the input of a trusted FSP are expenses worth incurring in the pursuit of one's financial objectives.

2. Passive with an FSP

There's hardly anyone in this quadrant today. It is the quadrant that I favour and it acknowledges that working with a qualified, trusted FSP is well worth the potential additional cost, but also that using active managers to implement the strategy is often a waste of time, energy, and money.

3. Active DIY

A somewhat curious quadrant, especially for those people using A Class mutual funds. The assumption here is that the consumer doesn't need an FSP for investment advice or advice regarding taxes, estate planning, or myriad other financial issues, but believes that active management adds value and that superior active managers can be reliably identified.

4. Passive DIY

A respectable quadrant if you are reasonably astute, have a simple situation, and are remarkably disciplined in your investment approach. Anyone with the time, temperament, and training to manage their own financial affairs *should* be in this quadrant and pocket the savings in the process.

The problem with the second quadrant is the presumptive nature in which investment products are sold today. Active investments generally come with embedded compensation and passive ones do not. Furthermore, research shows that FSPs generally add value, but since they will only recommend active products if they want to earn a living, emphasis is put on the value of active management as provided through the careful guidance of a trusted advisor. This is as if passive management accessed through the careful guidance of a trusted advisor wasn't an option. Practically speaking, retaining embedded compensation prevents passive management with qualified advice from ever becoming an option.

We have four possible combinations of approaches: active with advice, active without advice, passive with advice, and passive without advice. One conclusion would be that the passive with advice combination is likely the best, yet there's virtually no one in the country using that format.

Most people would agree that the majority of accounts in Canada are either managed in an active with advice (Quadrant 1) or passive without advice (Quadrant 4) format. What is one to do if they fall into one of the other two camps?

We've already discussed why active without advice makes little sense. Interestingly, the most likely defense for that approach is if the investor believes they can do it themselves and then uses no-load funds in constructing a portfolio or trades stocks directly using the same premise. Conversely, the passive with advice camp is the one which might well make the most sense when looked at dispassionately.

The point is that the active/passive debate is one consideration that needs to be resolved for many consumers and the advice/no advice is another *separate* decision. In an unbundled world, there is absolutely no reason why one decision should have any impact on the other and both can be contemplated strictly on the basis of merit alone.

The above chart is a simplification, since it assumes an investor is using either entirely active or entirely passive investment products. There remains a legitimate case to be made for both approaches. Similarly, there is a large number of consumers who use FSPs for the bulk of their net worth, but carve out a small amount of "play money" where they dabble on their own. This is fun to some people.

As a result, all four quadrants are at least somewhat oversimplified. Both decisions might be considered with a "blended" or "indifferent" approach. There's no easy way to accurately reflect these nuances and uncertainties.

Get Advice If You Need It

The power of habit and the charm of novelty are the two adverse forces which explain the follies of mankind.

—Comtesse Diane

Everyone has an opinion on the value of advice and the need for it. Not surprisingly, nearly all FSPs think advice is important. There are some people who are able enough or whose circumstances are simple enough that they can do things adequately on their own.

Reasonable people might differ on what percentage of the population needs advice, but since a lot of advising involves discipline, process, perspective, and similar things that are not easily quanitified, there's nothing close to a consensus profile of a person who should use an FSP as opposed to one who might be successful going it alone.

As a general rule, most people would say that most consumers would be well served to use an FSP, although it is probably fair to allow that there is a subset of the population in which it is well within their abilities and entirely justified to forgo these services. Whether the percentage of the population that should work with an FSP is 50%, 70%, 90%, or some other number isn't really the point. Perhaps the fairest thing to say is that many people should use an FSP, while others needn't.

The Tyranny of Overconfidence

I've mentioned the research showing that a large majority of the population thinks they're above-average drivers. Overconfidence is a common affliction that many of us suffer from and one that we would all do well to consider when investing our money.

Virtually everyone would be well advised to be a little more humble when it comes to stock picking, but stock pickers are typically anything but humble.

I have yet to meet a money manager who will admit to being below average. I've only met a handful of FSPs who are willing to acknowledge that their results have been no more than middling when trying to identify superior managers, even though we've already seen that the industry has a collective track record that is embarrassing. Every stock picker on the planet, it seems, thinks they're smarter than their average peer.

The bad news for many consumers and SPANDEX FSPs is that reliable outperformance is a doubtful proposition no matter who is doing the talking. The good news for STANDUP FSPs is that it doesn't matter. If there is only one concept that you take from this book, I believe it ought to be that good financial advice is not about security selection or market timing. Anyone who makes these their primary value proposition is likely a person who not only fails to legitimately add value but who also deliberately gets people to focus on unimportant things.

The Automatic MER Reduction

David Bach has made a name for himself with his simple, homespun approach to planning for and achieving financial independence. According to him, virtually anyone can become a millionaire by simply making relatively modest lifestyle adjustments that save a few bucks here or there and then investing those few bucks for growth. I agree with him. This is a modern-day "a penny saved is a penny earned."

Anyone can "run the numbers." A few dollars a day, invested for high single-digit long-term growth over the course of a person's working life could easily add up to over $1 million. Stated another way, if a latte costs about $3 and you were in the habit of picking one up daily, you could save yourself a little over $1,000 a year. If you simply invested those savings for your long-term future, you'd be better off for sure.

What I find curious is that the institutions that hire Bach and help to spread his gospel by giving away his books by the thousands are leaving one thing out in the equation: it doesn't have to be lattes. It could be anything. Taking public transit, for instance, or brown bagging it to work. There are myriad ways to save a few bucks here and there on a routine basis. As such, I find it curious that other simple methods are seldom used.

Since we're having a discussion about scrimping and saving our way to the retirement that we all want, why not link the saving and the investing aspects of the program? Why not save the money by buying cheaper investments? A penny saved is a penny earned, but I bet your friendly neighbourhood banker never told you about that one.

Most ordinary Canadians invest by using products that have an annual cost associated with them called a management expense ratio (MER). Many actively managed fund MERs in Canada are well over 2.5%. That's a $2,500 annual cost on $100,000 invested. Instead of buying active funds, consumers could just as easily buy competing products for 2% less in an unbundled format and about 1% less even with financial advice added in. That's a huge potential annual saving! If your portfolio is at the $100,000 level, there's $1,000 in annual savings right there.

Here's where it gets fun. A latte might cost $2.75 and increase with inflation, so it might cost $2.85 next year. However, the cost of your portfolio is linked to financial markets, so $70,000 this year might be worth $76,300 next year. This is because one might assume that inflation goes up about 3% a year and that markets go up about 9% a year. Not for sure, but on average. Since markets grow at a higher rate, your savings grow at a higher rate too.

A generation from now, a latte might cost $5.95. However, that $70,000 investment portfolio might have grown to $560,000. Giving up lattes would save you about $2,000 a year by that time, but using indexes to build your nest egg would save you about $8,000 a year. That's the great thing about the automatic MER reduction, it works better than other methods, plus you get to have your retirement and drink your latte too.

The Missing 1%

Let's apply Bach's logic to the services and products offered by FSPs. Here's the killer question that I think FSPs should be asking their clients: "If I could show you a way to add 1% to your annual investment returns—holding risk constant—would you be interested?" Stated another way, "If you had a time period of twenty-five or more years and a small six-digit portfolio that you were adding to annually, would you be interested in having an additional quarter million dollars of net worth at the end?"

This is the question FSPs can now ask their clients. As it now stands, FSPs who use mutual funds generally earn about a 1% annual recurring compensation on products that cost about 2.5%. If products representing an indexed approach to an identical asset mix were used, the product cost would be about 0.5%. Throw in an additional 1% fee (potentially tax deductible) and the total client cost drops to 1.5%. It is the FSPs who largely control the discretionary 1% and generally recommend that fund managers receive the money in the hope that they will add value after their fee comes off.

There's a real need for clarity here. The active managers that are hired might indeed add value. Then again, it is just as possible (actually, it is probable) that they might subtract value instead. On average, though, the most likely return on any investment is the blended asset class benchmark returns minus the cost. In other words, lowering product cost results in clear benefits to the consumer.

Other things will not be constant, of course, but they are just as likely to end up working against investors are they are to work in their favour. As such, the most rational approach to take is to presume that everything else is equal. That's what unbundling does. The "parts and labour sold separately" proposition that most FSPs steadfastly avoid not only perpetuates the myth that financial advice is free, it potentially leads to less than ideal product recommendations.

The decision all FSPs have to make now is whether they actually work on behalf of the investment product manufacturing and distribution companies or on behalf of clients. Assuming the FSP gets paid the same amount either way, the real choice from a client perspective might be: "Would I rather pay 1.5% or 2.5% a year for a combination of products and advice?"

FSPs could be doing a huge service to their clients by saying, "Lookit, there are three parties to this arrangement here: me, you, and the product manufacturers. I'm interested in working for your best interests. What if we fired the active fund companies and passed the 1% saving on to you?" This should be a no-brainer. Every FSP is expected to put their client interests first. Every FSP loves their family above their suppliers. Therefore, the fund company should finish third in this little contest every time. The question becomes one of relative merit: if the FSP makes the same money either way, who deserves the discretionary 1%, the client or the fund company?

Fair-minded people can differ, but it boggles my mind that almost all FSPs choose the first option, yet insist that they're putting their clients' interests first. However, it is FSPs who are in the position of control. They essentially decide whether actively managed fund companies get an extra 1% (adding 1% to client cost) or if the active fund companies should be squeezed out (saving the client 1%). Why not let the clients decide? If presented to clients this way, I'm sure that clients out there would prefer the unbundled passive approach.

There's even some room for maneuvering here. Some FSPs could quite properly say, "Since I'm adding value here and saving you some money, how about if I keep a portion of those savings for myself?" This is especially true with small, high maintenance accounts (perhaps less than $250,000). The FSP could say, "What if I charged you 1.4% on assets instead of 1%? True, I'd be getting more money, but you'd be getting someone who is more aligned and client-centred, and you'd still be saving 0.6% annually." On a quarter million dollar account, that still amounts to $1,500 in annual savings, so it's hardly chump change. It's a value proposition whose time has come and there must be plenty of consumers who believe they deserve at least some of the missing 1% way more than the actively managed mutual fund companies do.

Let's run down a quick list of overall benefits:

- greater overall professionalism
- transparency of product and service pricing
- elimination of bias in product recommendations
- clear delineation of services to be provided and reciprocal client obligations
- possible tax deductibility

- increased FSP compensation
- reduced consumer cost
- focus on what is important
- no more loads, transaction costs, or incentives to churn accounts
- clear alignment of FSP and client interests

Know Yourself

I never really do anything with my car other than drive it. It's not that I'm particularly slothful or negligent, it's just that I have no personal aptitude or training in automotive repairs and maintenance. But I do understand that it is important that my vehicle receives regular care and attention: tune-ups, winterization, tire rotation, oil changes, and so forth.

Sensing that I was more of an academic and less of a "work with your hands" kind of person, my parents insisted I take a basic car maintenance course when I was in high school. Their intentions were entirely good, but their money was entirely wasted. I quickly forgot everything I was taught. Use it or lose it.

This illustrates that in a world of different strokes for different folks, we can't all be good at everything. Generally speaking, people are good at what they know and know what they are good at. Not everyone wants to know about financial planning and portfolio management. Others do want to know, but their interest does not translate into aptitude.

Most people know intuitively whether they want to work with an FSP. Still, what sorts of things should be considered when deciding? When the price of advice is made explicit where it was previously hidden, some consumers will naturally reconsider the value proposition being offered.

Financial journalists tend to focus on FSP costs and all but ignore the very real benefits of qualified advice. Conversely, many FSPs only tell consumers their side of the story, which, not surprisingly, is the other half. They say clients *benefit* from advice in the form of improved discipline, reduced taxes, reduced stress, total integration, and a number of other important objectives. Since consumers should want these things for their portfolio, they should gladly pay what it costs and simply ignore the media noise about cost.

The truth is somewhere in the middle. Cost is one half of the story and benefit is the other. Ultimately, this is a discussion about value. Everyone needs to recognize that different people define *value* in different ways. A new compact Hyundai might cost $15,000. A new mid-sized Toyota might cost $25,000. A new full-sized BMW might cost $60,000. Which is the best value? The notion of "value" depends on whom you ask. All three models are profitable for their manufacturers because they serve different segments of the marketplace. People who buy the Hyundai focus primarily on cost. People who buy the BMW focus primarily on benefits. A large number of people fall somewhere in between. None of them are right or wrong, they're merely expressing a preference for their definition of value. What's your measuring stick?

If you think your FSP is adding value that is at least equivalent to what you are paying, keep your FSP. If not, have a clear and frank discussion about expectations. If they cannot or will not be met, find another FSP. The person you choose should meet all your criteria. If you can't find anyone who can add sufficient value for your purposes, then be prepared to go it alone. If you are correct, the savings will exceed the costs associated with the benefit of having an FSP and you will be better off.

But be sure you think about all the costs, including opportunity cost and the value of your time when making your decision. For instance, how many consumers consider the superficial loss rules when doing their investment planning? Consumers can sell an actively managed mutual fund and reposition the proceeds into another investment such as an index fund or ETF with a similar mandate and it is not considered a superficial loss. Similarly, they can sell one actively managed mutual fund and buy another similarly mandated fund and accomplish the same objective. But how many DIY consumers actually do it?

Earlier, we looked at how fee scalability offers considerable benefits, especially for accounts over certain thresholds. Once you get over larger thresholds, it can actually be cheaper to work with a fee-based FSP than to use most actively managed A Class mutual funds at no load. Scalability offers disproportionate benefits for larger accounts, but since we have already looked at fee scalability as one of the primary features of professional financial advice, what are the others?

Consumers need to be able to make a meaningful comparison between what they're paying and what they're getting in return for their advice dollar. The cost differential between using an FSP and going it alone as a DIY consumer will not likely be as great as the media would have you believe, even if you consider only investment management and set all other planning concerns aside.

While it will certainly cost more to work with an FSP than to do it yourself, it will often be worth that added cost. Without knowing what questions to ask, how will we ever come to the answers we seek? Professionals can help to identify those areas that require attention and ensure those areas are suitably addressed.

There are other benefits that clients need to understand about working with FSPs in a fee-based arrangement. The first is transparency. There is no direct economic benefit to working with someone who charges a direct fee to a client as opposed to being paid by a product supplier.

However, there is usually an added level of comfort in having all the cards on the table. When the only way an FSP is paid is directly by the client, you get a sense that reasonable efforts are being made to do the best job for clients. The mind tends to focus when the chequebook is pulled out. This, of course, is how most other professionals get paid, so consumer understanding and acceptance should be high once the transition is complete. Right now, STANDUP FSPs are effectively being penalized for being early adopters of a professional paradigm. This is because a large proportion of the consumer population seems to prefer to not have to have discussions about FSP payment, truly important priorities, and the alignment of interests.

Given that many FSPs genuinely want to do the right thing and that there's a clear opportunity for FSPs to finally do it, what needs to happen next? The answer is that FSPs have to decide once and for all that they will function using a model of professionalism and put the best interests of their clients ahead of corporate interests. Plan the work, work the plan.

What Can STANDUP Advisors Do?

To think is easy; to act is difficult; but to act as one thinks is the most difficult of all.
— Johan Wolfgang von Goethe

Above all else, STANDUP Advisors will now need to demonstrate in clear terms that they are working for their clients, not their product suppliers or employers. Actions speak louder than words. Consumers are becoming increasingly aware of the conflicts (some real, some merely perceived) that FSPs face on a day-to-day basis. Once the priority of loyalty has been clearly established, other elements of good advice are sure to follow.

If embedded compensation were eliminated, FSPs would finally be free to align their words and their deeds. Many adamantly believe in market inefficiency and would no doubt continue to recommend products that seek to capitalize on it. That is unequivocally their prerogative. There are some observers, however, that think product recommendations would change drastically if embedded compensation were to go. Of course, this is also a matter of opinion. Since it hasn't been tried before, no one really knows for sure what would happen.

The Difficulty in Implementing the Concepts

On top of the need for FSPs to explain this paradigm shift compellingly to their clients, there is the additional need to focus on the truly important aspects of a solid advisory relationship. Clients in turn need to understand that the problem is as old as the hills. Virtually the entire financial services establishment wants innovative, client-centred STANDUP FSPs to fail. To demonstrate not only the insidiousness of the problem but also how long problems like this have been around, here's an excerpt from *The Prince*, written by Niccolo Machiavelli in the 1500s:

> He who innovates will have for his enemies all those who are well off under the existing order of things, and only lukewarm supporters in those who might be better off under the new.

Information about asset classes, risk, return, co-variance, and standard deviation is nice, but it doesn't matter one bit to typical investors largely because the nuances are beyond them. They would rather buy into the investment pornography of forecasts, predictions, and guru worship. Sadly, they often leave the logic and portfolio design to FSPs, who are usually just as likely to buy into the prevailing paradigm.

More than anything else, this is why many investor advocates believe regulators and legislators need to step in to protect investors. After all, there are only so many STANDUP FSPs out there and they can only do so much. As it is currently constituted, the system puts too much power in the hands of manufacturers and distributors. The average FSP today still lacks the background and courage to stand up and do what is right, but that is now changing.

As we've seen, most major brokerage and financial services firms aren't in the business of truly educating the public, since a well-informed public would cut into their profits dramatically. They try to convey that financial advice is far too complex to try doing it on your own. In doing this, they also hide the ugly truth that their primary value proposition is first and foremost a personal revenue-generating exercise.

A physician who stubbornly refuses to use new procedures or medicines is considered unprofessional. Blatant refusal to stay current can lead to malpractice suits, since physicians are mandated to protect the health and welfare of their patients. Full professional disclosure is simply a part of how true professionals conduct their day-to-day affairs. Similarly, it would be difficult for an FSP to be considered a true professional if the advice they offered did not incorporate the fullest breadth of products and services currently available.

Scientific Testing And Necessary Disclosure Underpin Professionalism—STANDUP. That's the answer. What we need now is for FSPs to stand up to the financial services establishment, to stand up for their clients. In doing so, FSPs need to be clear about their role. I asked Dan Wheeler, Director of Global Financial Advisor Services at Dimensional Fund Advisors (DFA) for his perspective on the role of qualified advice. *Note that DFA is both a proponent of EMH and a proponent of qualified advice. Do not let the vested interests of the industry suggest that the two are mutually exclusive.* Here's what he had to say:

> The role of the advisor is really a defensive role. The advisor is there to manage expectations, to make sure that all the bad things that can happen to people and their capital do not happen—things like market timing and tactical asset allocation. If you're moving money in and out based upon some type of economic forecast, you endanger the person getting the capital market rate of return and getting to the point where they want to be years down the road.[1]

If Wheeler is right, then what kinds of defensive things can FSPs help with and what kinds of additional activities might a consumer want to have access to?

An Ongoing, Iterative Process

It needs to be noted that good financial advice is not a one-time event. Instead, financial advice giving is an ongoing, iterative process. People graduate from school, find work, get married, start families, pay off debts, take on mortgages, get promotions, acquire stock options, endure disabilities, buy second properties, suffer temporary setbacks, and experience myriad other things. Life happens. Circumstances change and so should the plan.

Consumers need to be able to change with the times in managing the various developments in their lives, and FSPs should enable their clients to focus on all aspects of their financial lives, with the most important things being addressed first. A financial plan is usually done at the beginning of a relationship in order for an FSP to win an account, but it is usually not reviewed. There isn't a formal plan, just a brief written action plan focused on narrow investment matters and perhaps the provision of insurance. Some commentators are fond of saying that if financial planners were charged with financial planning as a crime, most would be exonerated because there wouldn't be enough evidence in their files to support the charges.

Planners, advisors, brokers, and other FSPs who go by similar titles, should all be engaging their clients in regular processes and procedures to make sure they are on track with their plans. This assumes there are financial plans in place to begin with. The universally accepted six-step process to financial planning is:

1. Understand the client's situation.
2. Clarify goals and objectives.
3. Identify any particular barriers or unique circumstances.
4. Make written recommendations with clear alternatives.
5. Implement the chosen route.
6. Review the plan regularly.

Clients can work together with their FSP to complete self-diagnostic checklists on a wide variety of financial matters including client awareness, investment planning, investment policy statement monitoring, debt management, tax planning, estate planning, disability and income protection, and asset protection. A qualified, professional FSP has a pivotal role to play in this instance. Let's have a quick look at some of these matters:

Client Awareness

This is an extension of the six-step process. Clients need to understand that financial professionals cannot help without complete information. No one goes to the family doctor and says, "Doc, I'm sick and I need you to make me better," then when the doctor asks where it hurts, answers, "I'm not going to tell you." If clients want the full benefit of professional help, they need to understand that full disclosure is required. Of course, the information gathered should always be held in the strictest confidence.

Investment Policy Statement Monitoring

It has become a generally accepted practice to set expectations and parameters for portfolio design, monitoring, and evaluation. If financial planning is going to be more than a series of one-off ad hoc decisions, then a framework for portfolio construction needs to be a given. People get blueprints before they build a house and an investment policy statement (IPS) is like a portfolio blueprint. Like so many things in life, what gets measured gets done.

Pension funds and money managers the world over set parameters to ensure they have a clear mandate to benchmark their individual managers and the portfolios they design and manage. However, most people (including many who presently work with FSPs) make ad hoc investment decisions based on emotion and current events.

An IPS may one day become mandatory in all investment portfolios. An IPS is like a contract between the client and the FSP regarding the most critical matters of portfolio design and management, including expected real (after inflation) rate of return, return variability, asset mix, tax optimization, liquidity, frequency of face-to-face meetings, and thresholds for rebalancing. It is crucial for those FSPs who are serious about maximizing long-term, client-specific, risk-adjusted, after-tax returns that an IPS be used to maintain focus. People get respect when they inspect what they expect.

Other factors can be considered as well. For instance, to the extent that cost is a concern, steps can and should be taken to reduce or, at the very least, disclose them. Similarly, there may be a desire to have the family member in the highest marginal tax bracket pay all the fees associated with the account in order to make the best use of potential tax deductibility.

Debt Management

Debt management can be further subdivided into three areas: personal debt levels, interest rates charged, and tax deductibility. Not everyone has to worry about debt, but for those people who have debt, it certainly merits specific attention.

Tax Planning

Most people do most of their tax planning in April, long after the end of the calendar year. Ideally, people should aim for income that is as tax effective as possible. Are clients doing all they can to deduct, defer, and divide their respective incomes? What about RESPs for children? Are records being kept for matters such as capital losses, allowable expenses, and similar considerations? In many instances, an FSP can add value in these areas—areas that do not show up explicitly in portfolio performance reports.

Estate Planning

Estate planning is no longer seen as the preserve of the wealthy. It is important that consumers name proper beneficiaries on investment accounts, select and name guardians for their young children, choose an executor, set up trusts for minor children, and have powers of attorney in place in the event of incapacitation.

Disability and Income Protection

Would it be prudent to set aside a sum of money regularly in order to deal with the unlikely but potentially devastating impact of a premature death or disability? Consumers should give this serious consideration, since the correct answer is almost always yes. Practically speaking, this should be coordinated with benefits offered by employers, much like pension benefits. Critical illness coverage is also gaining considerable attention.

Asset Protection

For some, life insurance is part of an income replacement strategy, while others use it for estate creation, estate preservation, or tax minimization. Does the family in question have the right kind of insurance and the right amount of coverage? How flexible is the policy if circumstances change? Business owners have the added issues of succession planning, risk management, and creditor protection. These all need to be explored fully by those people who fall into this group.

Also, since financial advice is not free, consumers should quite properly consider what they're getting in return for the money they pay. We've already discussed the scalability of STANDUP FSP fees. However, when discussing FSP compensation, there are two other important attributes that consumers should consider: deductibility and directability.

Deductibility

This is a misunderstood and often improperly quantified benefit. The Income Tax Act (ITA) allows for the deductibility of investment counselling fees under section 20 (1) (ii). Although the matter is contentious and ill-defined, the prevailing and conservative view is that financial planning fees (e.g. those associated with a financial independence calculation and illustration) are not deductible. As a result, many FSPs have taken to doing their financial planning work for free, provided the investment counselling fees are sufficiently large.

The problem is that professional counselling fees are only deductible if they do not apply to registered accounts. Counselling fees for registered plans (RRSPs, RRIFs, LIRAs, RESPs and the like) are not tax deductible. Only the fees associated with non-registered accounts (also known as cash accounts or investment accounts) are tax deductible. If a consumer has both an investment account and a registered account with an FSP, the deductibility is prorated and allowed on a proportional basis. There are many people who feel the ITA needs to be rewritten in order to clarify the issue of deducting financial planning fees and whether deductions should be allowed when F Class mutual funds are used.

Both opponents and proponents of direct fees have been known to misrepresent deductibility. Opponents say that since there is a de facto deduction through the reduction of gains in an MER, there is no benefit whatsoever. This is true only if talking about instruments that earn interest income. Conversely, proponents imply that the benefit of the deduction is absolute and applies in all circumstances. This, too, is erroneous. As is often the case when two sides try to persuade relatively unsophisticated consumers about the merits of their way of doing business, the first casualty is truth.

It is true that products with embedded compensation already offer a de facto deduction through the reduced income or capital gains realized through MER deductions. This reality is ignored by some FSPs who overstate the benefits of deductibility in the furtherance of making a sale. A $100,000 investment in a bond fund that earns 6% (5.5% after backing out an embedded 50 bp trailing commission) leads to $5,500 in taxable income at the client's top marginal rate in a cash account. If the same fund is used in an F Class format and an identical fee is charged, there is no benefit to the consumer from a tax perspective because the deduction occurs at the same marginal tax and inclusion rates.

What about vehicles that earn capital gains? The recent lowering of the capital gains inclusion rate from 75% to 50% is a major boon to many people working with fee-based FSPs. Let's say we have a mutual fund that earns 10% before backing out the 1% trailing commission. A $100,000 investment would render a return of 9%, which would be taxed at 50% of the owner's top marginal tax rate, currently around 46% in most jurisdictions but varying slightly between each of the provinces and territories. In the embedded format, the gain (assuming the top marginal rate) is 9% x 50% x 46%. The total tax bill is therefore 23% of the 9% gain or 2.07%. This yields an after-tax return of 6.93% to the client.

Now let's look at the situation in which the fee is charged separately. Assuming an identical 1% fee, it can be charged as an expense against all sources of regular income. As a result, it is deducted at the full 46% rate, rather than at half that rate. This results in the following sequence: (10% x 50% x 46%) – (1% x 54%)—the reciprocal of 0.46%. In this instance, the client gets a gross return of 7.7% minus 0.54% for a real return of 7.16%. The difference of 23 bps is the difference between 1% deducted at the top marginal rate (i.e. against regular income) and 1% deducted against capital gains (i.e. at 50% of the top marginal rate). The larger deduction derived from claiming investment counselling fees against all sources of income leads directly to higher after-tax client returns. As we can see, there is a very real and substantial benefit to charging client fees directly, provided a number of factors are considered. These include:

• the fee needs to pertain to a non-registered account or deductibility is lost

- the fee needs to pertain to capital gains or dividends, which are taxed at a preferential rate, allowing the investor to capitalize on the inclusion spread
- the actual amount of the benefit depends on the client's marginal tax rate

If either of the first two circumstances exist, there is no benefit either way. If the third exists, the benefit of direct fees may be reduced if the client in question is not in the highest marginal tax bracket since the *spread* between any given rate and 50% of that rate goes down as the rate goes down. For example, at the 46% rate, the benefit is 0.46% - 0.23% = 0.23%. At the 38% marginal rate, the spread is reduced to 0.38% - 0.19% = 0.19%.

Directability
The final additional benefit of working with a professional, fee-based FSP is directability. Directing fees to be paid from outside one's account provides a major benefit to consumers that most people simply never think of tapping into. It is the flip side of deductibility and allows the consumer to decide who will pay the fee and from which account. If all fees are associated with a registered account, there is no benefit from a cost perspective. Transparency is nice, but does not add to the bottom line, since fees aren't deductible for registered accounts. While fees for a registered account cannot be deducted, they can be paid from an investment account or bank account. This can maximize tax-deferred compounding in a registered plan.

Let's say you're fifty-nine years old and have $600,000 in family RRSPs growing at 9% a year before fees. If you can pay a 1% fee from outside the plan, it will compound tax free until age sixty-nine at 9%, rendering a total portfolio size of $1,420,418.00. However, if the fees come from the investments while inside the plan, the de facto growth rate is reduced to 8%, rendering a portfolio worth $1,295,354.80. The amount paid by the consumer is essentially the same throughout (1% on the annual portfolio size), but there will be an additional $125,063.20 available when the RRSP is converted into an RRIF in a decade.

Of course, the benefits continue later in life. Even though the

RRSP matures and is converted into an RRIF once clients are in their seventieth year, the benefits continue for as long as the client lives; there is merely a need to redeem a small portion of that portfolio on an annual basis. Still, if the client lives to be ninety years old, there will be an additional twenty years in which the RRIF earns a de facto return that is 1% higher than it would be using conventional billing methods.

What if the client is much younger, say twenty-nine years old, with a forty-year time period before retirement and perhaps a fifty-five year time period before passing away? Two primary assumptions will likely change. First, the client is likely to be a little more aggressive, so the difference in return might be between 10% (paid separately) and 9% (paid within the account) as opposed to 9% and 8% for the older person. Second, the account is likely to attract a fee of more than 1% in the early years, but because of scalability and superior tax-deferred compounding, might still attract a fee that averages out to 1% per year over the life of the relationship with the FSP.

Let's say this client is starting out with a modest portfolio of $50,000. Taking a forty-year time period and using 9% and 10% as return assumptions, we get a portfolio differential of $692,492.

A simple way of approximating the growth rate is to use the "Rule of 72." This states that the rate of return divided into 72 gives you the length of time in years it takes to double your money. A portfolio earning 10% doubles in about 7.2 years, while a portfolio earning only 9% doubles in about 8 years. Big deal, you might say; after nine or ten months, both portfolios reach roughly the same point. But when the time period is forty years, that 1% difference in compounding is absolutely massive.

The 9% return doubles roughly 5 times, so the portfolio grows to about $1.6 million ($1,570,471). The 10% return doubles just under 5.5 times, growing to about $2.3 million ($2,262,963). This twenty-nine-year old with a modest portfolio just added about $700,000 to his retirement portfolio by paying his FSP fees separately.

Let's also assume that this young financial independence seeker is also maximizing his annual RRSP contributions. Since the limit is now being raised and will ultimately be indexed to inflation (how many financial plans have you seen that reflect this assumption?), let's assume that his annual RRSP contribution is $18,000. Now how does this young fellow fare? The results are staggering and well into the millions of dollars.

This even works for non-registered accounts. Not only can consumers reduce their tax bill by deducting fees, they can minimize portfolio shrinkage by paying fees from their bank account. There are also applications for income splitting. If one spouse is in the top marginal bracket while the other is a homemaker, the high-income spouse can pay fees for all family accounts (including children, trusts, etc.) and deduct the fees (where deductible) at her top marginal rate. This is really a combination of deductibility and directability, but you can see that there are potentially large benefits here too.

All this leaves more money in consumers' pockets. The best thing about fee directability is that it represents a win/win scenario for FSPs and consumers alike. In this case, the FSP is no worse off, having received an identical level of compensation, but the consumer is better off because there is more money left in the account at the end of the relationship.

Investment planning and tax planning are often seen as separate matters. Unfortunately, a recent online survey showed that 79% of all CFPs felt their clients regularly confused financial planning with investing.[2] It's got to be difficult to explain a value proposition if most of your consumers don't recognize it.

Taking a comprehensive approach can offer considerable benefits. The ever-changing landscape has made it imperative that people consider the implications of all decisions so that nothing is overlooked and maximum benefit is gleaned when choosing to work with a qualified FSP. Taken together, deductibility and directability are a powerful pair. Anyone who has registered accounts can benefit from improved tax-deferred compounding. Anyone who has non-registered accounts can claim tax deductions that would otherwise not be available.

There's a lot that a STANDUP FSP can do to help bring about positive change. The hope here is that STANDUP FSPs will recognize themselves in these pages and do the right thing as a result. There are substantial benefits that apply to virtually all consumers in all circumstances when working with a STANDUP FSP, but "virtually all" is not the same as "all." What sort of person might be as well off or even better off if the services of a qualified FSP were not retained?

Do-It-Yourself Advice

Nothing astonishes men so much as common sense and plain dealing.
                                        —Ralph Waldo Emerson

Having taken the time to go over the benefits of working with a STANDUP FSP, it would be inadvisable to overlook the alternative of doing things yourself. Unless you actually enjoy doing the work or unless you are exceedingly secretive about your personal affairs, the real "win" for DIY consumers comes from saving the money that would have otherwise been paid to the FSP.

Many consumers are likely being penny-wise and pound foolish by passing up on qualified advice. But it needs to be acknowledged that some people would indeed be better off if they simply fired their FSP, pocketed the difference, and did everything themsleves.

Unbundling for DIY Investors

One of the dirty little secrets of the financial services industry is that discount brokers aren't really offering discount products when it comes to most mutual funds. The term "discount brokerage" might be one of the great marketing ploys of our time. Simply put, if you're buying an A Class mutual fund at a discount brokerage, there's no discount. So if you're going to be your own investment manager, for goodness sake, whatever you do, don't use A Class mutual funds.

At the heart of this challenge is the fact that mutual fund companies consistently portray trailing commisisons as a sort of fee for ongoing advice. That portrayal is inconsistent with that of both the Investment Funds Institute of Canada (IFIC) and CRA. Instead, IFIC and CRA are of the view that trailers are a form of deferred commissions, not a fee for ongong service. Why would any person willingly pay a commission, deferred or otherwise, on a product that wasn't even sold by a representative? Given that most A Class funds at discount brokerages are bought on a no-load basis, there isn't even a deferral—the payment (typically 1% for equity funds) go on in perpetuity. The practice is nothing short of outrageous.

Nonetheless, when FSPs get letters from fund companies thanking them for their business, they often begin with phrases like: "Your service fees are detailed below...." The double standard in depiction is both self-serving and reprehensible.

With discounters, there's no doubt about what you get: no advice with the same embedded compensation going to a non-existent FSP. How's that for a value proposition? Of course, if one were to use other investment vehicles such as individual stocks, traditional no-load funds, bonds, royalty trusts, and ETFs, there would certainly be a cost saving associated with forgoing advice.

One of the major regulatory reforms that has to take place is that discount brokerages should no longer be allowed to operate this way. Clients pay FSPs a fee for advice. Quality advice is not free and should never be portrayed as being free. If there's no advice being offered, there shouldn't be an additional fee associated with buying or owning a product. My experience is that STANDUP FSPs are justifiably outraged by this continued form of legalized robbery. In stark contrast, SPANDEX FSPs don't mind at all. To them, it simply justifies their existence, as they tell their clients, "It costs no more to work with me." Consumers who ask their FSPs and potential FSPs for an opinion on this matter can probably separate the wheat from the chaff fairly quickly.

One way the discounters might be able to reconcile their stated position in the marketplace with what they actually do is to create yet another class of mutual funds with the help of some regulatory overseeing. These funds would only be available to clients of discount brokerages and not available to the wider public.

Since they would be manufactured exclusively for the use of DIY investors, these might be called DIY or discount units, so we'll call them D Class funds. If A Class funds feature embedded compensation, I Class funds offer a manufacturer's discount and reduced compensation, and F Class funds offer totally unbundled compensation, one might think another means of slicing and dicing compensation isn't necessary. But what about compensating the discount distributor of the product? It would be unreasonable to charge clients for advice not rendered (A Class), but it would be equally unreasonable to expect discount brokerages to sell funds without getting any money for their services. What if there were a smaller embedded compensation going to discounters for their trouble? Perhaps 25 bps (0.25%) would be suitable payment in this circumstance.

The cost of buying a mutual fund as an administrative transaction is the same whether that fund is offered in an A Class, F Class, or D Class format. Whatever system is ultimately adopted should be fair to everyone. Charging consumers for non-existent advice is contrary to most people's sense of decency, but allowing them to buy and sell mutual funds completely free of charge isn't a viable option for the discounter either.

At 25 bps, the discount brokerages would at least be getting something for their trouble of providing DIY investors with a reasonable alternative. They would be offering consumers real choice in the marketplace without feathering their nests. It would cost consumers more than F Class, but only modestly, and would still allow discounters to offer a real, credible value proposition to consumers who want to forgo paying for advice when none is required. This could be a justifiable exception to the objective of total unbundling.

Unless D Class funds are introduced, it is entirely possible that certain mutual fund investors will actually save money and gain a potential tax deduction by working a with a fee-based FSP as opposed to doing it themselves. For instance, a $1,000,000 all equity mutual fund account in A Class funds at a discount brokerage might involve paying the discounter $10,000 a year in trailing commissions. (In exchange for what?) If working with a fee-based FSP, the fee might be less than $9,000, but the consumer would also be getting *a potential tax deduction and qualified advice that could save money, time, and aggravation, not to mention coaching and behaviour modification.*

The Three Ts

There are two primary consumer segments in the financial services marketplace: delegator/collaborators and do-it-yourselfers. Many people have an intuitive gut reaction about which camp they fall into and work in accordance with that gut feeling. There are a number of consumers who simply don't need an FSP. Nonetheless, the generally accepted principle is that people should, at a minimum, possess the "Three Ts" necessary to manage their own financial affairs: time, temperament, and training. Here's a quick self-diagnostic exercise to help you determine which group you fall into:

Time
- Do you review your portfolio at least annually, even if you change nothing?
- Do you act without being reminded of major deadlines?
- Do you plan for your future in a meaningful way?
- Are you a "doer" who is not inclined to procrastinate?

Temperament
- Do you maintain your asset allocation in turbulent markets?
- Do you maintain your savings rate over time?
- Do you sleep as well as usual in turbulent markets?

Training
- Do you have the capacity to handle your own circumstances?
- Are you even aware of how complex your situation is?
- Are you aware of planning concepts beyond basic strategies?

If you honestly answered yes to all ten questions, you probably don't need an FSP. If you answered no only once or twice, you might already need an FSP. If you answered no three or more times, you almost certainly should be working with an FSP. There are certainly people who can honestly answer yes to all ten questions. Most people, however, cannot.

The need for qualified professional advice becomes even more clear when you consider account size. Since advisory fees can be scalable, there are disproportionate benefits that accrue to households with larger pools of investable assets. The bigger your port-folio, the less advice costs on a per-dollar-invested basis. Some people are delegators as a practical matter, rather than because of natural predisposition. Furthermore, the bigger the portfolio, the bigger the absolute dollar consequences of an unfortunate error or untimely oversight. There are many people who are wealthy but not particularly sophisticated. Going it alone might save a few dol-lars but won't make much sense, all things considered.

Many FSPs fear that some of their clients will leave to go to a discount brokerage if the artificially level playing field of mutual fund cost is eliminated, making it cheaper for DIY investors. Essentially, what these "professionals" are inferring is that their advice is worth less than it costs. Many SPANDEX FSPs fear that if it becomes evidently and *consistently* cheaper to go to a DIY envi-ronment, there will be a mass exodus of clients to discount houses.

I sometimes ask other FSPs if they do their own taxes. Some do, some don't. For those who use a tax professional, I ask them if they know they can save money by doing their taxes themselves. Of course they do, but they also find it both convenient and comfort-ing that they have a professional looking after their tax matters. For the record, I use a tax professional to assist me in my tax plan-ning. Financial advice, like tax preparation, is the sort of thing some people don't mind doing themselves, while others simply hate it. People are either do-it-yourselfers or delegators and chang-ing the price structure associated with the task is unlikely to alter that fact. Anyone who is a delegator by nature will likely continue to delegate even if there are cost savings that can be realized by doing the work alone. The fact that many FSPs are themselves del-egators with their own tax returns demonstrates this quite vividly.

Know Yourself Redux

People simply need to decide. Do they want cost savings or value-added assistance in arranging their financial affairs? It comes down to whether you believe an FSP can add value through planning, discipline, insight, additional services, or just peace of mind. It also comes down to whether the person you hire is worth what you pay.

Financial wisdom will soon be sold separately from financial products. If you already have what it takes to plan your affairs and manage your portfolio, then off you go. Consumers need to be honest with themselves. They shouldn't either rush off to find an FSP or blindly stick with an FSP if they believe they can do just as well on their own.

It would be wonderful if there was a simple, reliable way to determine whether any given individual would be better off working with an FSP or going it alone. There isn't. It comes down to whether they have the confidence in their own abilities to do the necessary work for their unique circumstances.

At $500,000, a comprehensive approach is usually required to make sure everything is addressed and coordinated. This might involve getting a team of related professional advisors working together to ensure they are all on the same page. Wealthy individuals are increasingly turning to qualified professionals precisely because of the complexity and interrelatedness of financial management.

Consumers need to know what matters to them and to know their own strengths, weaknesses, and tendencies. Given that most consumers have already decided whether to work directly with an FSP, it is unlikely many will reach a different conclusion when the cost of doing so is brought into the open. There will be a handful of consumers at the margin who switch, but generally speaking, the expectation is that those who are currently with an FSP will stay with an FSP and those who are DIY consumers will be happy to remain DIY consumers.

The reasons for this type of seemingly dysfunctional behaviour are rooted in behavioural finance, the study of how human emotions, biases, tendencies, and perceptions shape investment decisions, seldom for the better. To the extent that we know these quirky tendencies can checker our thinking, we need to take action to effectively curb them. You can tell people not to panic when markets are temporarily down, but this is something that is often easier said than done, especially when your life savings are at stake.

Anyone who is still uncertain about whether they should be working on their own or with an FSP might re-examine the chapter on behavioural finance. Think of market gyrations as the equivalent of a cheesecake buffet to a person on a diet. If you can resist its temptations on your own, then perhaps you don't need additional assistance. If, on the other hand, you think you'll need the financial equivalent of a personal trainer to keep you honest with your resolutions of disciplined good health, then hire one.

Consumers need to seriously consider the complexity of their personal financial affairs. Are they basic and predictable or complex and erratic? No matter how disciplined you are, there's no sense in doing things yourself if your situation requires a deeper level of preparedness. Think of the continuum we looked at earlier: moving from empowered do-it-yourselfer to collaborator to delegator to abdicator. Consumers need to determine where they fit. There is absolutely nothing wrong with being a do-it-yourselfer as long as you know yourself and can be certain there will be no regrets if you work this way.

It is ironic that FSPs generally make more money when markets are going up (when they are less necessary from a behavioural perspective) and less money when markets were going down (when they are actually more necessary). When markets are going down and clients are spooked by it, FSPs often have to work harder to keep clients from making "The Big Mistake." On the other hand, as long as things are going well, it might be argued that FSPs are less useful, since clients are naturally inclined to stick with the original plan. This is not to suggest that people should use an FSP when markets are headed downward but can feel free to do their own planning when things are all right. And it certainly doesn't mean that financial advice is only about investments either.

Another area where people might need qualified advice is insurance. More than anything, all this means is that some serious introspection is required before deciding whether to work with an FSP.

STANDUP Insurance Advice

It is the mark of an educated mind to be able to entertain a thought without accepting it.

—Aristotle

Until now, most of the discussion surrounding financial advice has revolved around investment options. Real integrated wealth management needs to cast a much wider net. It should encompass financial planning, estate planning, tax planning, risk management, and investment management. Any client of an FSP who is genuinely trying to integrate advice on all aspects of their financial life will find the process conspicuously incomplete if it does not consider the proper use of various forms of insurance.

Insurance provides financial risk management. It comes in various forms, but at its core is used to mitigate the financial risk associated with an unfortunate event such as a death, disability, or critical illness. Many consumers have come to think of insurance as either a necessary evil or an unnecessary money pit that offers nebulous benefits to the purchaser. Either way, few consumers have a high opinion of those people who recommend insurance as a viable planning tool. Insurance in its many forms is a product that offers fuzzy lifestyle benefits that are often difficult to quantify, largely because people have different impressions and values surrounding the notion of quality of life.

The poor cousins of the insurance world, home and auto insurance, are thought of in particularly unsavoury terms. They are seen as necessary evils imposed by governments as a means of mitigating liabilities that would otherwise almost certainly go unfunded. While these are certainly important considerations when engaging in life planning, they are beyond the purview of this discussion.

Those who make a living selling insurance are often thought of as anything but true professionals. When going through a life insurance illustration, much of the discussion surrounds emotional hot buttons associated with something going horribly wrong. The image of people crossing the street in order to avoid coming into contact with an insurance representative holds true. In spite of this, there are many people working in the insurance industry in a highly responsible and professional manner, offering solutions more appropriate than anything else available. These solutions are often complex and highly specialized.

The appropriate use of insurance is a vital part of integrated financial management. This is especially true for affluent people because the applications are almost endless. The wealthy might need to shelter money from taxes, protect their human capital (earning power), control the risks inherent in small businesses, make charitable gifts, or pass a meaningful estate on to future generations. Insurance is often the most effective and tax efficient way of doing so.

From a wealth management perspective, there are four primary types of insurance: life, disability, long-term care (LTC), and critical illness (CI). The first comes in various formats: renewable term, term to one hundred (T-100), universal life (UL), and whole life. These are all predicated on the inescapable fact that after centuries of medical advances, the long-term human mortality rate remains unchanged at 100%.

The last three types of insurance are somewhat less likely to be part of most people's planning, largely because they are relatively misunderstood. They are based on the probability of becoming disabled, critically ill, or unable to care for oneself later in life and provide financial assistance for those who ultimately come to need it.

It's a particular shame that critical illness insurance and disability insurance are not more widely accepted, but this is partly because they are more expensive than life insurance. There's a perfectly good reason for the cost: both outcomes are far more likely to occur than *premature* death. For both products, there is a return of premium option available. If you don't need the insurance but pay into the system long enough, you can get your money back. Try that with your local home insurance policy.

In many ways, LTC and CI policies are the easiest to understand because they offer what might be called "pure insurance" (i.e. insurance and nothing more). As a result of this purity, compensation is more predictable and easier to calculate and disclose before the sale is transacted.

Long-term care does two things: it protects the client's assets and quality of life. It pays out when it is determined the client is unable to care for themselves. The test lies in how well the insured can perform basic daily activities such as eating, dressing, and toileting. It is widely believed that by 2011, one-fifth of the Canadian population will be age sixty or older, and that 1.5 million of those people will suffer from some kind of disability during their retirement years.

Right now, elderly people who do not use long-term care insurance and are unable to live independently face two choices: they can either accept a very basic level of care offered through government programs or they can deplete their own savings in order to pay for additional support necessary to maintain a suitable level of human integrity. Where appropriate, LTC can bridge the gap. As a rule, LTC comes in three formats: per diem plans, reimbursement plans, and income plans. The exact services covered can vary widely, so be sure to ask about varying levels of institutional and home care, adult daycare, and respite and palliative care.

Much like LTC, CI insurance is a particularly vital product that is not often presented to clients. A high percentage of mortgage foreclosures in Canada are due to critical illnesses, while relatively few are due to death. Furthermore, there are only four critical illnesses that make up the lion's share of all claims: cancer, heart attack, stroke, and coronary artery disease. So before some FSP tells you about how the policy recommended has twenty-four different illnesses covered, simply turn to that FSP and say, "That's nice. Please tell me about the *definitions* the company you recommend uses in making payments to victims of the big four." That's not a question most people would think to ask, but it is far more relevant than rhyming off a laundry list of esoteric illnesses.

Insurance Issues

Standardization is also a big issue in the insurance industry. Almost everyone in the field agrees that we need identical and consistent wording around the definitions of ailments that can be easily understood in layperson's terms. If the terminology is easier to understand, it will be easier to explain and easier to help people get the coverage they need. Until now, every provider has had its own definition of the threshold needed to constitute a critical illness. Imagine having a mild heart attack (or "infarction") and having the claim denied because it was "too mild."

Consumers need to understand that there is no such thing as a free lunch. If one CI provider is cheaper than another, it is likely not that the company is ultra competitive or because the company actuaries have mispriced the product. The most likely explanation is that the company's definition of what constitutes a critical illness is narrowly defined and therefore less likely to trigger a payment. As in life, with insurance you get what you pay for. Professional conduct requires consistent, plain, and professional disclosure of the matter at hand.

The other contentious wrinkle in CI coverage is that there remains some uncertainty about whether or not the death benefit (paid out to a living person upon diagnosis of a critical illness) should be tax free. You'd think the tax people would be clear on this one way or another. In spite of this, CI coverage is rapidly becoming a major tool in the professional FSP's tool kit.

Even a passing consideration of disability, critical illness, and long-term care coverage would go a long way toward meeting the test of providing life management to people who need it. Life happens. People often make financial decisions without fully contemplating the consequences of things not going exactly as planned. Truly professional FSPs will insist that all bases are covered. On the whole, a good principle to apply when considering insurance is that there needs to be a genuine insurance need, otherwise it is almost certainly not right. The corollary of this principle is that insurance does have a valid place in many portfolios and might even offer the best possible solution to a person's financial problems. The appropriateness and type of insurance depends primarily on the situation.

Segregated Funds

The insurance industry features a mutual fund counterpart called segregated funds. They are similar to mutual funds because they offer investment options to clients, but different because they feature an insurance component offering a guarantee if held for ten years. At present, most insurance companies generally only protect 75% of the amount invested. Segregated funds also offer a 100% principal guarantee if the unitholder passes away in the first ten years with the ability to lock in and reset a (presumably higher) value with a death benefit if the unitholder passes away within ten years. Segregated funds also offer creditor protection in case of professional liability or insolvency and generally cost about 50 bps more than similarly mandated conventional mutual funds. Consumers need to consider whether the benefits outweigh the costs.

Unlike conventional investment products, however, licenced representatives are allowed to sell segregated funds without ever completing a "know your client" form to ensure suitability. In other words, there is no requirement to demonstrate that the funds being recommend correspond to the lifestyle or general objectives and needs of the person making the purchase.

This represents a massive gap in the overseeing and regulation of the financial services industry. There are simply no quality control assurances for how segregated funds are sold in the marketplace. Even more disconcerting is that there are no requirements for branch managers to oversee segregated fund recommendations and no requirements for audits to ensure suitability. There is also no such thing as an unbundled F Class segregated fund. Anyone who wants the product will have no choice but to purchase it in a bundled, embedded compensation format. Again, is this because FSPs don't want it or because insurance companies simply refuse to manufacture it?

Many life-licenced agents have little training in investment planning. The opposite is equally true: most investment specialists have little training in insurance. A little knowledge could be a potentially dangerous thing. Having a life licence allows people to sell segregated funds even though they are de facto mutual funds and require a rather different knowledge base.

Some FSPs with an insurance background have been known to recommend highly concentrated investment mixes in pursuit of maximum returns. This would almost certainly not be permitted in the more closely regulated investment industry. If putting 100% of your investment portfolio into the technology-heavy Nasdaq index in 1999 made little sense, how would doing so within the context of an insurance policy make it any better? As with investment planning, there is no one to make sure that client illustrations are reasonable, so recommendations like this can be and have been made with virtual impunity. Brokerage firms and mutual fund dealers have branch managers to review trading, but insurance managing general agencies (MGAs), the counterpart to an investment firm, have no analogous person in the hierarchy.

Incidentally, FSPs have a really tough time moving their practices between insurance MGAs. Insurance companies have now made it a requirement that new business be submitted through a carrier (insurance company) before that carrier will transfer existing policies on to the books of the new MGA. Clients don't like it and FSPs don't like it, but none of that matters. Insurance companies do what they want while showing precious little regard for other stakeholders.

On top of this, there is no mandate to complete segregated fund trades in anything other than a paper-based transaction system. This lack of mandatory electronic order execution means that trades can be placed many days after the original order is placed with potentially damaging consequences if investment options are moving up smartly. Unlike standard mutual funds, there are added problems when redeeming the annual 10% free units from segregated funds. This is one more reason why the insurance side of the financial advice industry will find it difficult to move to an unbundled, fee-based business model in a practical manner.

How Life Insurance Works

Anyone who thinks ordinary investment options are difficult for the average consumer to understand should look at life insurance. If you want to see convoluted products, applications, and marketing, then these products are for you, especially the complex and divergent bonus structures put in place by various companies as they compete for business on the life side. By trying to add value and flexibility, they often add cost and complexity. Perhaps most shockingly, many FSPs are at a loss to explain the terms and conditions associated with many bonus structures. If the person recommending a product doesn't truly understand how it works, what chance is there that the person buying it will ever understand?

Almost any meaningful comparison between competing universal life (UL) illustrations involves calling in experts to "reverse engineer" the options. Insurance companies actually like this because they can honestly say, "There's nothing else on the market like this product." Differentiation using complexity is good for insurance companies because there's no meaningful way for consumers to make apples-to-apples comparisons. Of course, these companies all say that the client comes first.

People are often left to make their final decision based on whether they trust their FSP, not on the relative merits of competing products. Similarly, there are often major problems associated with trying to rerun in-force policies (i.e. illustrate them again). The software that allows this is constantly being updated, making it difficult for conscientious FSPs to take meaningful information to their clients.

Right now, insurance is available only as a commission-based product. There are rare instances in which companies strip out all commissions and simply pay FSPs a fee, but the case size needs to be truly massive. When this occurs, it is difficult for competing FSPs to offer something comparable on a pure cost of insurance basis. Many feel a commission-based compensation format is appropriate, since the purchase of insurance is more like the purchase of real estate than any other financial product. When the planning implementation is largely predicated on a single up-front purchase, commission is widely seen as the most appropriate form of payment for the person assisting with the decision-making. Even this concept can be a delicate one to maneuver, since renewable term life policies offer pure insurance, while whole life and UL policies have embedded investment options that should be reviewed just like any other investment portfolio. Although real estate may be the best analogy, it doesn't quite capture the nature of the problem. Today, people can sell their homes without using the services of real estate brokers. Aside from whether this is a prudent course of action, it should be obvious that there is no analogous alternative for insurance.

Another matter to be considered is that insurance often involves the sale of a concept or strategy. In some instances, the FSP making the recommendation might have only a cursory background in the applied nuances surrounding the concept in question. Some insurance concepts are highly complex. Others might involve inherent conflicts. Although the concept in question might be entirely appropriate for the client's circumstances, care should be taken that perceived and real conflicts be acknowledged and explained.

As in real estate, where three or four agents might be representing different clients and only one can ever get paid, insurance is based on contingent outcomes. Real estate agents are paid shortly after the closing of a deal, even though the purchaser may well be making payments on the property for the next twenty years. With insurance, there's no guarantee that the purchase will be allowed to proceed since there are always underwriting issues that might prevent this from happening. The fact that approval is not automatic means a lot of spade work might be lost.

Here's how it works: after successful underwriting, the purchaser acquires a policy, signs a contract, and ultimately begins making installment payments until the policy is totally acquired. This is a lot like a mortgage. The person making the sale is paid in a lump sum shortly after the contract is signed and the first payment is received. Many people in the industry feel that offering an annualized compensation system for ongoing support and advice is inappropriate. Some would argue that there's still the matter of managing the investment side of the account, but since the primary role for insurance is risk management, commission advocates believe the primary compensation is quite appropriately placed on the front end of the deal.

Unlike most mutual funds, different insurance companies pay different commissions (remember, it all comes out of the client's pocket in the end) and the quantum of commission is seldom disclosed to the purchaser, even after the fact. Many companies are now revisiting compensation structures to level out and standardize FSP compensation, regardless of the concept solution presented. Otherwise, FSP motive can always be called into question, just as it is with investment products.

Permanent Insurance

Life insurance that has an investment component to it is sometimes called permanent insurance because it cannot be outlived (i.e. is certain to pay out) provided that the appropriate premium payments are made. Permanent insurance comes in two forms: whole life and universal life (UL), both of which essentially allow policyholders to overpay in early years in order to build up a cash reserve to be used to pay the premiums later in life. All policies have a number of common provisions, including provisions for suicide, loans, premium payments, reinstatement, and so forth.

When it comes to whole life and universal life policies, the surrender charges are directly analogous to DSC charges—they are punitive. The analogy extends to FSP compensation as well. Even if a client switches FSPs shortly after buying a policy, the FSP who sold the policy will continue to receive compensation. As with mutual fund loads, the "eat what you kill" mentality is alive and well in insurance.

Even more than with DSC mutual funds, there is little incentive for most FSPs to offer ongoing advice on insurance policies once they are in force. Consumers need to be mindful of this. Responsible FSPs will point out that UL policies still need to have their investment components managed and that term policies might need replacing. Replacement often makes more sense than most insurance companies let on. Many people who have purchased life insurance might also have an unmet need for living benefits and critical illness insurance.

Once the initial sale is made on a UL policy, there's not a lot for the FSP to do. There is a prevailing sentiment that post-sale service is not particularly important in the insurance business. In light of this, there's a related concern of switching FSPs if service or advice turns out to be poor. No matter how much a client wants to switch FSPs, the FSP who sold the original contract and the MGA they work for both need to sign off on the agreement to pass the client's account to a new FSP. Switching is a client right, but if the original

FSP refuses to return phone calls or provide basic service, the client will be stuck with that FSP forever unless the FSP consents to the switch. How's that for consumer choice and protection?

The insurance side of the financial advice business generally takes a dim view of replacement policies, but offers only nominal compensation to new FSPs who take over for the one who sold the policy in the first place. In terms of equity, this is a tough nut to crack because an argument can be made for paying the FSP more on the front end without harming a new FSP if they take over later.

The Ultimate Bundled Product

People in marketing departments long ago realized that insurance wasn't the easiest product to sell. This is a result of the complexity of the products but also because people are resistant to dealing with their own mortality and have difficulty dealing with intangible products, especially if they won't be around to enjoy the payoff.

The intellectual gap has been bridged somewhat with the release of life policies that combine life insurance with investment benefits. Known as whole life, these are a sort of black box investment where all the money seems to go into one pot to cover both investments and insurance. This is the original financial services version of bundling. The problem with these products is that they are highly inflexible. Consumers are paying for insurance and investments simultaneously. At any point, they can access the investment portion and forgo the insurance (if they live, for instance) or keep the insurance in place and forgo the investments (if they die). Since people are paying for both and haven't figured out how to be dead and alive simultaneously, the products have fallen into disrepute. This is a little unfair, since policyholders can always access the paid amount through the cash surrender value once the whole life policy is in force, but the general limitations remain a very real concern.

Whole life policies can be useful for affluent people who are certain they will not need to access the money they are putting into the policy over the course of their lifetime. Some people bought whole life in the past when it might not have been the most appropriate solution for their circumstances. In these cases, sensible

FSPs looking at the situation often advise policyholders to keep these policies but stop paying into them once there is sufficient cash reserve to meet future obligations. Whole life isn't a bad idea unless people continue to pump money into the policy.

This lack of flexibility has some roundabout benefits. The major benefit is that insurance is now self-funding and that no money will be required later, when insurance may be prohibitively expensive, if you can get it at all. The second reason is that there might be a modest amount of growth in the face amount, allowing for de facto protection against inflation. The third reason is that people can borrow against the cash surrender value of whole life policies, allowing them to leverage out a tax-free income.

Somewhat Unbundled Insurance

Not wanting to be depicted as dinosaurs, actuaries and marketing people got together to revamp their insurance products to make them more responsive to consumer wishes. The investment side fund that would ultimately be called upon to fund premium payments was separated from the insurance portion so that access to the money could be permitted while keeping the insurance in place. Unbundling! The new generation of insurance products, released in the 1980s, was called universal life insurance. It was far more flexible because it allowed policyholders to manipulate their funding patterns to better meet their needs and to have more say in investment options within the policy. In this respect, insurance representatives are light years ahead of their investment representative cousins. But just because the product's bells and whistles are unbundled, it doesn't mean the products are transparent in their compensation structure. The commissions for a "buy term and invest the difference" and a UL policy should be identical because one is effectively a bundled version of the other. Unfortunately, they are not.

Increased flexibility can also mean reduced discipline. The phrase "you can pay me now or pay me later" has truly frightening consequences when the choice to pay later means risking default.

Insurance contracts are like mortgages: it's generally best to pay as much as possible up front. Paying more early on mitigates the risk of vanishing premiums that don't actually vanish. A universal life insurance contract allows for premiums to be paid and growth to be credited to the policy in the form of the account value. That value can dwindle as monthly deductions and withdrawals are made. There are a number of options to consider:

- death benefits can be level or increasing
- cost of insurance can be yearly renewable term (YRT) or level
- investment options are available both as active and passive strategies
- premiums are flexible regarding amounts and timing
- the availability of withdrawals
- the availability of leverage
- riders to enhance coverage
- the ability to change any of the above once the policy is in force

The insurance industry would have us all believe that flexibility is the same as unbundling. Although the compensation aspect of insurance products is not unbundled, the industry would argue that the considerable flexibility of a modern-day UL contract is effectively unbundled because it involves exact charges for fees and mortality and exact charges for premiums and growth with a wide array of combinations and choices between them. This complexity can lead to a number of problems that are fairly unique to the insurance side of offering financial advice. These need to be considered fully and addressed in a way that dovetails with the red flags that have already been raised on the investment side.

Whole life and universal life policies give the insured person the ability to deliberately overpay premiums in order to establish a tax-sheltered investment account that will grow and ultimately pay the premiums at a later date, thereby offering "permanent insurance" once the policy is fully funded. It is this unique feature that has caused many wealth management experts to sometimes refer to permanent insurance as the last great tax shelter or the best kept secret in personal finance due to the preferential tax treatment of death benefits.

Compensation Disclosure

Just as FSPs tend to recommend equity mutual funds over fixed income funds when equity commissions are higher, there's a perception that the insurance advice being offered may not always be the most balanced and in the best interests of the consumer. Not surprisingly, commissions tend to be much higher for more complex products. Think of term insurance as insurance that is rented and other forms as insurance that is permanently owned. Which type do you think FSPs are more likely to recommend to their clients?

The inference of compromised independence is unfortunate because there are a number of circumstances in which a clear and compelling case can be made for a permanent insurance solution over a renewable term solution. For example, everyone acknowledges that term is cheaper. But think about it from a logical perspective. Renewable term insurance is designed to expire before the client and relatively few families ever collect on these policies. In contrast, permanent insurance policies, if used properly, are guaranteed to pay out potentially huge sums to the insured's next of kin. When approached from this perspective, isn't it entirely sensible that permanent insurance should cost more?

Technically, FSPs do not have to accept a commission and cannot reduce the premium to the client by the amount of the commission being paid. If they could only reduce the client's premium as an offset against not receiving a commission, there might be a way to charge ongoing fees for insurance in a way that is similar to ongoing fees for investments.

To further complicate matters of compensation and disclosure, insurance payments to FSPs depend not only on the type of coverage but also the quantum of coverage and number of lives being covered. As with the above premiums, there are overrides that might affect FSP compensation considerably but are seldom discussed or disclosed.

For instance, the FSP might recommend a term to one hundred (permanent insurance) option that seems to suit the client's needs very well. What might not be disclosed is that although the first-year commission might be 40% of the premium, there might also be an override from 100% to 200%. Overrides are like a hidden quota system. Companies pay them for increased business. As a result, an FSP might be given an incentive to put all business through one insurance provider in order to qualify for the largest override possible. That's fine if that company has competitive products in all fields of insurance, but what if there's another company that can provide superior coverage? In that instance, the FSP might recommend the company with the bigger override (what's best for him) rather than the company with the best coverage (what's best for the client).

The surest way to accurately disclose compensation for insurance at present is after the fact because there are a number of variables that affect compensation along the way. There is certainly an opportunity to offer a best guess of what the compensation will be with illustrated assumptions. Besides, if there is a perceived conflict that only comes out after the fact, disclosing it at that point is rather like putting up a "bump" sign on a road after you've gone over the bump—it's too late at that point.

Consumers can be shown what the anticipated FSP compensation is for alternative proposed solutions and can ask for an explanation from the FSP if the most strongly recommended solution is also the most lucrative for the FSP. If the FSP can make a compelling case for why that solution is being recommended, then the client should give it serious consideration in spite of the fact that the FSP stands to earn more. There are many examples in life when the best products cost the most.

In spite of the obvious benefits of compensation transparency, there is a very real concern in the industry that consumers might recoil in horror when they learn how much FSPs stand to make if placing a large policy. It would be a shame if people resisted a solution simply because they fear it is somehow wrong that someone could make so much money in meeting that need. If an FSP can demonstrate that the market will bear a high level of compensation for meeting a client need, you'd think the client would find that reassuring (it must be hard and meaningful work if it pays *that* much). The financial services industry needs to come to terms with the effects that "sticker shock" might have on consumers' buying patterns and product choices.

As with investment products, disclosure and full client education are vital in making an informed decision on placement or rejection of insurance. The average consumer, however, has no clue about how to read and understand an insurance quote. In spite of this, consumers are asked to initial and sign these applications and illustrations, verifying both the formal explanation and personal comprehension of the contents. There is usually nothing about the compensation of FSPs in these illustrations, yet the actual dollar amount could easily be included in the illustration.

Until the mid-1990s, FSPs could be licenced to sell either insurance or securities, but not both. Earnest people trying to solve financial problems on behalf of their clients by using the widest possible array of tools were constrained by regulators who insisted they could only go to work with half a tool kit. This is just another example of the traditional sales paradigm holding sway and FSPs having to play the hand they're been dealt by corporate interests.

The brokerage and insurance industries grew up as "silos," each disdainful of the other. Prior to the days of comprehensive wealth management, this adversarial approach was seen as being sensible. Until recently, FSPs had to choose what kind of products they would offer and often had to force a product solution on to their clients based only on what they were legally permitted to recommend. Insurance people sold insurance products even if investments made more sense. Investment people sold investment products even if insurance made more sense. Mutually exclusive licencing arrangements made for numerous inelegant planning solutions and needlessly forced consumers to work with multiple FSPs. How on earth did that help consumers?

Clients were largely oblivious to the silliness of separate licencing arrangements and the planning solutions they spawned. They simply assumed that the person they were talking to would recommend whatever was appropriate as opposed to what was expedient and what they were permitted to recommend. Ethical FSPs referred clients to other professionals if they were not equipped to deal with the situation properly. Many, however, did what they had to do to feed their families, and their clients were none the wiser. Even today, regulators still expect FSPs to have separate files for insurance and investments for the same client, even though member firms promote one-stop shopping for financial services.

Illustrations

Looking at how insurance policies are employed, cynics sometimes call the questionable use of assumptions "illustration games."

The trouble with illustrations and assumptions is that fair-minded people can differ. Although there is no single, unequivocal right answer, there should at least be a well-thought-out analysis that shows the client the alternatives in a way the client can understand.

For instance, if an FSP shows an illustration that features a level cost of life insurance, instead of a yearly renewable term, less money will be kept in the investment side fund for supplemental income in early retirement. As a result, the yearly renewable term (YRT) might be seen as the superior alternative from the client's perspective. Although YRT would be better for the client for the first fifteen years or so, the FSP's pay would be cut by about two-thirds if that option were employed. How many clients do you suppose ask to see a YRT illustration for comparison? How many FSPs take the initiative to illustrate the YRT option to the client?

Perhaps that's just as well. Critics of YRT suggest that it is a dreadful policy that illustrates well because it seems cheap at the outset. They also say that YRT is a ticking time bomb that may not be the most appropriate insurance option under any circumstances because term is better if you die early and level cost permanent insurance (either UL or whole life) is better if you die late. With YRT, costs rise in perpetuity, making insurance prohibitively expensive and highly prone to lapse later in life when it is most needed. Level cost permanent insurance allows the consumer to overpay in the early years of the policy being in force in order to save a gigantic amount later on. As a result, YRT almost never makes sense unless the client is very young, is not concerned about the death benefit, can significantly overfund the policy in the early years, and uses a conservative illustration to benchmark expectations.

So even illustrations can be deceptive and the problems discussed earlier about probabilistic forecasting and reasonable assumptions are equally applicable to insurance illustrations. Probably more so since no permanent insurance policy can be placed without an illustration signed by the client. Illustrations are also why costs matter. The additional fees within an insurance contract are applied to things like investment expenses, mortality costs, taxes, capital costs, and administrative costs. The 2% provincial new premium tax also applies to permanent insurance policies with an investment component. It's like a 2% front-end load on investments, meaning that only 98¢ of every dollar invested in an investment side account actually goes into that account.

Once again, it is of paramount importance that the assumptions used be reasonable. There are many people in the industry today who believe it inappropriate to illustrate returns higher than 5%. It is not unreasonable to expect returns of 2% less than what one might ordinarily expect a similar investment in a non-insurance environment to produce. If we assume a 4% cost (the MERs on insurance investments are also considerably higher in insurance vehicles), this means the investment would have to come in with a 8% nominal return in order for the illustration to be accurate at 4%.

An asset allocation in conventional mutual funds generally costs about 2% less than in an insurance contract using the same asset mix. The MER on index funds in Canada is usually a little below 1%. The MER on index pools in UL policies is usually about 2.85%. There are three reasons for these higher MERs:

1. Insurance companies have been known to pay a 1% bonus to clients who stay invested for sufficiently long periods.
2. Insurance companies have to pay investment income tax on the money in the UL policy (usually 50 bps to 70 bps), which is passed on to the policyholder.
3. Capital taxes are also due.

That's an extra 2% in insurance product MERs. Some of the more enlightened companies are finally getting on with the unbundling required. They're abolishing the bonus structure and reducing their MERs by 1% as an offset. These companies now charge as little as 1.60% for index pools in a UL environment.

Looking at the drag of an extra 2% MER, a portfolio that returns 9% in an investment account will show an insurance illustration for that identical portfolio of about 7%. How many actively managed investments can return 9% after taking off the 2.5% standard fund MER? If the expected pre-cost return is indeed 9% but total costs are 4.5%, the total return after costs will still only be 4.5%. Illustrations might do well to more fully explain the impact of costs. Some STANDUP FSPs working in insurance have been ahead of the curve in acknowledging cost as a factor in actual results.

Consumers will be better served if they can see a range of outcomes in their insurance illustrations, giving them a better feel for what they're getting into. Illustrations are nice, but remember that the consumer is buying a *contract*, not an illustration. There are many who believe that the key to good disclosure is to find, to the greatest extent possible, what the required gross rate of return is in order to fund a specified illustration rate. For instance, some policies pay guaranteed bonuses, while others only pay a bonus if the client achieves a positive rate of return or a return above a certain prescribed amount. Again, costs matter. So does disclosure.

Illustrated disclosure began a generation ago when the world was mired in a historically high interest rate environment. The term "vanishing premiums" became well known in many households. Whole life policies had been sold using the concept of a limited payment period with the notion that by paying more early on, there would be enough money in the contract to carry it until the policyholder's death. When rates dropped, the money being generated within the policy dropped with it, causing the vanishing premiums to reappear in order to prevent the policy from lapsing.

Today, no one would be so foolish as to offer an illustration where interest rates remain sky-high indefinitely. Still, the possibility of having to pay massive premiums in one's autumn years (when insurance often becomes prohibitively expensive) just to keep a policy in force is a frightening thought. Offering misleading illustrations is hardly behaviour that is becoming of a true professional. Just as with Monte Carlo simulations on the investment side, many believe it should be mandatory to offer a variety of illustrations to demonstrate that due consideration is being given to a variety of possible outcomes when using insurance. Illustrations should show a range of premiums, a range of payment periods, and different growth scenarios.

Keeping with the notion that financial planning is an ongoing, iterative process, illustrations should be rerun every few years to account for changes in circumstances and for comparison against the original plan. In essence, this is what the Canada Pension Plan Investment Board did when it increased premium payments over the past number of years; it allowed for changing circumstances and took those new circumstances into account when revising public policy. Citizens didn't like it at the time, but it represented sound thinking and purposeful planning.

Truly comprehensive FSPs will also want to offer IPSs for their permanent life products. The principles are identical to those discussed earlier in considering investment account IPSs. *In fact, a client might want to have a single IPS that governs both the life insurance contract and the investment accounts simultaneously. After all, the two should be combined when considering the holistic nature of comprehensive, professional wealth management advice.* In this case, the client would need to sign two copies of the IPS—one for the insurance file and one for the investment file.

Alternatively, if the consumer chooses to view the two accounts as separate silos, this can be accommodated with two separate IPSs reflecting different objectives (e.g. investment IPS for retirement income, insurance IPS for charitable giving).

People using permanent insurance vehicles are allowed to shelter potentially large amounts of money from the taxman. This option is especially attractive for people who have "redundant assets" (i.e. more money to their name than will be required to maintain their quality of life until they pass away).

Term to one hundred is also technically considered permanent insurance and is often an outstanding investment in its own right. For instance, a seventy-year-old might buy a T-100 policy, knowing his actuarial life expectancy is fifteen years. The odds are about fifty-fifty that this person will live to see his eighty-fifth birthday. Although the effective rate of return upon death on the eighty-fifth birthday might be a mid-range, single-digit return, the payout will be made in after-tax dollars, making the return equivalent to something in the low double-digit range when compared to other alternatives that are necessarily taxed at a higher rate. This is also the sort of disclosure that real professionals should make when discussing alternatives with clients.

As a general rule, people are allowed to purchase either market indexes or actively managed investments within a permanent insurance policy. There are variations on the theme because some index options cost substantially less than active investments. In these instances, the indexes often don't include reinvested dividends. As with so many things in life, it helps to check the fine print.

In general, an investment purchased within a permanent insurance contract costs 2% more per year simply to cover additional insurance costs. If the TSX 60 Index could be purchased for 50 bps as an investment, it would likely cost 2.5% if purchased within a permanent life contract. If it costs 2.5% to buy the Ivy Canadian fund as an investment, it might cost 4.5% within a UL contract.

Active and Passive Insurance Options

If a consumer invests in an passive option through an FSP in an investment framework, it might cost 0.5%, but the FSP receives no compensation unless they charge for it separately. If the consumer buys an actively managed mutual fund, it will cost perhaps 2.5%, but the FSP receives a 1% trailing commission. There's a 1% saving to the client when holding FSP compensation constant. In other words, an apples-to-apples comparison of active and passive investment options might involve a choice between an index at 0.5% and an F Class mutual fund at 1.5% because neither pays the FSP anything.

In an insurance environment, the FSP gets paid the same whether the client buys an active or passive investment vehicle within the permanent life policy, *but the client pays 2% more*. Passive investments in an insurance contract might cost 2.85%. Active investments in an insurance contract might cost 4.85%. We've already established that insurance products cost about 2% more than identical pure investment products. We've also established that unbundled active products cost about 1% more than comparable passive ones. Doing the math, an unbundled active investment might cost 1.85%. Add on 2% for insurance costs and we get an expected MER of 3.85%. But active insurance products generally cost about 4.85%. Why the extra 1%?

In the world of DIY investing, consumers are forced to pay a 1% trailing commission to discount brokers who offer no advice. In the world of insurance, that 1% trailing commission equivalent is found in the form of higher consumer MERs. The FSP gets the same compensation irrespective of the investment vehicle chosen. The net effect is that insurance companies are padding their pockets by comparing costs of active management *with compensation* to passive management *without compensation*. They keep the missing

1% as pure profit. Many FSPs recommend passive strategies within insurance policies even though they recommend active strategies in investment accounts. It is highly instructive that in an insurance environment, FSPs are happy to recommend the cheaper product and pass the savings on to their valued clients *provided it does not involve taking a personal pay cut.* Most UL products feature the use of indexes for the investment component. As a result, FSPs have some explaining to do. Why do they typically recommend actively managed products on the investment side but index investments on the insurance side? If the FSP sincerely believes that one format is better than the other, shouldn't that format be recommended in both cases?

Insurance companies need to be held accountable for their product pricing. One possible solution is to pay the insurance compensation and the investment compensation separately. This, of course, is another form of unbundling.

Other Considerations

Remember that investments inside an insurance policy grow tax deferred until withdrawn at a later date, exactly like an RRSP. Given the choice between both active and passive investments, in which a person has both a permanent life policy with a discrete investment component and an investment account (non-registered), the active portion of the portfolio should be held in the insurance policy. That way, the portfolio turnover associated with ongoing buying, selling, and rebalancing will not trigger tax liabilities that could be a potential concern in an investment account. This is not rocket science, but it is remarkable how few FSPs integrate the details of their clients' insurance policies with their various investment accounts.

Most insurance product purchasers never ask about the little "enhancements" that are often tied to bonuses. What they don't know certainly *can* hurt them. A person can buy the same policy with no bonus option. When this occurs, the potential for a bonus is forgone in exchange for the certainty of a lower cost. Most people prefer the unbundled, simplified approach, leaving the complex bonus structure out of the policy. Neither is right nor wrong, but the illustration clearly reflects the implied assumptions.

Today, universal life and whole life insurance products are perhaps more complex than anything else in the financial services world, with the possible exception of hedge funds and their underlying options strategies. Given the understandable reticence most people feel when discussing life insurance, there's a natural tendency to ask, "Where do I sign?" without looking at the fine print. It may not be a pleasant thing to discuss, but it certainly is important.

In many instances, the spadework for insurance requires even more due diligence (on the part of both the buyer and the FSP) than for other investment vehicles. What is the current status regarding buying insurance directly? It simply doesn't exist at the retail level in Canada. Rather than debate whether this should be the case, let's just accept it for now. If you know you need comprehensive planning anyway (and insurance is a part of it), you may want to work with a qualified FSP.

Insurance is the sort of financial product that is often purchased once and then forgotten about. This is often a mistake because insurance needs can change drastically with life events such as increased income through promotions, additions to the family, and gaining significant equity ownership in a company. Like other aspects of your life, it should be reviewed at least sporadically to ensure nothing has changed too much in the interim.

Leaving registered accounts aside for the time being, consumers should recognize that UL policies are tax shelters because the money inside grows tax free. That's not as good as an RRSP, where you also get a deduction for making a contribution, but tax-deferred growth can be very attractive.

Anyone who has money in both an investment account and a UL policy and wants to use both active and passive approaches should probably use active management in the UL policy since there are no taxable distributions on the securities traded within the account. Anyone buying life insurance with redundant (non-registered) assets should be using highly taxable assets such as bonds and GICs to pay the premiums because the money inside an insurance contract is tax deferred. If you can't stuff your fixed income investments into an RRSP or RRIF, an insurance policy is the next place to go.

DIY Insurance

Dealing with the need for insurance is far more complex than many people realize. Consumers have no real alternative but to purchase these products from someone who stands to earn a commission for recommending them. Nonetheless, I still encounter a wide variety of SPANDEX FSPs who are adamant that consumers should never be given the option of buying insurance without an FSP as the intermediary. This is an arrogant position to take. No matter how useful one's advice or services might be, consumers should always be allowed, when taking into account their own self-interest, to forgo those services and do it themselves. Even when SPANDEX FSPs are right, the market shouldn't deprive consumers of their right to be wrong.

There are no discount brokers for insurance. Potential client savings would be enormous if there were because virtually all of the premium a client pays in the first couple of years goes to paying the FSP. Wouldn't it be nice if a consumer could go to a website, answer a suitability questionnaire, compare relevant quotes, and ultimately get insurance coverage while saving the embedded commission?

A lot of room for human error remains and the consumer in question might buy the wrong kind or the wrong amount of insurance as a result. Of course, the same can be said for investment options, yet no one bats an eye when people buy investments without corresponding advice.

If the parts and labour are sold separately, then consumers should have the capacity to opt out of advice for any and all products and save the corresponding compensation for non-existent advice in the process. Consumers will have to understand that although they might save a considerable amount in premiums, they might do an even greater amount of financial damage to their personal affairs if they take this approach. Liability is like that; once you take matters into your own hands, you have no one else to blame if things go awry. Advice costs money. Forgoing advice, therefore, should cost less. Yet it sometimes doesn't. There is simply no truly unbundled insurance option available to consumers today.

A very real problem with disintermediation of specialized knowledge and services is one of information pilfering. For instance, since automobiles have been offered online through "no haggle, no hassle" providers, some cost-conscious consumers speak with their local dealership about the makes and models they are most interested in and then go online to buy that vehicle at a lower price. This is an abuse of the system and it's one of the ongoing problems with commissions and advice. No matter how much value is added along the way, if there's no sale, there's no paycheque for the person with specialized knowledge.

One area in which the insurance side of the financial advice industry is ahead of the investment side is in FSP taxation of purchases for the FSP's own account. We have already seen that with investments, FSPs often inadvertently charge themselves. They pay trailing commissions on mutual funds, earn those same trailers as income, and then pay tax on that income. The insurance industry has eliminated this silly circumstance. When FSPs buy policies for themselves or members of their families, the commissions on the purchases are tax free, as they should be. Accountants don't send themselves a bill when they do their own taxes. Why should insurance agents bill themselves when they purchase insurance?

Given that current tax law already reflects a more enlightened view of FSP compensation for disclosure, one would think FSPs who recommend insurance would also favour a similar tax treatment for DIY insurance purchasers. If it is unreasonable to pay tax on services provided by yourself, it should be equally unreasonable to pay for services at all if they are never provided. In spite of all the grand talk of integrated financial advice being a reality, the insurance and investment elements of financial advice are clearly not yet running on the same track. The logic of FSP compensation and consumer choice on the investment side seems diametrically opposed to the logic used on the insurance side.

There are still a number of clear inconsistencies between the logic underpinning FSP compensation when comparing insurance and investments. Many believe this is also an illustration of why the wealth management industry needs one single regulator and one single set of standards. Without common ground rules and a consistency of purpose, there will always be a disconnect between the rhetoric communicated to consumers and the products they are being offered. The products should be seamless and in order for that to happen, the compensation rationale behind them will also need to be seamless. Becoming an integrated profession will not be an easy transition.

Insurance Needs to Focus on Consumers Too

In Canada today, there are a number of associations that FSPs can join to promote their collective professional interests. Most would have the general population believe that they are practicing professionals, even though they are not members of these associations. There is a view that the insurance aspect of advice is a laggard within the industry regarding disclosure. It seems life agent FSPs are more resistant to compensation disclosure than any other type of FSP. That's a shame because the interests that are paramount should always be those of consumers.

When someone uses the services of a lawyer or accountant, that person knows how much the service costs because that person gets a bill for services rendered. There are still too many FSPs today that think and act like sales agents. This is especially noticeable in the insurance side of financial advice, where many FSPs believe it is none of their clients' business how or how much they get paid. The gauntlet is being thrown down here. A profession is evolving into existence from a sales-cultured industry before our eyes. What will FSPs do to answer the challenge?

Part Four
Professionalism

Be a STANDUP Advisor

Hold yourself responsible for a higher standard than anyone else expects of you.

—Henry Ward Beecher

There's no gun being held to anyone's head. There's absolutely nothing stopping FSPs from continuing to do business the way they have throughout their entire lives and no one has to change anything if they don't want to. But that's the funny thing about change—it will occur whether you want it to or not. Resisting it merely makes things more difficult down the road.

STANDUP or SPANDEX Advisor?

For years now, FSPs and the firms they work for have been talking about professionalism in financial services. To hear them tell it, virtually everyone who offers financial advice is a "professional." However, unlike the more established professions, the generally accepted attributes of professionalism are not yet consistently present.

There are many FSPs who are true professionals in every sense. By now, it should be clear that I believe the industry can be divided into two extreme types of FSPs: STANDUP Advisors and SPANDEX Advisors, with most falling somewhere in the middle. In comparing these extremes, there are three factors to be considered:

1. What evidence is the product or strategy recommendation based on?
2. Is disclosure being made regarding the pros and cons of the recommendation?
3. What is the impact as it pertains to professionalism?

Surgeons get their patients to sign a consent form before they go under the knife. This commitment requires that patients give their informed consent prior to a procedure being performed. It doesn't guarantee that the procedure will be a success, of course. It does, however, protect the professional from lawsuits stemming from alleged non-disclosure of real or perceived risks and limitations associated with the course chosen.

Certain FSPs make absolutely no disclosure of the fact that the majority of actively managed products and strategies end up underperforming asset class products (especially on an after–tax basis) in the long run or that future outperformers can't be reliably identified at the time of purchase. Most make no disclosure that all pure index-based strategies underperform their respective indexes. Unfortunately, there are still some who recommend products based on things like compensation considerations, which products have the best short-term numbers, or which wholesaler took them golfing most recently.

Offering financial advice is an important and noble calling. However, this calling is currently being sullied by a subset of the industry with a mindset that prizes sales volumes and non-disclosure over qualified advice and professionalism. That has to change and until it does, FSPs have no business referring to themselves as professionals.

The Professionalism Dividend

In 1989, there was a lot of talk in public policy circles about the so-called "peace dividend." The idea was that since Communism and the Berlin Wall had fallen, the world (both the eastern and western blocs) could divert money and energy that had gone toward the Cold War to more useful initiatives—things like health care, environmental protection, and so forth. Notwithstanding whatever you might think about how this peace dividend was ultimately spent, it might be time to take a look at a similar concept as it applies to financial advice. Let's call it "the professionalism dividend."

Rather than diverting copious financial resources for some societal aim, the notion here is that disproportionate amounts of goodwill, new client accounts, and, ultimately, riches may well accrue to those advisors who demonstrate a clear and unambiguous commitment to professional conduct. By diverting energy from sales pitches toward those activities that are viewed by society as being representative of professionalism, we could get to a clear win/win situation for both clients and FSPs. Imagine that—a world where the STANDUP Advisors win out precisely because they are conspicuously good.

In an interview that appeared in the March 2006 edition of *Advisor's Edge* magazine, industry veteran Doug Macdonald was asked, "How would you respond to the argument 'You're either an ethical advisor or you are not. How you are paid has nothing to do with it'?" Macdonald responded that he would agree and that one could be an ethical advisor regardless of how one is paid.[1] Most others, myself included, would also agree, but with a caveat. We've already examined how FSPs are not homogeneous. Most are ethical, but a handful are not. For the ethical ones, the method of payment is of absolutely no consequence. For the unethicial ones, however, the temptation of making a quick buck might be too strong to resist. *The point is that the payment method doesn't indicate either the existence of ethics or a lack of ethics in and of itself. The real issue is in regard to perception and opportunity. The mere possibility that compensation considerations could skew the recommendations being given shows that bias, including the perception of bias, still exists. If that perception could be altered, why wouldn't we all band together to do it?*

If there is one thing that comes across loud and clear in my conversations with most consumers, it is that they are quite open to working with an FSP they can trust to look out for their best interests. As it stands now, most are skeptical. A cynic might even say that the few consumers of financial products and advice who are not skeptical are merely naive. Wouldn't it be great if consumers were neither of those things and justifiably content with that status? Wouldn't it be absolutely fantastic if consumers trusted FSPs implicitly because the way they went about doing their work was transparent, aligned with the clients' highest, most motivating values and of the highest quality in terms of both competence and ethics?

Clearly, FSPs want to be thought of as professionals. Unfortunately, most consumers think of most FSPs as rather less than that. Imagine if it were different. Imagine if there were a level of trust that existed between a client and an FSP that was comparable to the trust between a patient and a surgeon. It would be implicit. It would be absolute. It would be marvelous!

Trusted professionals should recommend products based not on compensation considerations, but on what works best for their clients. While most do recommend what they believe is best for clients, why do we allow the possibility of higher compensation to cloud the issue? People in the business all know that compensation is a very serious, loyalty-warping consideration.

Of course, everything worth explaining could also be disclosed in writing and in advance of any work being done. FSPs could offer professional and independent advice irrespective of the products used to implement that advice. This eventuality is coming whether we like it or not. Regulators might make meaningful and transparent disclosure a pre-condition of all account opening procedures going forward in the near future. The Canadian Securities Administrators' (CSA) Client Relationship Model (formerly known as the Ontario Securities Commission's Fair Dealing Model) is looking to enact something along these lines.

This disclosure would need to be written in terms any competent layperson could understand. This might include the use of letters of engagement, compensation disclosure letters with transparent fees, written investment policy statements (IPSs), and so forth. With client sign off, clients cannot say these details were not set out clearly at the beginning, making it awfully hard to sue FSPs.

Furthermore, certain industry associations are now raising the bar in areas where regulators have been relatively silent. Those who have widely accepted designations like the CFP will have a huge professional advantage over competitors doing the same work but without the designations. Add in a mandatory commitment to best practices throughout the industry and we're well on our way to creating a real profession. It's coming and everyone knows it. Will FSPs be ready? The time has come for FSPs to STANDUP for professionalism. The best FSPs have chosen to change before they have to. It is also time for consumers to demand a much higher degree of professionalism from their FSPs.

The Feeling is Mutual

Presently, FSPs suffer as the "ham in the sandwich" between corporate interests and consumer interests. True professionals will always respect those who have a different view and encourage their clients to invest accordingly. If they disagree, however, they also have a duty to say so. Some vertically integrated financial services companies have gone so far as to request that their FSPs change the disclaimers in newspaper articles to include the sentence: "The views expressed are the personal views and opinions of the author and not those of [the company] and are not endorsed in any way by [the company]."

I know of at least one firm that took this highly unusual step, but then did not allow the FSP to make a reciprocal disclaimer to his own clients. It should be obvious (and only fair) that if companies are going to insist on a disclaimer like the one above, advisors using a disclaimer could also write to their clients saying something like: "Please be advised that the views expressed by [the company] are the personal views and opinions of the people expressing them and not mine." After all, liability and the need for clarity should cut both ways.

Are Professionalism and Entrepreneurship Mutually Exclusive?

Is it possible to be a "professional entrepreneur"? Both perspectives have attractive attributes, but FSPs' actions belie their words—and actions speak louder than words. Most FSPs likely fall somewhere in between the two extremes.

On one hand, we have a culture of championing high sales volumes and bringing in new clients, incentives for doing so, business plans that focus on profit margins, and a clear focus on the bottom line. On the other hand, we have a need for compensation disclosure and rate cards, meaningful and rigorous training, peer reviews with an ethics component, and consistent minimum standards for practitioners. Is it possible to reconcile these disparate objectives? We've already looked at a similar continuum regarding compensation models exclusively. When we did that, we acknowledged that the quality of advice was a separate matter and that no compensation model had a monopoly on competence.

What about the related question of entrepreneurship? Specifically, what if we tried to guess where the total population of all FSPs might fit on this continuum between hardcore entrepreneurs and hardcore professionals. Before proceeding, a reminder:

There's nothing inherently right or wrong about either entrepreneurship or professionalism. However, since this is a book about converting a sales-based industry into a profession, we would be remiss if we didn't at least take stock of where we are now.

Many observers feel that the industry skews to the left and that practitioners in the arena of financial advice are simply more motivated by sales and marketing than they are by offering quality services with dispassionate advice. If I were to venture offering up likely psychographic allocations for these two extreme views and the points in between, it might go something like this: A 30%, B 25%, C 20%, D 15%, E 10%, F nearly 0%. Of course, this is just one person's opinion, but no one has statistical data on the subject. Besides, it's just subjective at this point anyway.

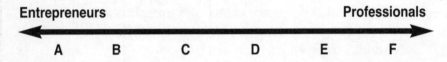

It likely just comes down to a question of preference. If you want to be an entrepreneur, then be an entrepreneur and say so clearly and proudly. Similarly, if you want to be a professional, then be one and say so clearly and proudly. Many FSPs talk about their professionalism, yet act like entrepreneurs. For the FSPs reading along, if you've gotten this far, please consider this my invitation to move rightward to become more of a STANDUP FSP. By the way, I am not implying that 30% of FSPs are SPANDEX FSPs either. One can be an entrepreneur without being a salesperson.

The two extremes are not mutually exclusive in the eyes of most people. After all, law firms have rainmakers that bring in new business. Accountants and dentists have to gather a steady stream of reliable clients and manage their practices accordingly. Given the current breakdown, as a consumer, where would you want your FSP to be on this continuum if you had the choice?

I believe most consumers would likely want their FSP to move more to the right too. In spite of this, financial services companies continue to have points programs where FSPs can get rewards points (like Air Miles) for entrepreneurial sales results, yet receive none for using letters of engagement, compensation disclosure, investment policy statements, written financial plans, or suitable training designations. In management as in life, what gets rewarded is usually what gets done. Corporate Canada rewards those activities that suit Corporate Canada's agenda. In essence, I'm encouraging FSPs to do the right thing in spite of what their employers and/or product suppliers would have them do. The best FSPs put their clients first.

Perhaps the above continuum can serve as a good starting point for consumers in determining your FSP's mindset. Why not take it with you the next time you have a meeting and ask your FSP to place themselves on one of the six points from A to F. Next, ask your FSP's rationale for doing so. Finally, ask for tangible evidence from those who purport to be professionals to demonstrate a clear commitment to the principles of professionalism. Accountability can be a wonderful thing, and you may be surprised by the conversation that follows.

Don't Blame FSPs for Scandals

There is a real need to clarify something that annoys many STANDUP FSPs. We've all heard the phrase "don't shoot the messenger." There's a similar line of thinking that should apply when discussing the recent mutual fund market timing scandal with your FSP, not to mention other examples of corporate malfeasance.

Your FSP almost certainly had nothing to do with it, so it is almost certain that you shouldn't blame them. With the exception of the handful of FSPs who were directly involved, it is the fund companies alone who betrayed your trust on this one. Although it is not publicly known at this time how widespread this activity was with these brokers, the rest of the advisory community was oblivious to what was going on.

There have certainly been instances in the press where FSPs have engaged in unbecoming and unethical conduct in the past. However, this isn't one of those instances. The market timing scandal is about having mutual fund companies allow a small minority of sophisticated clients to take advantage of time zone differences by exploiting pricing anomalies to the detriment of long-term unitholders. It has been said that time zone pricing differentials allowing people to engage in market timing is like betting on

306 — John J. De Goey

a horse race after the race is over. Most FSPs found out about this practice at the same time and in the same way unitholders did: they read about it in the press when the story broke.

The problem is that financial services industry representatives have a "you are what you sell" image with the public. "If the product manufacturers engage in unethical conduct, then maybe the people who recommend their products are unethical, too" is how the thinking sometimes goes. People often judge others by who they associate with.

It's unfortunate that fund companies drone on and on about their "partnership" with FSPs when times are good only to fall silent on the matter of who takes the blame when times are not so good. There's a certain constituency out there who think that FSPs are somehow lining their pockets in all this. And the fund companies are doing nothing to dispel that perception.

FSPs end up being tarred with the same brush that is applied to the fund companies who were caught with their collective hands in the proverbial cookie jar of client investment accounts. Real professionals would never condone such conduct and would want the record to be set straight and pronto.

Wouldn't it be nice if, just once, the fund companies who did this to their "valued clients" would at least offer an apology for their behaviour? Wouldn't it be even better if they stood up and in their *mea culpa* and said something like, "Your advisor had absolutely nothing to do with all this. The responsibility for the market timing activities that took place in your account rests solely with the fund companies you placed your trust in." That's not really the way the media portrayed it.

After the story became public, FSPs received correspondence from the companies in question acknowledging that, although what happened "was not in the public interest," "our job…is to assist you in any way we can to maintain the trust of your clients." Perhaps they should have thought of that sooner. After all, the best way to maintain trust is to not betray it in the first place. As is so often the case, the regulators only swoop down after the fact, once consumers have already been hurt.

What if there were twenty "bad apple" FSPs all in one firm doing something that is unbecoming to the industry? Would the compliance department in that firm make an example of only five (if so, which five?) and let the others off with a warning? Or would the company say that the conduct of the rogue FSPs was universally unacceptable and impose sanctions on all twenty of them? I think it's fair to say that most people would expect the latter outcome, and rightly so.

It's funny how the outcome changes if you change just one variable. With the market timing scandal, it was generally thought that at least twenty mutual fund companies were aiding and abetting the practice of market timing. Unfortunately, the OSC only saw fit to impose sanctions on five of them. It is generally accepted that at least fifteen other companies had their hands in the same cookie jar, but that those companies got off without paying a dime in restitution.

In contrast, exchange traded funds (ETFs) don't have many of these drawbacks. While it is true that one could still buy a Japanese ETF after the Nikkei has closed, the price paid would be a real-time price in a different foreign market rather than a stale price that would be associated with a mutual fund with a similar mandate. ETFs trade like regular securities, so it is impossible to engage in market timing with them. Limitations include ETF availability for certain asset classes and the inability to make systematic monthly contributions or withdrawals.

Consumers could even force the issue. They could ask their FSPs why they haven't recommended passive options in the past, especially if at least some of the mutual funds currently in their portfolio that are doing worse than their benchmarks. Couldn't those be replaced with ETFs? If the FSP counters that they need to be paid, the consumer should calmly agree and offer to do so directly.

Limits and Blame

Most people would agree that limits are a good thing. Whether it's speed limits on highways, spending limits on credit cards, age limits on alcohol consumption or salary caps on hockey payrolls, society has found lots of useful applications for limits. The very first section of the Constitution Act of 1982 makes it clear that the rights and privileges set out in our Charter of Rights and Freedoms are guaranteed only to such "reasonable limits prescribed by law in a free and democratic society."

In the mutual fund industry, the firms that recommend these products often have a curious viewpoint. They are opposed to having legislation enacted that would limit the fees they can charge, arguing that a vigorous free market should set those prices. Conversely, when advisors want to charge "whatever the market will bear" for their advice, product distributors have no problem in setting both maximum and minimum fee limits. The manufacturing and distribution sides of the financial advice business need to get their stories straight.

There are many people who believe cost limits have a role to play in financial services, but how can companies justify putting a limit on FSP fees when there's no limit on manufacturer fees? Shouldn't it be both or neither? As it is now, the industry is rife with double standards.

Notwithstanding the fact that basic tenets of capitalism call for an unfettered market, there's a good case to be made for putting limits on both. No matter how libertarian one's views are about elements of social welfare, it seems there's a consensus that sometimes limits are necessary simply because of the abuse that would likely occur if there were none. For instance, I know of one company that has a 1.5% (of household assets) annual fee limit for FSPs who charge directly, yet allows FSPs who use proprietary products to earn up to 1.65%. Shouldn't compensation limits at least be product neutral if they are going to exist at all?

The industry mindset is to pin the blame on the FSP. It has to stop. Distributor companies can terminate FSPs for pilfering client assets, but FSPs have no reciprocal recourse if product manufacturers engage in market timing. The Portus fiasco has compliance departments pointing each way internally but generally avoiding direct responsibility while trying to pin responsibility on FSPs. Manufacturers don't need to limit what they charge, but FSPs do. Where does it end?

Helping people achieve their financial goals is fulfilling and important since many people have been known to make unduly emotional decisions with their money. Advisors need to shoulder their fair share of the burden in ensuring the system offers a reasonable degree of balanced commercialism.

We're all in this together. Consumers should demand more. Product manufacturers and distributors can do more. Politicians can do more. Regulators can do more. Enforcement officials can do more. Until now, FSPs have been asked to make disproportionate sacrifices to improve the system. It's the time for the other stakeholders to step up to the plate and show a real commitment to converting the business of financial advising into a real profession.

Was That Wrong?

If limits are a good thing, then culpability is a curious thing.

Since there are so many sneaky ways that a corporation or FSP could hurt a client, the industry has given up trying to enunciate all the permutations of all the possible transgressions. Instead, the industry is increasingly opting for principles-based approaches to enforcement and regulation. If any individual or company engages in behaviour that is contrary to the public interest, then sanctions may be applied.

You may remember an episode of the popular television series *Seinfeld* that illustrated this kind of approach. In the show, George is working late in an office tower one night when he finds himself alone with a cleaning lady and the two become amorous. The problem with what happened next only became apparent to George when they were discovered.

The next morning, George found himself in the boss' office as he is asked to explain his conduct. With mock-innocence, George, the new employee, asks his boss if what he did was wrong. He then claims to have checked the company's code of conduct and hadn't found anything prohibiting employees from having sex with the cleaning staff and that if he had, he wouldn't have done such a thing. The old adage "It's easier to ask for forgiveness than it is to ask for permission" was alive and well.

This little vignette also shows how the financial services industry has come to act when dealing with corporate indiscretions. Again, let's consider the market timing scandal that came to light in 2004. There was nothing in any rulebook prohibiting hedge funds from getting in and out of mutual funds in mere hours to take advantage of global pricing and timing disparities, even though the wilful acquiescence regarding this kind of abuse of the system was clearly contrary to long-term unitholders' best interests.

After considerable investigation, it was determined that restitution needed to be paid, although payment came by way of a "negotiated settlement." But paying restitution is not the same as being found guilty. Even as the restitution was quantified and even as the cheques went out to unitholders, the companies found to have engaged in market timing always pointed out that "market timing is not illegal." There are two things to think about here: First, did the restitution payment bring a fair closure to this sordid tale? Second, is the lack of explicit illegality a source of concern?

With regard to closure, it is generally accepted that the payments made fall well short of the money that was skimmed by hedge funds. Mutual fund companies point to the fact that they only profited to the extent that they charged hedge fund companies fees in exchange for their speedy in-and-out shenanigans. However, if long-term investors had over $400 million in fund valuations stripped out and fund companies paid only $205.6 million in restitution, then unitholders are still out $200 million. For those keeping score at home:

Hedge Fund Companies: Up over $400 million
Mutual Fund Companies: Down $205.6 million (less fees earned)
Mutual Fund Unitholders: Down about $200 million

If, as the industry keeps on telling us, the client comes first, why were clients out of pocket $200 million even after the improprieties were "reconciled"? There's obviously some concern regarding public relations and public perception. Since fund companies are repeatedly pointing out that what they did is not illegal, consumers might be led to believe that they are being well-served and well-protected by the system. Regulators point to the "best interests of consumers" phraseology of a principles-based system as providing a wide enough net to catch unbecoming conduct that might otherwise have avoided retribution. However, if perpetrators are allowed to claim that they broke no laws, then the stench of their misdeeds can still go largely undetected. When the punishment is seen to be grossly inadequate, the overall system can be called into question.

For instance, what's to stop mutual fund companies from devising some devious but technically legal kickback scheme where fund companies get to keep somewhere between the restitution amount and the profit and the hedge fund companies keep the rest? Both the fund companies and the hedge funds could be about $100 million better off, for instance. If one ignores the consumer, the basic principle of fairness shows there's room for corporate profits to be made, even after restitution. Putting this even more starkly, if the punishment does not fit the (non) crime because it is too lax, there's a good chance that the (non) criminals will become repeat offenders. Corporations seek to maximize profits and under the current system, there's still plenty of room to do that. Some of the companies caught in the "time arbitrage" scandal denied any wrongdoing in their annual reports as well.

Posing a basic word problem that even a regulator can understand, if person A steals $1,000 from person B, gets caught, is found guilty, and is ordered to repay person A $500 dollars, has justice been served? *Wouldn't anyone agree that at the very least, person B should get all of his money back?* And shouldn't person A also be asked to pay a fine or do jail time or perform some kind of community service to pay the overall debt to society? Should person A get off any more lightly if he gives the stolen money to person C or loses it on the way home?

If an individual FSP found a way to skim millions of dollars out of client accounts, they would be fired on the spot for a clear breach of fiduciary responsibility. That's the "micro" application of a principles-based approach. The "macro" (corporate) perspective is rather different. What hedge fund companies and mutual fund companies colluded in perpetrating would be tantamount to robbery if an FSP did it. But the principles-based system assumes this conduct doesn't break any laws. There you have it. Product manufacturers were colluding to effectively legalize robbery...and they stole from the very people whose interests they insisted were a top priority.

There are many consumer advocates who do not believe justice even came close to being served. Many agree with a principles-based regulatory framework. However, any system, whether principles-based or rules-based, needs to have the punishment fit the crime, or transgressed principle, as the case may be, in order to be a credible deterrent that protects consumers. The application of a principles-based approach remains very much open to interpretation. The approach holds much promise, but is off to an disappointingly poor start, given how puny the restitution settlements have been in light of the conduct in question.

Not protecting the public interest can take a number of interesting forms. Cigarette companies were forced to disclose that their products are carcinogenic long ago. Mutual fund companies, however, make no disclosures regarding the improbability of actively managed products beating their benchmarks. If public welfare and the public interest were paramount, that kind of disclosure would exist. Many feel that disclosure, if it is ever going to have its desired effect, needs to be made simpler and more "in your face." Comprehensive disclosure made in the fine print on the bottom of page fifty-four of a prospectus is not the kind that engenders informed consent.

What if a "distribution" company (the kind that offers financial advice) were to encourage its advisors to buy company stock before doing an IPO, then publicize a business plan that it intended to convert other companies' products into the higher cost (to the client), higher margin (to the company) products? What if the FSPs from that distribution company disclosed to their clients that they were owners of the company whose products they were recommending? And what if there was no disclosure at all that the "wealth creation" strategy from the beginning was to leverage their role as trusted advisors to get clients to switch from high-priced third-party products to egregiously priced in-house products that produced a profit margin that was eight or ten times higher?

This becomes an exercise in defining "informed consent." Even if tens of thousands of clients signed disclosure forms that spelled out that the advisor was a shareholder in the company whose products are being recommended, is that enough? It has long been suggested that mutual funds are sold, not bought. If the disclosure documents merely state the fact that the advisor has an equity stake without also disclosing and explaining the bias-inducing implications, most consumers would be ill-equipped to make the connection. If you ask a client to explain what they just signed, chances are you'd get a garbled response. Given the avalanche of associated legal terminology, many people have come to believe that "less is more" regarding disclosure.

If you had the power to recommend consumer products to a client and the products you recommended all paid the same, but one set of products helped to boost the share price of a company where you had a significant portion of your net worth committed, would that be an example of bias? Many people think it might be.

Many of the people involved would no doubt answer the way George did on *Seinfeld*. Critics will point out the compromise of fiduciary responsibility and distributor firms and the FSPs they employ will say in their most earnest tone, "Was that wrong?" Many fair-minded people would suggest that this practice is indeed wrong, even though the regulatory requirements for disclosure were technically met. If an FSP recommended a product to you, ostensibly because it was best for your circumstances but was also good for that FSP's bottom line, would a certain level of trust have been breached? Would the principle-based test of putting the consumers' best interests first still have been served? Rather than simply contemplating your answer, perhaps you could take this up with your regulator.

Ethics, Professionalism, and Change

The only rational way of educating is to be an example.
—Albert Einstein

Grappling with change is never easy. Change is especially difficult when powerful corporations resist it because it undermines their own interests. We've all heard the cliché: the more things change, the more they stay the same. There are justifiable reasons for people to harbour this kind of cynicism. Inertia often seems like the safest way to go.

For over a decade, consultants have been earnestly telling FSPs to change their business model from commissions to fees and to get the credentials necessary to have true legitimacy with consumers as bona fide professionals. Many STANDUP FSPs have done precisely these things. Sadly, many others have chosen not to. No matter how logically and compellingly applied, moral suasion can seldom overcome human nature. For the sake of all stakeholders involved, more forceful actions may be required. Leading by example only allows for modest progress.

The financial services industry is by no means alone in this, but the situation is dire. There are many in the industry who feel that at least one industry association that was established to champion the interests of all FSPs is firmly in the hands of SPANDEX Advisors. That same organization has seen membership dwindle from nearly twenty thousand FSPs at the beginning of the millennium to only about twelve thousand today. It's the STANDUP FSPs that are leaving. They want more and are bitterly disappointed that the organizations that are supposed to be representing them have essentially sided with the SPANDEX FSPs.

We expect many things from our professionals, including a dedication to clients' best interests, real independence, professional training and ethical integrity. In spite of generally high standards, these expectations have often not been met in the financial services industry.

Doctors have been hit with malpractice suits. The Governor of New Hampshire recently banned tied selling because physicians were getting free trips tied to their prescriptions and calling them due diligence trips. Lawyers have been sued for a number of reasons. Accountants are currently held in wide disrepute due to a string of recent corporate malfeasance scandals. With Tyco, Enron, Adelphia, WorldCom, and others, people only got up in arms after it was too late and far too many innocent people were hurt. We shouldn't let this kind of catastrophe happen again.

We see the signs of societal wear and tear in the other professions already. Lawyers are dealing with increased divorce rates. Doctors are treating more people due to stress brought on by financial concerns. Clergy all over the world have to deal with stresses, many of which are financial in nature. Newspapers are full of stories of seniors getting bilked out of their life savings. Those with large sums are even bigger targets, yet regulators continue to equate the possession of capital with the possession of a sophisticated investment mind.

People get hurt and lives are ruined. As with any ailment, prevention is the best prescription. To date, no one has replaced the policy of buyer beware with one of full and necessary disclosure. That needs to change.

Being a professional means being held to a higher standard than other members of society. Virtually every MBA program and professional school has courses on ethics and many have become mandatory for graduation. Still, the temptation to "fudge the rules" in order to pad the bottom line remains as inexorable as ever.

We all know how it works. You take a buddy out to lunch to talk about old times and then, just as the bill comes, say, "So, do you think we could do some business?" just so you can "honestly" claim a deduction for the meal. You pay a contractor less money in cash to do some work on your kitchen and he either falsifies his tax return or it's treated as though it were never earned in the first place. It happens all the time. Some financial advisory firms even go so far as to put out newsletters encouraging their clients to "get it in writing" before engaging the services of a building contractor even though they see no reason to have their own FSPs put their own obligations and fees in writing. It's this "do as I say, not as I do" attitude perpetuated by product manufacturers and advisory firms that has caused the industry to fall into disrepute.

That's the thing about ethics: they cannot really be imposed. Integrity is either earned through years of reputational diligence or not earned at all. Every industry and profession has some bad apples. The intent of this book is to offer clear examples of what the more established professions practice and to uncover some of the inherent inconsistencies in the field of financial advice. This way, the most appropriate concepts can be applied in the hope that a new profession might be born.

The stakes are often higher and more personal with financial advice than with other professions, so it's only natural that some consumers will be surprised at certain elements of how the industry works. Similarly, there will be resistance on the part of many FSPs, but it is FSPs who are in the best position to effect change. Corporate governance is a very real issue. People are rightfully wary of what professionals are saying and doing. They've been burned too often in the past. Some within the industry don't feel a sense of urgency. "It's not about how people are paid, it's about how people are made," they sniff—as though integrity can be discerned a mile away. The situation has become as dire as it is precisely because of how people are made. It's human nature to look out for number one.

As a society, we have done little to meaningfully address the inconsistencies in the field of financial services and advice. We have come to tolerate FSPs who have passed a course or two, allowing them to sell certain products, to consider themselves true professionals. We've done a poor job in other ways too. We teach our children about sex at a young age in our homes and schools, yet do virtually nothing to teach them to be savvy consumers of financial products and services. Is it any wonder, in this context, that salespeople can call themselves professionals and get away with it?

There are two possible solutions: either FSPs can call themselves salespeople or FSPs can act like the professionals they consider themselves to be. However, this brings us back to a "change imposed is change opposed" conundrum. The truly professional (STANDUP) FSPs of the nation have transformed themselves, but virtually no one has noticed. At the corporate level, profit margins continue to drive conduct, so the focus has been placed squarely on the bottom line, sometimes at the expense of conduct and best practices.

The rationale behind all financial advice needs to be reconsidered. In the current environment, it is important for clients to have some choice regarding FSP compensation and absolutely vital that proper disclosure is made before transacting business. Consumers should also have the right to both understand the differences in various compensation models that exist today and to choose which one best meets their needs. All models have some degree of merit, but some are simply more consistent with the generally accepted princples of professionalism than others.

There can be little doubt that the industry is evolving. The primary disagreement seems to revolve around how to get to where virtually everyone agrees we are heading. But if everyone pretty much agrees on the state and shape of the industry at present and the approximate shape of the industry in the future, isn't this the ideal time to get all stakeholders involved in a purposeful dialogue?

Disclosure is a difficult thing to do with verifiable evidence when people don't want to acknowledge what you are trying desperately to tell them. FSPs are often guilty of not correcting obvious misconceptions and misunderstandings. Industry players could do more to disclose exactly how and how much they are paid. Right now, the financial services industry is resisting transparency because it is convinced it will cost in terms of income. The opposite may be true.

At the corporate level, the Sarbanes-Oxley Act in the U.S. was passed to strengthen corporate disclosure and certitude in stated company metrics in order to reduce investor uncertainty and vulnerability. Capital markets need trust to be restored and that applies as much to other industry stakeholders as it does to FSPs.

What FSPs Can Do

Any FSP who is serious about being a STANDUP FSP needs to get with the program immediately. This means implementing as many of the best practices employed by other professionals as soon as possible. It means getting credentials that demonstrate a capacity to offer advice and no longer making do with merely having licences to sell products. It means talking to clients frankly to explain how the industry is changing and that positive, necessary, and long-overdue reforms are coming. Most of all, it means that FSPs will need to put consumer interests ahead of corporate interests in a way that is clear, persuasive, and unimpeachable.

Up to now, it has seemed that almost no one has had the courage to stand up and categorically do the right thing voluntarily. Many who have tried have been labelled heretics and have been made to suffer financially and emotionally for their efforts. As other stakeholders become more comfortable with how the industry works and what needs to change, these FSPs will be rewarded. Newly informed consumers of financial services will gravitate toward those FSPs who demonstrate true professionalism.

Regulators have put "snitch lines" in place to allow FSPs to come forward when they believe their peers are engaging in unsavoury practices. Where are the snitch lines where FSPs can divulge the unsavoury practices of manufacturers and distributors?

Coleen Rowley, Sherron Watkins, and Cynthia Cooper were *Time*'s "Persons of the Year" in 2002 for their willingness to step forward about wrongdoings at the FBI, Enron, and WorldCom respectively. No one, least of all STANDUP FSPs, should have to apologize for having high standards and for not tolerating the conduct of those who do not share them.

Former OSC representative Julia Dublin agrees with the view that corporate cultures and compensation structures tend to reward bad behaviour. She also notes that the three-way tug-of-war between consumers, FSPs, and corporate interests is under way, having attended a conference recently where some corporate interests referred to FSPs as "free-range chickens." One might have sought clarity in that statement; did corporate people think it was STANDUP FSPs or SPANDEX FSPs that were the problem?

What Consumers Can Do

More than ever, an informed consumer is a good consumer. This ancient Chinese proverb is more appropriate today than ever before: *Tell me and I forget. Show me and I remember. Involve me and I understand.*

Consumers need to get involved. They need to force the other stakeholders to give them more meaningful information for decision-making. This information also needs to be presented in a more understandable and accessible manner. Consumers need to look closely and to know in advance what it is they should hope to see.

There are already enough FSPs in the marketplace who espouse professional principles that finding one shouldn't be difficult. This is particularly important for people who are dissatisfied with their current FSP.

As everyone knows, the business of offering financial advice is predicated primarily on relationships. Relationships, in turn, are predicated on the usual hallmarks of professionalism: honesty, integrity, experience and a genuine concern for the welfare of the client. If the FSP you're working with today possesses these qualities, you would probably be well advised to stick with that person. Of course, constructively encouraging that FSP to get credentials, unbundle and disclose fees, and implement a number of professional best practices wouldn't hurt either.

Don't be too surprised if your FSP who has historically talked almost exclusively about investments is a lot more interested in insurance over the next little while. If insurance makes sense, have a serious look. After all, more holistic services and products are where the industry (soon we'll be able to call it a profession) is heading.

Perhaps most important, consumers need to understand that any FSP who begins a conversation by talking about professionalism will likely be making a huge financial sacrifice that might take many years to overcome. How many consumers would be willing to take a pay cut that lasts a number of years in their own careers?

It should come as no surprise that the financial services industry is less than credible in holding itself out as a true profession. The litany of malfeasance occurrences over the past number of years has caused virtually everyone to become at least a little jaded about how the industry works—sort of like politics. Let's consider this an opportunity to implement positive and meaningful change by making improvements to restore investor confidence.

Since an ounce of prevention is worth a pound of cure, disclosure at the point-of-sale needs to be overhauled considerably. This is especially true with regard to so called "manufactured" investment products: mutual funds, segregated funds, structured notes, universal life insurance policies, and hedge funds. Most people don't understand the risks they're taking because the risks are couched in legal language in the middle of an imposing technical document called a prospectus. The cigarette industry dealt with this problem by putting stark wording about risks and limitations on product packaging. Investment products would be well advised to follow suit. This way, no one would be able to say they weren't aware of the risks involved when buying one of them.

Consumers need to address the industry's tarnished reputation head on. Concerned stakeholders including the Small Investor Protection Association, the Consumers Council of Canada, and the Canadian Association for the Fifty-Plus have long been making helpful suggestions. These groups use their resources to ensure that consumer interests are heard. A number of prominent consumer advocates are also lending a hand.

One of the reasons consumer issues are seldom addressed in the political arena is that consumers are just too disparate and disorganized to work together. The diverse hodgepodge of consumer concerns often lacks sufficient focus to be clearly articulated and acted upon. That's not likely to be the case for much longer. The groups listed above, among others, are organizing to press for meaningful change. There are also some websites listed at the back of this book where consumers can go to either learn more or do more.

A number of consumer advocates have pointed out that while there are well-entrenched groups that represent other stakeholders (FSPs, member firms, product manufacturers), there is no analogous organization for ordinary consumers. This has led to a number of observers and at least one public policy advocacy group (Democracy Watch) asking for the establishment of an Investment Clients Association.

Such an organization could be publicly funded with seed money coming from advisory firms and/or proceeds of crime penalties. It has recently been established that at least one prominent lawyer who wrote a report for the government was paid $500,000 to write it. Why not divert a similar amount of government funding to establish an investor advocacy group? Legislation could be enacted where relevant matters could be disclosed in starker terms in order to help consumers combat against SPANDEX FSPs and inappropriate conduct by corporations.

Consumers need to confront older commission-based FSPs now to determine what the long-term plan is for the relationship. After all, long-term planning and meaningful relationships are what these FSPs are supposed to be all about.

What Regulators Can Do

To begin, regulators should get their collective acts together and do something tangible rather than simply write reports that end up collecting dust. Canada's balkanized regulatory framework is the laughing stock of the industrialized world, while the political wrangling and petty turf protection seems to go on forever. For years, there has been a debate about the regulatory form and structure that would best suit the Canadian marketplace. A debate between those favouring a single national regulator (led by Ontario and typically backed by the federal government) and those favouring a so-called "passport" model (led by British Columbia, Alberta and Quebec and favoured by the smaller provinces). The longer the quibbling goes on, the more Canada falls into disrepute. Meanwhile, consumers suffer.

Prior to the turn of the millennium, lawyer Stephen Erlichman of Fasken Martineau released a report entitled "Making It Mutual: Aligning the Interests of Investors and Managers." It addresses many of the issues discussed in this book. Many of his concerns are justified because the things he warns about came to fruition in the following years. In spite of this, precious little has been done to prevent malfeasance from rearing its head in the future.

The most recent of many blueprints for a single national regulator was offered up by Purdy Crawford, Counsel at Osler, Hoskin & Harcourt LLP. The Crawford approach goes to great length to insure that no one province (read: Ontario) has a dominant role. The idea is that one province could adopt a new Securities Act and that other provinces could follow suit by simply repealing old leg-islation. It's an opt-in approach to building a nationwide consen-sus. Of course, previous reports, such as the one submitted by Michael Phelps, have made the point that the federal government could always act unilaterally if need be.

In the meantime, corporations and individuals alike are left wondering who is minding the store. There's a sense that gover-nance, disclosure, and consumer protection are all rather lax in the current environment. If regulators are as committed to transparen-cy as they claim to be, then why weren't the concepts now found in the new Client Relationship Model adopted a decade ago? Aside from the provisions for performance reporting, all other dis-closures now on the table could have been made then. It seems the only thing holding anyone back was the will to make the dis-closures in the first place.

Too often in the past, white-collar crime and professional wrongdoings have gone lightly punished. When a person steals from another while wearing a conservative suit and using a line like, "Trust me, I'm a professional," the victim is often just as badly harmed as if the thief were wearing a ski mask and saying, "Your money or your life." There's just an overarching and pervasive perception that's held by a wide variety of consumers, STANDUP FSPs, and advocacy groups that regulators are failing to live up to their investor protection mandate. The sense is that whenever con-sumer interests are pitted against corporate interests, it's the cor-porate interests that always seem to come out on top.

Former OSC Commissioner, government report-writer, and present-day consumer advocate Glorianne Stromberg has often criticized regulators for not doing enough. She has made a number of constructive suggestions that have essentially fallen on deaf ears. She believes that the registration, compliance, and enforce-ment processes need to be looked at as a continuum. Presently, they operate as silos. She wants to improve the competency stan-dards that FSPs are required to meet. She even goes so far as to suggest that there is a need to introduce independence and objec-tivity into the process of setting the curriculum. Finally, Stromberg suggests that regulators establish an effective means to settle dis-putes between consumers, FSPs, and their firms. In her opinion, what's needed is a system that allows disputes to be dealt with fairly, expeditiously, and affordably. Like many others, she fears the current system has caused consumers to lose confidence in regulatory enforcement as it pertains to the public interest.

Presently, regulators are using an "access equals delivery" perspective regarding financial information. This actually does very little to help ordinary investors make informed decisions about financial products. Meanwhile, nothing has been done to increase regulatory oversight even though hundreds of millions of dollars have been squandered in the form of scandals in the past several years. Again, note that these scandals were perpetrated by large corporations, not FSPs.

There are also problems at the provincial level. In August 2004, the Ontario Standing Committee on Finance and Economic Affairs released a report after the mandatory five-year review of the Ontario Securities Act. The committee asked that a task force be set up to review all aspects of SRO conduct and also recommended that "the Government work with the Ontario Securities Commission to establish a workable mechanism that would allow investors to pursue restitution in a timely and affordable manner, and that the government report on its progress in this regard within twelve months." It's now been nearly two years and still no report has been issued.

What might come as a surprise to many consumers is that many STANDUP FSPs are hoping that these sorts of reforms are brought in—and soon. Helping consumers to separate the wheat from the chaff is the sort of thing that STANDUP FSPs would heartily endorse. Not only is it good for consumers, it's also good for business if you're a STANDUP FSP.

Regulators can also do their part in assisting with a transition to financial advising becoming a profession by making some attitudinal adjustments of their own. For instance, in the March 2006 edition of *Advisor's Edge Report*, Richard Corner, the VP of Regulatory Policy at the Investment Dealers Association (IDA) was quoted in the context of allowing FSPs to incorporate, something other professionals have able to do for some time. He said, "There certainly is a lot of demand for it. It's seen as an issue in terms of trying to bring over *salespersons* who are currently using the MFDA (Mutual Fund Dealers Association) platform."[1] Many observers didn't think *salespersons* needed an SRO. They had always been of the impression that SROs were for professionals.

Incidentally, the same issue of the same publication also carried news of regulatory disharmony, where administrators acknowledged that they still haven't agreed on the most appropriate way to regulate financial services. Of course, FSPs who work in insurance (who have their own regulators) have their own opinions on the matter too. At the very least, regulators could insist on a more purposeful level of disclosure.

The concern here is one of degree. The Canadian Securities Industry has five specific Standards of Conduct:

Standard A: Duty of care
Standard B: Trustworthiness, honesty, and fairness
Standard C: Professionalism
Standard D: Compliance with the law
Standard E: Confidentiality

It might be added that FSPs who offer financial advice but are not securities licenced are generally bound by lower standards. Unfortunately, and in my view, even the highest standard that an FSP might be held to is likely nowhere near high enough.

To my mind, the industry simply isn't doing a good enough job. Here's why: Standard B enshrines the priority of client interests, the protection of client assets, the giving of complete and accurate information, and insistence on meaningful (full, true, and plain) disclosure. It does not say what needs to be happen in order to meet these lofty objectives.

The industry's primary SRO, the Investment Dealers Association (IDA), was split into two groups on April 1, 2006. One group, now known as the Investment Industry Association of Canada, promotes the interests of the industry as a whole. The other group, which did not have a name at the time of this book's printing, has a mandate to maintain self-regulation, including the enforcement of rules and regulations.

To date, the IDA has always insisted that the bar has been set appropriately. Then again, the major reason why the IDA split in two was the perception that it lacked credibility as both an industry advocacy group and a regulatory body. There was a perceived conflict of interest. Perhaps we should revisit the question of requisite disclosure of material facts. What was seen as adequate in the past (when the IDA was effectively making its own papers) might no longer be good enough.

Imagine if a provincial industry association representing physicians were to suggest that getting an "A" in your final year of high-school biology was considered sufficient training to hold yourself out as a qualified physician. No one would doubt that there's a standard, it's just that few would believe that the chosen standard was adequate. If physicians were to try such a stunt, consumers would likely feel the federal government would have no choice but to step in and impose unilateral changes to the Canada Health Act to make it more stringent. Presently, there is no financial services industry requirement to:

- Disclose that product manufacturers make more money on actively managed funds (i.e. through mutual funds) than on passively managed ones,
- Disclose that it is improbable (but not impossible) that an active approach (i.e. through individual security selection) will lead to more favourable outcomes, or
- Disclose that trading securities often results in higher annual tax liabilities.

The financial services industry depends on maintaining the trust of the people who hand over their life savings in the hope that the industry is transparent and ethical enough to conduct itself in a matter deserving of that ongoing trust. In my view, many of the industry's non-disclosures pertain to material factors that could very well cause investors to make different decisions if these disclosures were made.

I wonder what the industry is afraid of. If more upfront disclosures were not material, they would not cause people to alter their choices. Accordingly, why not make them in the name of completeness? On the other hand, if, in making the disclosures, investors altered their decision-making, it would essentially prove the materiality of the things that were being withheld in the first place. Making this kind of disclosure should have two primary aims: to maximize consumer understanding of what it is they are buying and to ensure its suitability. The only way we'll know for sure if it works is to make the disclosure mandatory and then see what happens.

What Product Manufacturers Can Do

Manufacturers need to stop effectively "buying" business from FSPs. For example, in April 2006, AIC Ltd. increased trailing commissions to FSPs on both low-load funds and on DSC funds at the end of their seven-year redemption schedule in an attempt to stop net redemptions. This is far from a new development because Brandes Investment Partners began the trend in 2002. Nearly everyone agrees that embedded compensation skews advice and compromises independence, yet no one is doing anything to reverse and ideally eliminate this kind of independence-compromising practice.

Product manufacturers could agree amongst themselves that subsidized advertising is a form of legalized bribery that needs to stop. As has been suggested previously, product manufacturers could also insist that only F Class funds be sold at discount brokerages. If nothing else, it would be a show of solidarity with STANDUP FSPs as compared with SPANDEX FSPs.

Better and clearer prospectus disclosure would help everyone understand the business better. An executive summary explaining the various elements of an MER will help many consumers to more clearly understand how these products work. Mutual funds remain suitable products for most people, but more could be done to illustrate just how they work, especially as it pertains to how FSPs get paid and how much of the MER goes toward the company, the FSP, costs, and taxes.

Insurance companies could offer similar levels of transparency. Specifically, the ridiculous systems of bonuses and caveats that so often finds its way into universal life policies should be stripped out and the fees stripped down. Even the most experienced players in the insurance industry acknowledge that the terms and conditions associated with bonus features are impenetrably difficult for most consumers to understand. Stripping out these gratuitous bells and whistles would go a long way toward simplifying and enhancing the lives of people buying insurance products.

What Advisory Firms (Distributors) Can Do

By now, it should be clear that some firms simply have no interest in making reasonable products and services available to reasonable FSPs in a timely manner. Every advisory firm should have a proper fee-based platform in place by now. Given that F Class funds were first released in October 2000, it is unconscionable that there are still national firms that cannot accommodate these professionalism-enhancing products and business models. To have those same firms turn up the rhetoric about simplifying and enhancing FSPs' lives and putting the client first borders on being reprehensible.

Points programs should be next to go. Who ever heard of real professionals getting points (with cash values) for selling stuff? For all that is said about the sales culture clinging to FSPs, it needs to be said that that culture is strongly encouraged by the majority of companies in the advice business. If consumers knew how bad it was, they would almost certainly be outraged.

Distribution companies could end the hypocrisy too. The points offered for sales need to stop. All the corporate interests needs to show that they are serious about financial advising becoming a profession.

I know of one FSP who made multiple attempts to forward a letter of engagement to his dealer in an attempt to get that dealer to use it as a template for all FSPs. The "win" for the company was corporate consistency and the adoption of a professional process. The alternative was either having every FSP in the company submit a unique letter of engagement for compliance approval (way more work with zero consistency) or not requiring FSPs to submit their letters of engagement for compliance approval at all. The company chose the easy way out and decided not to request that letters of engagement receive compliance approval before going into use. The STANDUP FSP who tried to simplify and enhance his employer's lives got a nasty letter put in his file after he became frustrated by corporate inactivity after making four constructive requests for consistent action.

Furthermore, corporate interests tend to be hard on STANDUP FSPs. I know STANDUP FSPs who have been forced out of the business. I know STANDUP FSPs who have quit in disgust. I know that confidentiality agreements with liquidated damages clauses are part of what corporate interests extract from FSPs in order to allow them to get on with their lives with their dignity intact. All of this has to stop. If giving financial advice is ever going to become a true profession, then stakeholders are going to have to praise and promote those FSPs who do what is right for the consumer. At present, the opposite is true.

What Bankers Can Do

Over time, FSPs will come to be accepted as true professionals. One of the very practical hurdles that will need to be faced is the financing of a professional practice. Our chartered banks will play a vital role in the delineation of salespeople from true professionals. Most banks will employ salaried salespeople at their branches, although many will also have qualified professionals on staff. These people will have a mandate either to offer advice directly or to do a quick set of diagnostic tests and then refer the client to someone in the bank's brokerage or planning arm for more specific advice. In either case, the clear delineation between bare-bones advice and true professionalism needs to be transparent.

This is especially true because there are many advisory firms that will need banks to step in to facilitate an orderly transition from one FSP to another as the professional emerges and matures largely through the retirement of SPANDEX FSPs. Just as banks offer mortgages to allow people with modest equity to acquire suitable housing, they will increasingly be asked to step in and offer lending services to fledgling professional FSPs who have considerable skills but a modest income.

Critics have said that the problem with the financial services industry today is that it favours size over competence. Those who have built up a big enough practice will be financially viable as independent business owners under virtually any circumstances. On the other hand, newly minted graduates with the best and most current training in financial advice will be practically precluded from getting started because they won't have the financial resources to compete against established FSPs

Again, it is instructive to examine what other professions do to get around this problem. There are thousands of doctors, many from modest socio-economic beginnings, who have massive student loans on the books when they graduate. They gain access to this money precisely because bankers understand that medical school students are excellent credit risks; they tend to pay off their loans promptly and often go on to become excellent clients. The same goes for dentists, lawyers, accountants, architects, engineers, and other professionals.

Dentistry is a particularly useful example. There are plenty of young dentists who graduate dental school with zero clients and the need to spend $250,000 or more on office space, equipment, and hiring receptionists, hygienists, and the like. They often have massive student loans as well. How do they get started? They go to their friendly neighbourhood banker and show them their DDS degree. That's about it. After a few questions and a couple of routine forms, the vault is opened and another fledgling dentistry practice is underwritten. Banks know that their young dentists will pay them back in no time.

This presents another example of why the financial services industry needs to unbundle its product offerings in order to become a true profession. As long as the industry survives on commissions, bankers will quite properly guard the vault. Salespeople are high-risk clients. Professionals are low-risk clients. Just ask any salesperson what kind of experience they had going to a bank to get the business started. No matter how sound the business plan, no matter how necessary the product, there's a very real chance that the clients might never come. The surest way to pass the torch from old-school salespeople to young, bright, forward-looking professionals is to provide the seed money that will get the them started and send the salespeople packing.

The only way to gain certitude about cash flow, revenue, cost, net profit, and all the other metrics that bankers quite properly look for is to have an established business model based on *recurring revenues*. Salespeople don't have it; professionals do. No reputable banker will lend to someone who will only pay the loan back if sales are made, but virtually any reputable banker will lend based on a predictable recurring cash flow based on an established clientele that pays regular, ongoing fees for professional services. The industry calls the conversion to fees "annuitizing your book of business." It is a vital precondition of being able to have banks facilitate the buying and selling of a practice. Otherwise, FSPs will come together to do transactions based on "best guess" estimates and highly uncertain assumptions.

Converting from commissions to fees is akin to converting a "book of business" into a bona fide "practice." Even as FSPs begin their conversion from sales commissions to unbundled advisory fees, banks will need to develop profiles on the attributes of FSPs who might be deemed a good credit risk. Factors might include age, geography, product mix, specialization, and maturity of the practice. Most important, the practice will already have to be fee based, otherwise the retiring FSP will not have an asset (client list) that can be reliably passed on to another FSP.

Some FSPs will simply have to move up or move out. Within a few years, they will either be relegated to the lower status of salespeople or pushed out of the industry altogether. These FSPs will cause the most sizable shift seen in financial services in some time and they should begin their transition immediately.

Perhaps even more tellingly, research done by Stratos Wealth Management in 2006 showed that investors clearly want to work with FSPs that offer fair fees, transparent pricing, and unbiased advice. Stratos hired Decima Research, a well-known market research firm to do the actual polling. The found that 48% of Canadians feel they are paying too much in fees and that 43% believe that the industry lacks clarity and transparency. In short, there's a huge constituency out there waiting for STANDUP Advisors to come out of the woodwork and make themselves known.

If FSPs want any kind of residual value for a business they may have spent their entire life building up, they will have little choice but to convert to a fee-based model. Either that or they can continue to earn commissions until the last possible moment but will have no one to buy their practice from them when they want to ride into the sunset. On the positive side of the ledger, mature practices are generally the easiest to convert to fees since DSC penalties should be the lowest and relationships should be the most entrenched.

No reputable professional retires from an industry without a practicable succession plan for their valued clients. Any FSP who wants to hang around for "just one or two more RRSP seasons" and then lets their clients scatter is not a real professional.

What *You* Can Do

In the end, change will come. If we ("we" being all the stakeholders in this discussion) sit back, it will continue to come slowly. However, if we take action, it *may* come more quickly. It only seems reasonable to choose the second path since the finality of the outcome seems so inevitable. Practically speaking, we're now at the point where almost everyone agrees on where we're going. Although we haven't agreed on how to get there, a consensus is emerging.

Many stakeholders are in a state of denial, given how many of them act as though everything is fine as it is. Others do nothing simply because they have no idea about how bad things are. Presently, there are a number of observers who would likely have no alternative but to conclude that the situation is desperate. There is a popular saying that suggests knowledge is power. I disagree; it isn't that simple. I believe knowledge only becomes powerful when combined with deliberate, purposeful action. The time has come for everyone involved to put their knowledge into action and come to terms with the changes that will be necessary to move the rendering of financial advice forward and into the realm of a true profession.

There are many problems that could be avoided if only the parties had a clearer and more reasonable set of agreed-upon expectations to begin with. In general, better client statements are something the industry should be striving for. Allowing end-users to get a clear sense of what has been invested or withdrawn and how the account has performed since its inception through a client-specific rate of return should not be rocket science. As our society ages, there will be an increased need for statements that are clear, consistent, and easy to read—even for people with limited eyesight. Apart from the usual concerns about jargon and legalese, this is another reason why the industry's "fine print" simply has to go.

Meanwhile, course textbooks repeatedly tell FSPs and their

managers that most disputes stem from simple misunderstandings at the outset. As such, I've believe that virtually everyone would be in favour of tools that would minimize misunderstandings. Sadly, many such tools have been slow to gain acceptance.

There are many who believe that various forms of malfeasance will not go away and that meaningful dispute resolution is still unavailable. Most advisors are still unaware of the existence of their own arbitration rights, alternative dispute resolution options, and potential recourse offered by the Ombudsman for Banking Services and Investments (OBSI). There are a number of consumer advocates who would suggest that the pursuit of justice through these means is effectively useless anyway, given how few complaints result in rulings that favour consumers. The industry is not seen as being responsive to repeated pleas for increased and improved consumer protection, and any industry that fancies itself as a profession but has dispute resolution mechanisms that are viewed as tantamount to kangaroo courts clearly has a credibility problem.

A related matter regarding both disclosure and the improvement of the FSP-client relationship is performance reporting. The industry has long resisted giving clients a personal annualized rate of return on statements. The stated reason for the resistance is that the mathematics required is cumbersome. Apparently, this is not the case. Warren MacKenzie of Second Opinion has developed a website that does precisely that.

The site www.showmethereturn.ca not only offers people a chance to plug in real world data to derive customized return data, it also features an online petition where people can sign up to request that this be made manditory. There are more than a few skeptics who fear that the real reason behind this suppression of individualized performance reporting is that most companies and FSPs do not want to be held accountable for performance that lags benchmarks. I am one of those skeptics.

The time has come to create a new profession. If we're respectful of everyone's legitimate interests, we just might find a way to get this done to maximize the advantages for all concerned.

Is Anyone Doing Enough?
No matter what various stakeholders might insist about the

progress that is being made, there can be little doubt that more can and should be done. In the mid-February 2006 edition of *Investment Executive*, Glorianne Stromberg wrote a column entitled "While the World Changes, We Dither." In the opening, she writes:

> Canada's financial services industry has a tendency to study problems to death but never solve them. There are many examples of this: fund governance, meaningful and timely disclosure, financial intermediary proficiency, meeting clients' personal financial planning needs, modernizing securities regulation, and effective enforcement of securities laws—to name a few.

It might be added that Stromberg's first report on how to deal with many of these same issues was submitted well over a decade ago. There are also a number of people who feel we are approaching what Malcolm Gladwell would call "the tipping point," essentially the spot where everyone "gets it" and changes their behaviour accordingly.

This is a call to action. If you are involved in the financial services industry in any way—as a consumer, FSP, industry executive, legislator, regulator, or journalist—do not simply put this book down and move on with your life. Instead, do something to encourage meaningful change in an industry that desperately needs to embrace substantive change in order to become a profession. If you really care about the future of financial advice in Canada, here are a few groups you might wish to contact in order to effect positive change:

Provincial Regulators
Alberta Securities Commission 403-297-6454
www.albertasecurities.com
Alberta Insurance Council 780-421-4148 www.abcouncil.ab.ca
British Columbia Securities Commission 604-899-6500
www.bcsc. bc.ca
Insurance Council of B.C. 604-688-0321
www.fin.gov.bc.ca/ inscounc.htm
Manitoba Securities Commission 204-945-2548
www.msc.gov. mb.ca

Manitoba Consumer and Corporate Affairs 204-945-2542
www.gov.mb.ca/finance/cca/index.html
Insurance Council of Manitoba 204-988-6800 www.icm.mb.ca
NB Office of the Administrator 506-658-3060 www.gov.nb.ca
NB Superintendent of Insurance 506-453-2541
Nfld. and Labrador Securities Division 709-729-4189
www.gov. nf.ca
Nfld. and Labrador Insurance Division 709-729-2571
Nova Scotia Securities Commission 902-424-7768
www.gov.ns. ca/nssc
Nova Scotia Superintendent of Insurance 902-424-6331
www.gov.ns.ca/enla/fin/super.htm
Ontario Securities Commission 416-593-8314 www.osc.gov.on.ca
Financial Services Commission of Ontario 416-590-7000
www. fsco.gov.on.ca
NWT Securities Registry 867-873-0243
NWT Superintendent of Insurance 403-873-7308
Nunavut Legal Registries 867-873-0586
www.gov.nu.ca/j ustice.htm
Quebec Securities Division 514-940-2150 www.gov.qc.ca
Quebec Insurance Division 418-528-9140
PEI Registrar of Securities 902-368-4551
www.gov.pe.ca/securities/
PEI Superintendent of Insurance 902-368-4550
Saskatchewan Securities Commission 306-787-5645
www.ssc.gov.sk.ca/investors.html
Saskatchewan Superintendent of Insurance 306-787-5550
Yukon Registrar of Securities 867-393-6251 www.gov.yk.ca
Yukon Superintendent of Insurance 867-667-5940

Miscellaneous Financial Services Contacts
Advocis 416-444-5251, 1-800-563-5822 www.advocis.ca
Canadian Banking Ombudsman 416-287-2877, 888-451-4519
www.bankingombudsman.com
Canadian Institute of Financial Planners 1-866-933-0233
www.cifps.ca
Canadian Securities Institute 416-681-2215, 1-866-866-2601
www.csi.ca

Canadian Venture Exchange/Toronto Stock Exchange
416-947-4670, 1-888-873-8392 www.tsx.com
Certified General Accountants Assoc. of Canada
www.cga-canada.org
Canada Life and Health Insurance Assoc. 800-268-8099 (English),
416-777-2221, 800-361-8070 (French), 514-845-9004, 613-230-0031
www.clhia.ca
Canada Deposit Insurance Corp. 800-461-2342 www.cdic.ca
Chartered Accountants of Canada 416-977-3222 www.cica.ca
Credit Union Institute of Canada 800-267-CUIC (2842)
www.cuic.com
Financial Planners' Standards Council (FPSC) 416-593-8587,
1-800-305-9886 www.cfp-ca.org
Institute of Canadian Bankers 800-361-7339 www.icb.org
Insurance Brokers Assoc. of Canada 416-367-1831, 613-232-7393
www.ibac.ca
Investment Counsel Assoc. of Canada 416-504-1118
www.investmentcounsel.org
Investment Dealers Assoc. of Canada 416-364-6133,
1-877-442-4322 www.ida.ca
Investment Funds Institute of Canada 888-865-4342, 416-363-2158
www.ific.ca
Investor Learning Centre 888-452-5566 www.investorlearning.ca
Montreal Exchange 800-361-5353 www.me.org
Mutual Fund Dealers Assoc. 416-943-5827 www.mfda.ca
Office of the Superintendent of Financial Institutions
800-385-8647, 416-973-6662 www.osfi-bsif.gc.ca
Quebec Deposit Insurance Board 418-643-3625, 1-888-291-4443
www.igif.gouv.qc.ca
Society of Management Accountants of Canada 905-949-4200, 1-
800-263-7622 www.cma-canada.org

It also wouldn't hurt to contact your local MP, MPP, MLA, or
MNA to request immediate action on various regulatory matters.
Contacting premiers, ministers of finance, and the Prime
Minister's Office works even better. If you're an FSP, why not press
your company's management to put meaningful professional stan-
dards in place? If you're a consumer, why not do the same and

copy your FSP? Furthermore, anyone can write letters to branch managers (and ultimately the editor of the local paper) when they are made to endure services that are less than professional.

For their part, FSPs should show some real initiative and start using letters of engagement and compensation disclosure before being asked to do so by their clients and/or employers. Much needs to be done for rhetoric to catch up with reality. FSPs can set a good example for their peers and their industry so that the confidence that is currently waning can be re-established with honour and integrity. Bringing about constructive reform of the financial services industry and reinventing it as a genuine profession is everyone's business, so do your part. Stop reading investment pornography. Focus more on those elements of your financial life over which you have direct control—things like cost, taxes, planning, risk management, and personal behaviour. Most important, do not think that the manufacturing companies, distribution companies, and regulators have the matter well in hand. They're the ones that created this mess in the first place.

Notes

Part One: Preparing FSPs
Efficient Markets
1. William F. Sharpe, "The Parable of Money Managers," *The Financial Analysts Journal* 32, no. 4, (July/August 1976): 4.
2. P. A. Samuelson, "Proof That Properly Anticipated Prices Fluctuate Randomly," *Industrial Management Review* (Spring (6) 1965): 41–49.
3. *Barron's*, 2 April 1990, 15.

Education or Indoctrination?
1. *Funk & Wagnalls Standard Desk Dictionary*, 4th ed., s.v. "indoctrinate."
2. Michael Nairne, interview by the author, Toronto, Ontario, 25 April 2006.
Funk & Wagnalls Standard Desk Dictionary, 4th ed., s.v. "charlatan."

Part Two: Scientific Testing
Get an Investment Policy Statement
1. Gary P. Brinson, L. Randolph Hood, and Gilbert L. Beebower, "Determinants of Portfolio Performance," *Financial Analysts Journal* (July/August 1986): 39–44.
2. James Daw, "OSC Avoids Debate on Asset Allocation Report," *Toronto Star*, 24 September 2005, p. D2.

Scientific Testing
1. Rob Carrick, "The Financial Industry by the Numbers," *Globe and Mail*, 3 January 2006, p. B9.
2. Amin Mawani, Moshe Milevsky, and Kamphol Panyagometh, "The Impact of Personal Income Taxes on Returns and Rankings of Canadian Equity Mutual Funds," 7 March 2003 [cited 14 August 2006]. P. 8–9. available from http://www.ifid.ca/pdf_workingpapers/WP2003.pdf.
3. Bill Bachrach, *Values-Based Financial Planning: The Art of Creating and Inspiring Financial Strategy*, Aim High Publishing, San Diego: 2000.
4. Mark Hulbert, "Same Portfolio, Higher Cost. So Why Choose It?" *New York Times*, 9 April 2006, sec. 3, p. 11.

Part Three: Necessary Disclosure
Necessary Disclosure
1. Michael Ignatieff, *The Rights Revolution*, House of Anansi, Toronto: 2000, 171.
2. "Ontario Minister Wants Cigarettes Banned," *24 hours*, 10 April 2006, 8.

What Adds Value?
1. "Your Fund Manager Likely Is Overpaid," 2 April 2006 [cited 14 August 2006]. available from www.fund-manager.org.
2. *Funk & Wagnalls Standard Desk Dictionary*, 4th ed., s.v. "bribe."

What Can STANDUP Advisors Do?
1. Dan Wheeler, interview by Brad Steiman, 3 May 2006.
Survey, Financial Planners Standards Council, *Advisor's Edge*, February 2006, 11.

Part Four: Professionalism
Be a STANDUP Advisor
1. Deanne Gage, "A Consumer's Perspective," *Advisor's Edge*, March 2006, 5.

Ethics, Professionalism, and Change
1. Steven Lamb, "IDA Moves on Advisor Compensation," *Advisor's Edge Report*, March 2006, 2. (italics added)

Acronyms

BPS—Basis Points: there are 100 basis points in 1%.

CAPM—The Capital Asset Pricing Model: an early empirical framework for describing risk and reward. The three-factor model has since overtaken it as the best way to explain risk and reward in securities markets.

CFA—Chartered Financial Analyst: a designation devoted to rigorous security analysis.

CFP—Certified Financial Planner: the premier designation for financial planning.

CI—Critical Illness: insurance that pays a lump sum if you get sick, but live.

CRA—Canada Revenue Agency: the Canadian tax department.

DFA—Dimensional Fund Advisors: a mutual fund company dedicated to developing products based on academic research and empirical evidence.

DIY—Do-It-Yourself: a term used to describe people who prefer to forgo advisors and do their investing using discount brokerages.

DSC—Deferred Sales Charge: also known as "back-end load," it is a compensation structure that pays an FSP upfront but locks the investor into a redemption schedule lasting six or seven years. It also features annual trailing commissions.

EMH—Efficient Market Hypothesis: an academic theory put forward by Eugene Fama that posits security prices as always providing a highly accurate depiction of all available public information.

ETF—Exchange Traded Fund: a security that tracks an index at a low cost.

FSP—Financial Service Provider: a term created to capture the myriad forms that can be taken by people who offer financial advice.

FSPC—Financial Standards Planning Council: a Canadian organization dedicated to the promotion and acceptance of the CFP designation.

GIC—Guaranteed Investment Certificate: a bank product that offers a set interest rate over a prescribed time frame.

GST—Goods and Services Tax: Canada's primary consumption tax.

IDA—Investment Dealers Association: an SRO dedicated to the policing of the securities industry that, until April 2006, was also a trade association promoting the interests of the securities industry.

IFIC—Investment Funds Institute of Canada: the trade association for Canadian mutual funds.

IIAC—Investment Industry Association of Canada: the new name for the regulatory portion of what was formerly known as the IDA. The new promotional trade association has had no name confirmed at the time of this book's printing.

IPS—Investment Policy Statement: a written document that sets out the primary details of a client's portfolio, including the strategic asset allocation.

KYC—Know Your Client: a common advisory industry phrase the entrenches suitability as the "cardinal rule" of investment advice.

LTC—Long-Term Care: insurance for people for personal care, typically when they become elderly.

MER—Management Expense Ratio: the total annualized cost of owning a mutual fund, expressed as a percentage. An MER of 2.5% costs a $1000 client $25 per year.

MFDA—Mutual Fund Dealers Association: an SRO that is the mutual fund counterpart to the IDA.

MPT—Modern Portfolio Theory: Nobel Prize–winning research originally done by Harry Markowitz that shows how risk-adjusted returns can be improved by combining weakly or negatively correlated assets.

OSC—Ontario Securities Commission: the most prominent of Canada's thirteen securities administrators.

RRSP—Registered Retirement Savings Plan: a federal government retirement program that provides deductions for contributions and tax deferral for as long as the money remains invested.

SPANDEX—Sales Pitches And Non-Disclosure Elminate Excellence: a phrase concocted to characterize FSPs with a sales orientation.

SRO—Self-Regulatory Organization: an industry association with a mandate of self-regulation.

STANDUP—Scientific Testing And Necessary Disclosure Underpin Professionalism: a phrase concocted to characterize FSPs with a professional orientation.

UL—Universal Life: a form of permanent life insurance that has an investment component added.

YRT—Yearly Renewable Term: a form of simple life insurance that features annual premium increases as one ages.

Recommended Reading

Part One: Preparing FSPs

The Prudent Investor's Guide to Beating Wall Street at Its Own Game
by John J.Bowen with Dan Goldie

The Power of Index Funds by Ted Cadsby

The New Investment Frontier III by Howard Atkinson with Donna
Green

A Random Walk Down Wall Street by Burton Malkiel

Innumeracy by John Allen Paulos

Unconventional Success by David F. Swensen

Active Index Investing by Steven A. Schoenfeld

Common Sense on Mutual Funds by John Bogle

The New Finance: The Case Against Efficient Markets by Robert
Haugen

The Empowered Investor by Keith Matthews

"The Arithmetic of Active Management" by William F. Sharpe,
Financial Analysts Journal Vol 47, No. 1, Jan/ Feb 1991, (7-9).

"On Persistence in Mutual Fund Performance" by Mark M.
Carhart, *The Journal of Finance*, Vol. LII, No. 1, March, 1997

www.ibbotson.com

www.ishares.com is the site run by Barclay's Global Advisors.

www.dfacanada.com is the Canadian site for Dimensional Fund
Advisors

www.globeinvestor.com and www.globeinvestorgold.com are
useful sites if you enjoy research on securities and mutual
funds.

Part Two: Scientific Testing

Global Investing by Roger Ibbotson and Gary Brinson

Asset Allocation by Roger Gibson

The Intelligent Asset Allocator by William J. Bernstein

Winning the Loser's Game by Charles D. Ellis

Fooled By Randomness by Nassim Nicholas Taleb

Why Smart People Make Big Money Mistakes by Gary Belsky and
Thomas Gilovich

The Ten Biggest Mistakes Canadians Make by Ted Cadsby

Beyond Fear and Greed by Hersh Shefrin

Determinants of Portfolio Performance, Gary P. Brinson, L. Randolph Hood and Gilbert L. Beebower, Financial Analysts Journal, July/August, 1986, (39-44)

Determinants of Portfolio Performance II: An Update by Gary P. Brinson, Brian D. Singer and Gilbert L. Beebower, Financial Analysts Journals, May/June, 1991, (40-48)

Does Asset Allocation Policy Explain 40, 90 or 100 Percent of Performance? By Rober G. Ibbotson and Paul D. Kaplan, Association for Investment Management Research, January/February 2000, (26-32)

Part Three: Necessary Disclosure

Who's Minding Your Money? By Sandra E. Foster

The Professional Financial Advisor (First Edition) by John J. De Goey

Insurance Logic by Moshe Milevsky

The Facts of Life by Paul Grimes

www.insurance-canada.ca is the Federal Government site on insurance.

www.ccir-ccrra.org is the Canadian Council of Insurance Regulators' site.

Part Four: Professionalism

True Professionalism by David H. Maister

The Trusted Advisor by David H. Maister, Charles H. Green and Robert M. Galford

How Good People Make Tough Choices by Rushworth Kidder

Saving The Corporate Soul by David Batstone

The Corporation by Joel Bakan

Winning with Integrity by Leigh Steinberg

Leading Change by John P. Kotter

Creating Equity by John J. Bowen

Effort-Less Marketing for Financial Advisors by Steve Moeller

The Naked Investor by John Lawrence Reynolds

www.osc.gov.on.ca is the site run by the Ontario Securities Commission and features good background regarding regulatory principles and procedures.

www.investored.ca is run by the Investor Education Fund, a part of the OSC

www.investoradvocates.ca is a discussion forum on securities enforcement and investor protection issues

www.cegworldwide.com is a useful and influential site for FSPs

www.davidmaister.com is by a guy who writes and consults on professionalism

www.fin.gc.ca is the main site for the Federal Department of Finance

www.showmethereturn.ca helps people calculate returns for their own portfolios

www.canadianfundwatch.com covers major news in the world of mutual funds

Index

Acknowledgements

I was never really certain where this project would take me. Nonetheless, I wanted to see if the people who complain about the industry really cared enough to do something tangible about their complaints. I also took the challenge because I felt someone had to call corporate interests on their conduct—and no one else seemed to want to do it. In the end, I was angry enough at the way people think and act that I felt I had no real option but to try my hand at setting the record straight. In essence, I felt it was the sort of thing that I was born to do.

Having embarked on this journey, I felt I had no choice but to see it through. It became my mission to demonstrate the inconsistencies I have found in the financial services industry over the years to ordinary consumers, other advisors, financial writers, and clients. Being an impatient fellow with high ideals, a reforming disposition, and an inquiring mind, I also thought that change was "just around the corner" when I started my first edition. Today, I admit that there have been times when I thought that perhaps I should have listened to those who were counselling me not to even start down this path. Inertia can be an easy foe to underestimate.

Over the years, I've been fortunate to be able to draw on insights and inspiration from a number of truly remarkable people. One of them, Michael Nairne, taught me to "change before I have to" back in the mid-1990s. I took the advice to heart, while the industry did nothing. To this day, it astonishes me that the change I was hoping I would encounter "any day now" still hasn't materialized. There was once a time when I actually expected change to come swiftly. I am no longer that naive, but I remain just as determined. Steve Moeller and Andy Lank taught me how to take solid principles and apply them in an everyday practice. Sandra Foster taught me that writing books and having a practice are not mutually exlusive pursuits. Although we only met face to face recently, John Bowen has had a key role in shaping my thinking.

Thank you, Mario Frankovich, for believing in STANDUP Advice. You have affirmed my belief that there's plenty of room for independent companies that do the right thing in an increasingly corporate industry.

For a number of years, I have been writing in national publications as a means of getting the message out on professionalism. I like to believe I have made a small difference. As such, a sincere thank you goes to all the people who have called me or written to me over the years to either thank me for pointing something out or for telling it like it is or for fighting for what is right. You know who you are, and without your encouragement, I might have given up.

Thanks also to the many people who assisted in proofreading this book to catch the various flaws that escaped my own attention. Hugh Lewis, John "Jazz" Szabo, Craig Swistun, Camille Wilson, Joe Madill, Dietmar Niehaus and Ken Kivenko have all assisted me in maintaining accuracy and readability.

My parents, Neil and Mary De Goey, have been instrumental in giving me my roots and wings. The predisposition to get involved and work toward making a difference comes from them. If dictionaries carried phrases like "salt of the earth," their pictures would be there as defining examples.

My daughter, Sophie, is a constant source of joy and amazement. I am certain that in time, her wisdom and intellect will humble me.

My wife, Marina, continues to keep me grounded. Were it not for her support, I would have likely given up on championing positive reforms long ago.

About the Author

John J. De Goey, MPA, CIM, FCSI, TEP, CFP is a Senior Financial Advisor with Burgeonvest Securities Ltd., a member of CIPF. John enjoys a national reputation as an authority on professional, unbundled financial advice in Canada. A frequent commentator on financial matters, he has written for a number of media sources including *Advisor's Edge*, *Canadian MoneySaver*, the *Globe and Mail* and the *National Post*. He has made numerous appearances on a variety of personal finance television programs, including CBC's *Marketplace*, *ROBTv*, and *Canada AM*. John has won the National Multi-Media Award conferred by the Canadian Association of Financial Planners and he has spoken at numerous conferences throughout Canada as well as in Ireland, the United States, and the Caribbean.

A former employee at Consumer and Corporate Affairs Canada and a passionate voice for consumer interests, John believes in aligning the interests of financial advisors with the interests of their clients, not their employers or product suppliers. This includes fee transparency, consistent professional training, a focus on independent research, and unbiased financial advice. He also believes that qualified financial advisors are a valuable resource and that people should willingly pay for good advice.

John decided to become a STANDUP Advisor in 1999 after growing tired of waiting for the industry to transform itself voluntarily. Today, he rather enjoys pointing out the many inconsistencies within the industry but has never yet rolled his eyes at an interviewer when asked about investment pornography.

John is also the President of STANDUP Advisors Ltd., a company committed to bringing all industry stakeholders together to transform the financial services industry into a profession. He lives in Toronto with his wife, Marina, and daughter, Sophie. Although he is an avid hockey fan, it has been many years since he has accepted tickets from product suppliers as a means of "enhancing the relationship." He invites everyone to get involved in the business of transforming the financial services industry into a bona fide profession.